What is the role of the monarchy in Britain today? Is the Queen really a non-political figure? How much does the Crown exist in the interests of ordinary people, and are they receiving value for money?

All these and many other pertinent and impertinent questions are discussed in Mr Hamilton's penetrating and enlightening analysis of an institution about which he holds strong and well-known views. He is concerned to strip away the myth, sentiment and secrecy which surround the monarchy, and argues that if we must have one it should at least exist on an open and honest basis.

Openness and honesty certainly characterize Mr Hamilton's approach to his sensitive subject. The facts and figures upon which he bases his conclusions are clearly laid out in the appendices to this abrasive, entertaining book. They form a wealth of fascinating material which will surprise those who may previously have regarded his arguments as a wayward polemic.

MY QUEEN AND I

WILLIE HAMILTON, M.P.

QUARTET BOOKS LONDON

First published by Quartet Books Limited 1975
27 Goodge Street, London W1P 1FD

ISBN 0 704 32053 3

Printed in Great Britain by The Anchor Press Ltd
and bound by Wm Brendon & Son Ltd
both of Tiptree, Essex

To my late and deeply loved wife, Joan

'It could have been no difficult thing in the early
and solitary ages of the world, while the chief
employment of men was that of attending flocks and
herds, for a banditti of ruffians to overrun a country,
and lay it under contributions. Their power being
thus established, the chief of the band contrived to
lose the name of Robber in that of Monarch; and
hence the origin of Monarchy and Kings'

– THOMAS PAINE, *The Rights of Man*

ACKNOWLEDGEMENTS

My grateful thanks are due to those few who were willing to grant me personal interviews. Sir Alec Douglas-Home, ex-Tory Prime Minister and Foreign Secretary, was as courteous as he was uninformative – but he *did* give me some of his time. Mr Harold Wilson as Prime Minister granted an audience to one of my young research assistants, again with negligible results. But the gesture counted. Michael Foot was helpful in suggesting further reading and in reminiscing about the 1952 probe into the royal cash mystery. The late and much lamented Dick Crossman, who as a Minister in the 1964–70 Labour Governments came into frequent contact with the Queen, promised me access to his royal memories. Unfortunately he died before the promise could be fulfilled. His diaries on these and other matters when they are published should be among the most exciting political reading for generations.

I had informal chats with other ex-Labour Ministers. All had amusing stories to tell. Most had kissed the royal blarney stone. Many were anxious to kiss it again – and after the February 1974 Election, they did. Be that as it may, I was glad they would talk.

Three young men gave me valuable assistance in research – Mike Newman, Tony Hilton, and John Howe. One of them gained access to Mr Wilson, and another to the Palace itself.

No interviews were conceded by any member of the Royal Family, though Lord Snowdon would have liked to before he was warned off such a dangerous escapade. My *written* questions *were* answered, and one must be thankful for that. But correspondence courses with the Palace are fairly barren exercises. Courtesy is ladled out by the bucketful – hard information comes by the thimbleful.

The House of Commons Library research staff are one of the most underrated and self-effacing bodies of public servants we have. Their help was invaluable. Both the young and beautiful ladies and the older men ferreted out information which I could not have hoped to unearth myself. My eternal thanks to them. Occasionally they must have felt I was the plague in their lives.

My gratitude, too, to Mrs Jean Douglas, for typing out my almost illegible manuscript. Her patience, punctuality and cheerfulness were characteristics I cherished all the more as I have so little of them myself.

To those newspapers and magazines which have allowed me to use their photographs, cartoons and other material, I say a simple thank you. That goes, too, to my editor Peter Ford, who gave invaluable assistance in improving the quality and reducing the quantity of my verbiage so effectively – as well as protecting me from the laws of libel.

Last, but by no means least, thanks are due to those thousands of old-age pensioners, vicars, trade unionists and other ordinary mortals all over the world who continuously urged me on, with their letters and telegrams of encouragement, to *tell the unvarnished truth*. I hope my debt to them has been repaid in part at least by what I have written in this book.

Any errors of fact in the script are, of course, entirely my responsibility. So, too, are the opinions expressed. They may hurt a lot of people, and anger more. I'm genuinely sorry about that. No harm is meant to anyone. But no politician or writer worth his salt is unwilling to tell the truth as he sees it. 'Say it and be damned' – or risk elevation to the House of Lords. We shall see!

The author and publishers wish also to express their thanks for permission to reproduce extracts from the following newspapers: The Associated Newspaper Group (12 March 1974); the *Daily Mirror*; the *Evening Standard* (issue of 8 March 1972); the *Financial Times* (issue of 3 December 1971); the *Observer* (issue of 5 December 1971); *The Times* (issue of 3 December 1971), 'reproduced from *The Times* by permission'.

John Masefield's poem 'Prayer for a Beginning Reign' is

reproduced from *The Times* by permission of *The Times* and the Society of Authors.

The photograph of Willie Hamilton, M.P., aboard H.M.Y. *Britannia* is Crown Copyright and reproduced by permission of the Controller of Her Majesty's Stationery Office.

The cartoon on page 39, by Eccles, originally appeared in the *Morning Star*, and the cartoon on page 160, by Peter Fluck, originally appeared in *Labour Weekly*. Both are reproduced by permission. Royal portraits are by John Kent.

AN OPEN LETTER TO HER ROYAL HIGHNESS QUEEN ELIZABETH II

Your Majesty,

You know me solely by ill-repute. Yet I cannot recollect that I have ever said a cruel or critical word against you *personally*. You may well not believe me if I state that I feel no personal animosity to you or your family as individuals. On the other hand, some among your relations seem to be paid each year what would to millions be a fortune, and also seem to do very little to earn their £100 a day or more. So occasionally I have said hurtful things about members of your family, and sometimes I have regretted what I have said. But, if I have used harsh words, it has been because I feel that you, your family and the class you represent have grievously hurt the class to which I belong and which I represent in our sovereign Parliament.

You must surely agree that, by birth and upbringing, by the surroundings in which you live and the company you keep, you cannot possibly understand the feelings and the way of life of the millions of ordinary people it is claimed you keep united in one big happy family. It is a claim you have never contradicted, but in your heart of hearts, deep inside yourself, you must know how absurd it is.

You are known to be among the wealthiest women, if not the wealthiest woman, in the world. It is not wealth that has been created by any business acumen of your own, or even of your financial advisers (though they have helped). It is wealth that has been built up by invaluable, fabulous and unique tax concessions granted by Parliament, and never refused by you. You do not even pay taxes on the profits of your private estates at Sandringham and Balmoral. Whatever many of your people believe, you pay no income tax. You receive a refund of any taxes deducted from dividends on investments. You pay no capital gains tax. You pay no death duty. What do you do with it all?

You were badly advised when you declined to disclose to the 1972 Select Committee the actual extent of your wealth. Very many of 'your' people have to reveal such details to the Supplementary Benefits Commission and other means-testing bodies before they get one extra penny piece. But not you. You deliberately chose to go against the wishes of your ex-Prime Minister, an ex-Chancellor of the Exchequer, an ex-Chancellor of your own Duchy of Lancaster, an ex-Minister of Public Building and Works. You may still live to regret the day. As you must know, some future more radical Parliament could insist that you pay *all* these taxes. Indeed, if the Monarchy is to be genuinely, as opposed to superficially, 'democratized', the payment of taxes 'like any other citizen' becomes the logical outcome.

It has been suggested by some that because, as a Member of Parliament, I must have taken the Oath of Allegiance to you and your heirs, some of the things that I say come very near to treason. And, it is true, taking the Oath of Allegiance is one of the conditions for taking one's seat in Parliament. But that does not mean that I have to dote on every or any member of the Royal Family. It cannot mean that I must thereafter stifle my criticism or play false to my personal convictions. Nothing I have done or said is as treasonable as the activities of certain right-wing politicians, Tory government Ministers included, who have consistently supported the Rhodesian rebels against the Crown. None of them has been packed off to the Tower.

Large numbers of those known as 'your people' share the views I hold – many more than you are led to believe. They regard the *institution* of Monarchy as an instrument used to make respectable to the unthinking and the irrational a social and economic class system which is unfair, divisive and often cruel. From your own knowledge of Britain's history, you will know how your own ancestors on the throne were, almost without exception, foreign, conservative, reactionary and supporters of the *status quo*. Such freedoms as Britons enjoy today had to be taken forcibly from the Crown and the suppressive forces with which it naturally aligned itself.

There are still a few people around who think that the divine right of kings lingers, that you still retain some real political power. But whatever else you have – as a person or as part of an institution – it is not *political* power. The so-called royal prerogatives, the 'right' to appoint your own Prime Minister, the 'right' to dissolve or to decline to dissolve Parliament, are now no more than ritual play-acting.

Meanwhile, you are to be seen at your radiant best at annual high-society horsey events, and, quite frankly, at your most uncomfortable among factory workers, or even children. Why not try going to the Durham Miners' Gala, or the Tolpuddle Martyrs celebration, one year? That is where you will find your people of real worth, rather than in the Royal Box at Ascot. You might even start to enjoy yourself.

I suspect you to be the willing victim of circumstance, that you are suffocated by hoards of sinecured hangers-on. We may not know what any of these are paid or what they do. Questions about their salaries are courteously turned aside. Almost all members of the Royal Households are titled nonentities, drawn, it seems automatically, from one narrow section of the community. It is no wonder that so many feel that the Royal Households and their functionaries are little more than the tip of the social heap and the pinnacle of the British pecking-order, all closely committed to the beliefs and philosophy of the Conservative Party.

But then your daily round, your common task, furnishes you and yours with even more than you need to ask. Your sense of financial security and well-being is a dream yearned after by millions of your people. They cannot understand why you and your family should be so privileged and they so deprived. They look to you for genuine moral leadership, but do not hear from you or your husband one unequivocal word on the evils of racial prejudice when two million of your subjects in Britain alone are coloured. You encourage cruel blood sports, yet remain President of the Royal Society for the Prevention of Cruelty to Animals.

Many long to hear from you one occasional speech that contains not just colourless, negative clichés, but a forthright and passionate sincerity, a personal conviction. If, for instance, you would subject yourself to the kind of spontaneous interviews recently given by Queen Margrethe of Denmark, the result might be a dramatic revelation. Think, moreover, of the effect that an imaginative use of some of your wealth might have: encouraging foundations to, say, undertake research into alleviating the ever-growing problems of mental health or old age, or to enrich the cultural life of the nation. Your son, the Prince of Wales, could also be encouraged to set aside some of his own fortune for similar purposes. Your two younger children might be sent to a London comprehensive school, and so be better equipped to understand and cope with the world in which they are growing up.

It would only take a few such gestures for people to feel that a genuine unity of purpose does exist, that they have a Monarchy that is doing more than fighting a rearguard action to grab what it can and hang on to what it already has before its time runs out.

I remain,

Your wayward subject,

W. W. Hamilton

INTRODUCTION

The British Monarchy thrives on flattery and adulation, offered in large measure by the media and by the ordinary people. Nothing of that will be found in this book.

I have met the Queen on two formal occasions only, both connected with my less enjoyable parliamentary chores. I feel no sense of deprivation at not having met her informally. I found each of these events – the opening of the Kincardine Power Station (which is in my constituency) and of the Forth Road Bridge – tedious and demeaning: lined up to touch the gloved hand as if about to enter the gates of Heaven to meet my Maker. The Queen's representative in Fife then, quaintly called the Lord Lieutenant, was Lord Elgin. When he introduced me at the Forth Road Bridge, he could not even remember what constituency I represented. There was nothing for me to remember in the brief inane exchanges, except that Prince Philip asked me if the power station was on my stamping-ground.

Apart from that, I have not met any other members of the Royal Family, and so my sources of information for this book have been largely secondhand. I have, however, been able to engage in some kind of irregular, and no doubt for them reluctant, correspondence with Prince Philip, the Queen's Press Secretaries, and other personages connected with the Royal Households. And, of course, I served on the most recent Civil List Select Committee.

During the lifetime of the 1964–70 Labour Government it was

made fairly clear to me, through the Party Whips Office, that my views on the Monarchy would preclude me from ministerial office. Retrospectively, I have no regrets about that. But I do regret missing the opportunity to attend one of the 'meet the people' lunches that have been a recent feature of the Queen's public relations. I was approached by the parliamentary go-between and asked if I would accept an invitation to such a lunch. I said I would consider the invitation when it came. That was not good enough. Such an invitation would be in the nature of a Queen's Command, and the risk of a rebuff could not be taken. So the opportunity was missed. A pity in a way. My acceptance might have been misunderstood, but the lunch conversation would have been worth recording. What the Royal Family lacks is any healthy blast of face-to-face criticism. Affection no doubt exists – and most of it is genuine. Few Britons are *actively hostile* to the Monarchy. But there is a massive apathy and a mindless feeling that, whatever their faults, we could get something worse.

In 1849 a poverty-stricken Irishman from Limerick made one of the several attempts on the life of Queen Victoria. 'The stolid brute was arraigned at the Central Criminal Court on the 14th June, when he pleaded guilty and was sentenced to be transported [to Australia] for seven years.' His 'pistol' had been made out of an old tea-kettle spout and a piece of wood. His name was William Hamilton – no relation!

Today's Willie Hamilton is in no danger of transportation – though he has been invited to transport himself to the Soviet Union and threatened with assassination by some of Her Majesty's most loyal and bloodthirsty subjects. Judging from the many thousands of letters I have received in the course of the last twenty years, it seems a general rule that the more illiterate are the more loyal. On the other hand, royal critics are well represented among country vicars, college and university lecturers, students and other young people. Invitations to speak on the Monarchy come thick and fast each year from universities, schools and other debating societies. Only a fraction of them can be accepted, but all the indications are of a pent-up demand for anti-royalist speakers. This at least ought to be cause for *some* concern to the monarchical Establishment.

Even though overt republicans may be thin on the ground in Britain today, there is another side of the picture to be set against the continuous cascade of books replete with royalist bilge. Some of these are motivated by curiosity about the personal lives, idiosyncrasies and influence of particular monarchs;

but many are little more than collections of Women's Page tittle-tattle about the Queen's hats, the Duke's swear words or the Princess's pranks.

Kingsley Martin's book, *The Crown and the Establishment* (1963), has been the only recent work which has come remotely near to abrasiveness. Yet, in retrospect, it reads more like gentle banter and ridicule than bitter and critical contempt. Mildly provocative or satirical writers of magazine articles on the Monarchy, like Mr Malcolm Muggeridge and Lord Altrincham (John Grigg), have had to face the anger of a few royalist oafs. Grigg had his face slapped in public; for a while, Mr Muggeridge was banned from regular BBC appearances. Neither had done more than make harmless if critical fun and comment at the expense of the Crown.

Writing a book dealing exclusively with the present reign presents formidable obstacles. So much remains secret. Should there be a suspicion that an author is up to no good (for the Monarchy), cooperation from those who could probably provide original information is, not surprisingly, lacking. Courtesy comes by the bucketful – especially from the Court authorities. Written answers to written questions are tolerated, but requests for personal interviews are refused. Elected representatives are called on just to foot the bills.

Many of the principal actors of the last twenty years are still alive. The Queen, not yet 50, has seen six Prime Ministers come and go. All but Sir Winston Churchill are in 1974 still alive. All but Sir Alec Douglas-Home have written their autobiographies – the most unreliable sources of history you are likely to find. None of them throws much light on Prime Ministers' relationships with the Crown. Harold Macmillan, for instance, is very coy about the part *he* or the Queen played in dishing R. A. Butler for the Premiership! Nor do we know for certain the extent to which the Queen was a willing or unwilling appendage to the 'Magic Circle' that carried the aristocratic Sir Alec into No. 10 in 1963. Such subjects are still taboo.

As for Harold Wilson, his well-known taste for royalty has prompted me to devote a chapter to the kaleidoscopic history of the attitudes of Labour Party leaders to the Monarchy over the past seventy years. It's a pitiful story of retreat from red-hot republicanism to unalloyed sycophancy. What was it that changed in those years – the Labour Party, the Monarchy, or both?

It would be foolish not to admit that, during the last 100 years, and especially during the last seventy, the British Monarchy has not merely survived while others all over the world were toppling. It has also probably *grown* in esteem and affection, in direct proportion as its power and political influence have diminished. Queen Victoria sought actively to influence Governments, chastised Ministers, and made no attempt to conceal her Conservatism and conservatism. Queen Elizabeth II compares with Victoria only in her conservatism. And that is kept as discreetly out of the public gaze as possible. Victoria wrote letters. Elizabeth gets to know her people by watching a lot of television; and she does the crossword puzzles in the *Daily Telegraph.*

A 100 years ago, the dictum of the great constitutional expert, Walter Bagehot, that the principal role of the Monarch was to advise, warn and encourage her Ministers, was probably true. Today, it's as dead as cold mutton. It would be nearer the truth to say the boot is on the other foot: Ministers advise, warn and encourage the Monarch. The wheel has come full circle. Prince Philip was told by the Government to go to Portugal to attend the 600th anniversary of our oldest alliance – albeit to an obscene and repressive dictatorship. The Queen was told, 'advised' or encouraged to go to France and mouth the phrases that *her* Government put into *her* mouth about how much *her* people were looking forward to British participation in the Common Market – even though she must have been aware that a majority of her people were looking forward to no such thing.

Thus, politically impotent, the institution has survived two world wars and an abdication crisis within a space of two generations. It seems more firmly entrenched than ever: buttressed, at worst, by the British people's apathy, conservatism and love of tradition; and, at best, by the fervent belief that it works better than any other form of State Headship; that, like local rates, there's no acceptable alternative; and that we get it at a bargain price. Moreover, it keeps the Commonwealth together, or so we're told. And inside Britain, our Royal Family is the very model and guardian of a national and personal morality fast on the wane. The wicked waves of the permissive society crash on the rock of Windsor, yet it stands firm.

Few of the myths that pour out are demonstrably untrue. All have a sufficient ring of credibility to make them acceptable to a people that instinctively dislikes change. I seek in this book to explode the myths. It is not hard to show how the British Empire, held together, we were told, by the bond of Monarchy, has been torn apart by the raging torrents of nationalism and anticolonialism. The Commonwealth of today bears no resemblance to the Empire of yesterday; and the changes have been wrought by forces that had nothing to do with the Monarchy.

Internally, the story of our democracy has been – certainly over the past century – a story of capital against labour, of wealth and privilege against poverty and deprivation. Essentially, our two-party political system has grown out of that very clash of economic interests; and there was never yet a king or queen on the side of the poor and the deprived. None of them would have claimed to be. And, if they had, nobody would have believed them. Our democratic system, such as it is, owes little to the existence of the Monarchy. If anything, the presence of the Monarchy has sharpened the class conflict.

But the object in writing this book is not to destroy the Monarchy. It may destroy itself – sooner than we think. If Queen Elizabeth keeps her health, she could be on the Throne for another thirty years. By then, the Prince of Wales will be in his mid-fifties. No fresh young Monarch to go soft over. Just a multi-millionaire with middle-aged spread.

Already by the 1960s there was evidence, especially among the young, of an intensified questioning of existing institutions. The Church was becoming an irrelevance. The House of Lords was something to be laughed at: a political geriatric unit. Parliamentary democracy at large has come to be regarded with a good deal of scepticism and cynicism. Part of my purpose is to try to sharpen the focus of that criticism. And, particularly, to bring the Monarchy into the full glare of public scrutiny; to challenge the validity of the hereditary principle in a modern democratic society. Over the past ten years, no Prime Minister, Labour or Tory, has created one single hereditary peer. How much longer, then, will we continue to accept a hereditary king?

In that context, the question of money and cost is relatively unimportant. But to millions of her people, the pay claim that the Queen put in on behalf of the Royal Family in 1970 was an arrogant display of insensitive greed. It was nevertheless met in full by a Conservative Government. One can only conjecture how a Labour Government might have handled the situation. Certainly, as the official Opposition in 1972, it showed no great ardour in resisting the royal claim.

My own motivation is simple. I believe the Monarchy and its privileges to be immoral. I am a Democratic Socialist. A Christian Democratic Socialist. That means a belief in the equal dignity and worth of *all* human beings, whatever their birth or wealth. I have no time for what is called 'the cult of the individual'. Hero-worship is for spotty schoolboys and giggling schoolgirls. A class society such as ours, still based largely on inherited wealth, privilege and the power that goes with it, is indefensible. And, for me, the Monarchy symbolizes that system and gives it an undeserved aura of respectability.

In the course of writing this book, I have tried to avoid personalizing the issue. I am told that the Queen is a nice, pleasant person. Her family life would appear to be normal. She seems to do her job adequately, if not with inspiration. She must often be bored, and she sometimes shows it. Thousands of other women would probably have done the job as well, if not better. It is impossible to say, for there are no standards by which to judge. One plumber's work can be compared with that of another plumber. Nobody can be compared with the Monarch, except a *previous* monarch from a different age. The same difficulty applies to the present Queen's husband, mother, sister, children, uncles. None of them was born to rule. Only the genealogical wheel of fortune brought them to where they are. There is no need to be envious. Still less is pity called for. The Royals bear their burdens with great fortitude, and show no burning desire to quit the stage. Whatever happens, however long Queen Elizabeth may reign, she will go down in the history books as a good monarch. They mostly do.

I have traced the story of the Civil List Committee's proceedings in some detail, and hope I have committed no misdemeanours that will ensure my incarceration in the Tower of London or my expulsion from the House of Commons. No matter if they do.

The correspondence which I have had with members of the Royal Family is unique, despite its limitations, and has been fully recorded in the Appendices. These also contain various documents and accounts, and will amply reward close study, so I hope that readers will not ignore them just because convention demands that they be tucked away at the end.

My basic hope is that this book may inform some, provoke others and make all *think*, as objectively and as critically as they can, about what should be done to reform, modify or abolish some of our older and more revered institutions.

1. HOW THE MONARCHY SURVIVES

'In the Crown we possessed a symbol of patriotism, a focus of unison, an emblem of continuity in a rapidly dissolving world. There was a satisfaction in feeling that the Sovereign stood above all class animosities, all political ambitions, all sectional interests' – Harold Nicolson, *George V*, p. 526

During the past twenty years there have been many criticisms of various members of the present British Royal Family, both inside and outside Parliament. The press has often made cutting comments on the activities, and the frequent non-activity, of Princess Margaret. Attacks have been made on Prince Philip by such organizations as the Lord's Day Observance Society, for playing polo on Sundays, or the League Against Cruel Sports, for his regular shooting of defenceless grouse and other birds, or of wild animals when he's been on safari in far-flung corners of the Commonwealth. Politicians have joined in too, particularly when Philip has made provocative speeches on such controversial matters as the need to limit the size of families, the benefits of National Service, and lectured industrialists about 'getting their fingers out'. The Prince has cultivated the role of a royal bull in the democratic china shop. The exploits of his daughter, Princess Anne, have raised the ire of the anti-fox-hunting lobby, and of others who felt she was spending too much time in the exclusive company of horses and fresh young soldiers. Public opinion was further incensed when she was allowed to go scot-free after committing two motoring offences. Equality before the Law is not for the Royals.

The Queen herself, with her mother, Prince Charles and the Gloucesters, has been kept relatively clear of snide remarks. Lord Altrincham did once get into hot water for commenting adversely on the timbre of Her Majesty's voice and the quality of her speeches – with the result that he was effectively shut up. But the late Richard Crossman, a former Crown Minister, had among others been relentlessly scathing in his attacks on the Queen and her advisers for their arrogant refusal to disclose to Parliament the size of the private royal fortune. It is a mark of the Queen's personal popularity, combined with an indication of massive public indifference, that the Monarchy has got away with its courteous but ruthless resistance over this question, though the full story of that belongs in Chapter 2.

If the Crown continues to sail on with scarcely a ripple on the waters, it is because it thrives in our deferential, class-conscious, irrational society – a society laden with snobbery, humbug and hypocrisy. We are all expected to be eternally grateful for the Monarchy's presence. From the tiny tot to the tottering old lady, Britons are conditioned to revere and stand when the dirge of their imperialistic National Anthem is sung or played. The Queen's profile is there on every coin they spend and every stamp they lick. Yet, beneath the surface, there are unmistakable signs of restiveness and downright hostility towards the institution. Harold Nicolson may have seen in the Crown 'an emblem of continuity in a rapidly dissolving world', but an alternative viewpoint sees it as a cornerstone of reaction, conservatism and privilege in a world of revolution, change and challenge. For the moment, the British Monarchy may look safe and impregnable. But how long can it survive in its present form in a world of ever-rapid social and economic change?

In 1966, in his book *Long to Reign Over Us? The Status of the Royal Family in the Sixties* (1966), Leonard M. Harris made use of two sample surveys taken from people representative of the British population as a whole, categorized in terms of sex, age-groups, social and economic status, religion, regional distribution and political views. It is not surprising that the most ardent Royalist was found to be typified in an over-65-year-old lady who was Tory, Church of England and upper class. Not so surprising either was the fact that nearly two out of three in the 16 to 24 age-group thought a republic would be more progressive and forward-looking than a monarchy, and that half of the 25 to 44 age-group thought the same. Even among the over 65s, one in five believed a republic would be more progressive, and half of the 45 to 64 age-group held a similar view. And even though the Monarchy has a far stronger hold over women than over men, over all one in four women had reservations while one in ten was largely or entirely unfavourable and another one in ten couldn't have cared less.

No one can therefore honestly pretend, as foreigners often do, that the British are all wildly enthusiastic about their Monarchy. Americans and Frenchmen, with republics at home, are probably more ardently Royalist than most Britons. The grass on the other side of the fence always looks greener, and the museum-piece aspects of our Monarchy provide good tourist fodder. But if the republican tradition in Britain today does not feature in any party's political manifesto, it is far from being a dead issue. At any time a serious constitutional crisis could fan the sparks into red-hot flame. Only half the Labour Party's members throughout the country are reckoned to be 'entirely favourable' to the Monarchy, and one in three of Labour sympathizers' views vary between 'largely unfavourable' and 'complete lack of interest'. Naturally enough, the more 'left' a man's politics, the more anti-royalist are his sentiments. Within the Parliamentary Labour Party – usually regarded as being to the 'right' of its outside supporters – my own estimate is that at least one MP in three would vote for a republic given the chance. A majority of Labour MPs and Liberals certainly regard the Monarchy with a mixture of tolerance, healthy contempt, ridicule and apathy. The theme of apathy will, in fact, occur from time to time throughout this book, and I can personally vouch for the fact that bored indifference towards the Monarchy is not unknown among parliamentary Conservatives. Monarchists should not cosily assume that if the establishment of a republic were to become a radical issue in the near future, it would be doomed to failure.

The Monarchy itself is aware of the fragility of its hold on the public. That is why its image must be constantly burnished, why its public relations have become increasingly professionalized, and why news about the Royal Family is feverishly doctored and censored. The Monarchy in Britain today gives the impression of being on the defensive and of conducting a rearguard campaign. It is also, in itself, anxious to appear inoffensive and capable only of good: so, to many, we endure an uninspiringly dull institution. It is hard to imagine any present members of the Family achieving anything strongly individual or creative in their personal lives if they were to be stripped of their social advantages.

In his book *The Crown and the Establishment* (1943), Kingsley Martin attributed people's feeling that they needed a king to the individual's need for a 'father figure': to the yearning in each of us for someone to look up to; the craving for something which seems stable, simple and good in a world which is unstable, complex and strife-torn. And one aspect of the British character (against the equally important dissenting and sceptical aspects) has been a love of deference within the hierarchical tradition. Hereditary status is thought to convey magical qualities of worth, and these feelings still run strongly in parts of the national character. No matter if a hereditary Monarch is the biggest fool in Christendom, only a hereditary he or she can be brought up from birth trained to the task of kingship. That this is an irrational sentiment everyone knows if they are honest, for the *facts* have usually been otherwise. Queen Victoria was an ill-educated, reactionary busybody, who certainly didn't train her son for kingship – if she did, she was singularly unsuccessful. George VI was pushed unwillingly and unexpectedly on to the Throne, and survived the ordeal only because he had nothing to do while nothing he could say or do made any difference to anybody. Similarly, no one could seriously claim that Britain's present Queen was actually educated and trained to *know* her people. On the contrary, she lived almost as sheltered a life as any nun in a convent until she was pushed into the limelight, and the media and the Palace public relations machine began in 1952 desperately to create the dream of a New Elizabethan Era. The Coronation in that year was a striking pageant in which the Establishment worshipped God and Mammon simultaneously while satisfying the craving of the people to look up to somebody of exalted rank. It was a curious mixture of medieval feudalistic ritual and an ancient aristocracy brought out of mothballs for a day of 'Moss Bros.' magic. The total cost to the Exchequer was about £2 million. It was a sound investment in that it vastly helped to consolidate the tribal *status quo*. Moreover, the new Queen had the great advantage of being young and the first woman on the Throne in fifty years. People are naturally interested in a new situation – and here was a young lady who, beside providing that, was the 'divine' inheritor of her station in life, and who might lift the nation's eyes from the toil, thraldom and penury left by the wake of a cruel war. It offered an opiate at a time when opiates were needed.

It all seemed to work – more or less. Nothing untoward happened even remotely to suggest that an alternative kind of Head of State might be a better prospect. While wars and revolutions happened elsewhere, Britain, with its Queen enthroned, would remain steady as a rock, the very model of a nation wedded to the unquestioning acceptance of the civilized principles of law and order.

This myth – that the very existence of our Monarchy *guarantees* the continued acceptance of the principle of the rule of law – was, and is, assiduously fostered. Present events, both here and in the Commonwealth, have shown the danger of such nonsense. In fact, the opposite is probably nearer the truth: that the Monarchy continues to exist only *because* people accept the principle of the rule of law rather than the other way round. Quintin Hogg (now Lord Hailsham and former Lord Chancellor) in *The Case for Conservatism* (1947), attributed the fall of France and the survival of Britain in 1940 to the 'fact' that *we* had a Monarchy and the French had not. You would surely need to be hard-pressed to find a more absurd defence. Russia survived in the 1940s when all seemed lost. And what had happened to *their* Royal Family?

The common flaw in all these theories is that they view British society as deriving its stability, happiness and unity, such as they are, from the top downwards. The facts are otherwise. The inner strength of the British nation lies, above all, in the character of its people, with or without a monarchy. The form of political organization, the nature and extent of our natural resources and how they are used, our geographical position relative to our trade routes, the quality of our educational services, the family ethic – all these and many other factors are what matter in the end. The Monarchy has become an irrelevant ornament except for those who have a vested interest in its survival.

Meanwhile, to many people, the Queen still seems an emotional focal point for their sense of patriotism. In Britain the people prefer to have a king or queen, rather than a president, as a figure-head embodying their combined individualities and aspirations. Men simply cannot live by reason alone, any more than they can bear too much reality, as T. S. Eliot said. You don't have to *explain* the Monarchy on *reasonable* or *logical* grounds, because it can't be done, anyway. You can only say that it seems to work better than any other known form of state headship.

This links up well with the theory of inertia: that the British people are simply *used* to their Monarchy. They have been suckled on it, and have known nothing else. The British character is averse to change, which it suspects and even fears. It is a form of conservatism rooted in an innate distrust of the unknown. Better hold on to nurse, for fear of getting something worse. As D. W. Brogan put it in *The English People* (1943), 'The same archaic exterior covering modern interiors marks all aspects of English politics. Change anything except the *appearance* of things is the favourite English political method.' So the British monarchy is the ultimate pinnacle of British conservatism.

But there is still more to it, not least a love of the theatrical and a passion for colour, pomp and pageantry. The functions of both Crown and peerage to exploit the British craving for pageants, fancy dress, fairyland coaches and diamond-encrusted crowns are now far more important in ensuring the continuation of Crown and peerage than their now non-existent ritual and political functions.

Yet would not a circus do as well? Colour, pageantry, glitter and lots of coaches, clowns in ridiculous clothes and prancing horses? The difference is that the British people must also soak up a lifelong brainwashing about the value of the Monarchy – in schools, in the rapidly emptying churches, in a press which is largely and sycophantically pro-monarchist. If we are a conformist, conservative society, it is because life is easier that way. We derive a lazy satisfaction from accepting things as they are, and the Monarchy crystallizes and ossifies that smug contentment. We avidly display our deference, and we subconsciously recognize our dependence on the Queen in a kind of muted servility. When she does one of her well-publicized 'walkabouts' among the common herd, the people feel that *they* are on display to *her*, in a sort of culturally expected and socially sanctioned exhibitionism. It is deeply satisfying to those on display, hoping to be smiled at by however waxen a royal face, waved at by however mechanical a royal arm movement.

There is little doubt that many *believe* that our Monarchy *does* give Britain stability and unity. The papers, radio and television, the Church, teachers and authors, duchesses and peers, all tell them so. Britain's monarch is still 'Defender of the Faith', even though few of the Queen's subjects today think that faith worth defending or protecting. In the Monarchy is said to reside moral and gracious perfection: a model family with impeccable standards of behaviour, dedicated to serving the people.

The British Empire, they once told us, was held together by the Crown – as the Pope provides unity for Catholics all over the world. But, like Humpty Dumpty, the Empire has broken apart. So now, they say, the Crown keeps the *Commonwealth* together. True, it may *appear* to do so; but only provided the conditions for unity are already present. How long, for instance, will Ulster stay even in the United Kingdom? How long will Uganda or India remain in the Commonwealth? Pakistan has left. South Africa has gone her own racialist road. The unifying influence of the Monarchy is thus a gigantic hoax. Monarchical sentiment is learnt, like any other social custom. It is taught as we are taught to speak English and to say 'please' and 'thank you'.

The process of indoctrination starts early. History teaching in our schools is still often taught by reference to reigns of kings and queens. Royal photographs appear daily in newspapers, in women's magazines and on television. There are, endlessly, parades of brassy toy soldiers on beautiful horses – horses which live better than old-age pensioners. We have our national slogans: 'For King and Country' when soldiers are needed for savage wars; toasts 'To the Queen' at every business dinner or Tory nosh-up. We talk about 'The King's (or the Queen's) English' – which is no more than another dialect among many. Big rugby and football matches are preceded by brass-band renderings of the National Anthem – to the great irritation of fans in the terraces and players in the field. But still they conform. It's the done thing – and who the hell cares, anyway? Not so long ago, every cinema in the country had to play the National Anthem at the end of each day's programmes. The rush to get out of the doors before 'The Queen' came up on the screen grew too embarrassing and the rule was relaxed. And, every Sunday, those who attend an Established Church Service must pray for the whole of the Royal Family. The House of Commons does it every day. Less than a dozen MPs attend.

The influence of the Established Church as a powerful buttress to the Monarchy should not be underrated. The Church of England is the only Church which has permanent representatives in the House of Lords. And the personal oath of allegiance which every newly appointed bishop takes is vehemently anti-Roman Catholic. Bagehot wrote in *The English Constitution*: 'The English Monarchy strengthens our Government with the strength of religion . . . the Monarchy by its religious sanction now conforms all our political order.' If that was ever true, it is certainly not true today. But the Archbishop of Canterbury and his lesser fry have played meddling and often decisive roles – as in the crisis of Edward VIII's abdication in 1936.

Knowing they are vulnerable to the charge that they are now largely irrelevant and anachronistic, the Royals of today, as we have indicated, take their public relations very seriously. The more they have become exposed to the all-embracing mass media and a critical, questioning and articulate younger generation, the more the need has grown to project a new image. The Royal Family must be *shown* to be human, with a deft touch of humility and humour. However contrived, the strings must be pulled and manipulated by *professionals* who can gauge the audience.

The Royal Press Secretary, like all members of the Royal Household, is appointed by the Queen. The recommendation is made by the Lord Chamberlain, the senior member of the Queen's Household. The job is never advertised, but the man appointed has to know his way round the world of newspapers and the 'media' at large. The Press Office at Buckingham Palace stays on call twenty-four hours a day.

The PR side all began back in the reign of George III, when a Mr Doane was appointed to be Court Newsman. The appointment had been made on the advice of the Chief Metropolitan Magistrate after George III had grown angry about newspaper stories concerning his 'goings-on'. Mr Doane's job was to distribute daily to the morning papers an official version of royal movements, and this was called the Court Circular. It now appears as a curious anachronism only in such top 'establishment papers' as *The Times* and the *Daily Telegraph*.

From 1864 to 1886, a Mr Beard, who was Mr Doane's grandson, was Court Newsman. Mr Beard had to attend at Buckingham Palace twice daily – afternoon and evening – when Queen Victoria was in town, and once a day, Sundays included, when she was away from London. He also had to attend at Windsor Castle when needed, as well as at St James's when Court functions demanded it. His annual fee was £450. A Mr Phillips took the job over in 1886, and passed it down to his son, Mr W. Phillips, in 1899. In 1909, when Mr H. C. North took over, the annual fee was cut to £20, but it was recognized that the Court Newsman could take a rake-off from newspapers for information which he felt able to supply on his own responsibility.

After the First World War, in 1918, the first full-time, salaried Press Secretary was appointed to liaise with the press and feed them official announcements and information free of charge. In 1931, the office of Press Secretary was abolished and press matters were then for a time dealt with by the Assistant Private Secretary – part of the economy drive of the day. But, by 1944, the increased work-load led to the appointment of a new Press Secretary, and the Press Office at Buckingham Palace was opened under Captain Sir Lewis Ritchie with the help of one lady clerk. In 1947 Commander Richard Colville took over, plus one assistant press secretary to cope with the growing press interest in the Royal ladies – notably in Princess Elizabeth and her sister Princess Margaret. A part-time lady clerk was hired, who became full-time in 1952.

From that year the 'big sell' was on. In March 1958 a male Assistant Press Secretary was appointed from Canada – no doubt with the 1959 Royal Tour of Canada in mind. The Commonwealth flood now moved into full spate. In May 1959 a Ghanaian Assistant Press Secretary was temporarily employed in connection with the royal trip to Ghana later in the year.

Until 1959, the Queen's Press Secretary had been responsible for the press affairs of the Queen herself, her Consort, the Queen's children, and, of course, of Princess Margaret, besides advising all members of the Royal Family in general. It was no doubt a lot to handle, and after Commander Colville nearly ran the ship on the rocks over Princess Margaret's affair with Group Captain Peter Townsend, a bluff Australian cobber, Bill Heseltine, was brought in as a 'temporary' Assistant Press Secretary in February 1960. Meanwhile, in September 1959, Major John Griffin had assumed duties as Press Secretary to the Queen Mother, been given an office at Clarence House and taken over all press matters relating to the Queen Mother and Princess Margaret.

Mr Heseltine, after two separate periods as Assistant Press Secretary, finally took over from Sir Richard Colville (as he then was) on his retirement in 1968. Then, early in 1972, he handed over to his successor, Mr Robin Ludlow, previously on the staff of *The Economist*. But Ludlow lasted in the hot seat only until April 1973, when the job was passed to Mr Ronald Allinson, a former BBC sports commentator. The interesting thing about all this is that while the department's strength has remained virtually the same for the last fourteen years, the kind of person appointed has changed dramatically. We have travelled a long long way since Sir Richard Colville. With its appointment of Ludlow in 1972, the Palace had shown it recognized the importance of its image by getting a press man in to handle its public relations. The selection of Allinson, a lifelong journalist, was a further significant step in that direction. It was rumoured that Ludlow had had differences of opinion with the Palace, that he had wanted to ditch some of the starch and stuffiness and had failed.

What exactly does the Press Office do? My own attempts to get a personal interview with the Press Secretary himself have all been skilfully and diplomatically turned aside. On one occasion, the date and time were fixed. I had even been advised that I should use the tradesmen's entrance! Then, at the last moment, someone had to attend a funeral. A new date was fixed, but this time the State Visit to the Duchy of Luxembourg had been overlooked. What could be more understandable? No further dates were forthcoming, so as a last resort I put my questions in writing. The Palace *does* answer letters.

In fact, the Palace's handling of the media today reveals its string-pulling techniques at their most deftly skilful (see Appendix A). One of the main functions of the Press Secretary is to know *in advance* everybody the Queen is likely to meet on each official engagement: to answer any questions about the third man in a row whom she happens to smile at. He must also know how much time will be spent touring a factory, or the sort of dress the Queen will be wearing. For future reference, the Press Office enters all this information in an index roughly equivalent in size to the London telephone directories, and so makes instant access to such details available. The system works, as it is meant to work, entirely to the Palace's advantage. The press is fed only as much as the Palace wishes to feed it – and, like the Queen's usual formal little speeches, it's mostly painfully predictable and boring.

While, in theory, official royal engagements are open to the press at large, in practice journalists must work on a 'pool' basis. There are, claim the Palace, no 'ground rules' that must be followed by press or broadcasting organizations when royal visits are being covered.

> When arranging the facilities, the Press Secretary and his office always attempt to make sure that the press on the one hand are given adequate facilities to see, photograph and report on what is going on and, on the other hand, they attempt to make sure that facilities are such that they do not interfere with the dignity or propriety of any formal royal occasion. The only other 'rules' that exist are designed to facilitate this process by limiting the total number of photographers and cameramen present in close proximity to members of the Royal Family at such events. This is done by arrangement with the various newspaper or other organizations.

To put it crudely, the presentation is 'doctored'.

When the Queen boarded the famous flying white elephant, the Concorde aircraft, no copy journalists were allowed and only two photographers were permitted to go on the plane with her, one shooting in black and white, the other in colour. So the BBC and ITV camera crews tossed a coin. The BBC won and chose the plane, and ITV took all the outside shots. At the end of the day they swapped films.

The Palace censorship is gentle and subtle, but determined and effective. The gagging of the press is at its most expert on state visits overseas. On a recent South-East Asia tour, the Press Secretary went out two months beforehand to talk to Ministers of Information – in effect, his opposite numbers in the host countries. The purpose was to work out those engagements that would be free from the press altogether, those that would be open to a *few* press men, and those that would be a free-for-all. He also arranged the block booking of hotel accommodation for the camp followers, the telex lines to each country and other related matters. By the night before the Queen's arrival, most of the press were already there. The Press Secretary summoned them to a 'briefing' and laid down the 'ground rules': how close they were allowed to approach on official engagements; what transport would be available; the necessity for everybody to respect embargoes. British journalists on the whole wearily knew the form; the pep talk was mostly for the benefit of disrespectful foreigners.

The system is defended on the grounds that it works in everybody's interest. In fact it exploits the traditional laziness of the British journalist. What could become a hard, competitive overseas slog is transformed into a fairly easy joy-ride as everybody bands together. Twenty press passes may be available between sixty journalists. Those who attend functions brief those who don't. No one competes. There is no real pressure, everybody toes the line, and everyone is fed their ready-made copy fodder so long as they behave themselves.

The charade goes so far as for the *Daily Express* to publish photographs taken by *Daily Mirror* photographers and vice versa. And if there is an odd-ball (like a certain photographer called Bellasario) who doesn't play the game, the Palace simply takes away his reporter's accreditation. Apparently this happened on the 1967 New Zealand tour when two reporters got into the grounds of a house where the Queen was at a private reception. They were discovered. Their accreditation was removed. Their privileges were lost. They could no longer stay in the 'press' hotel, or use the 'press' bars, buses, planes or any other laid-on transport or the officially installed phones and telex. They were no more able to deliver the goods than neutered tom-cats. So they were packed off home, probably banned forever from any future overseas royal tours by their Editors.

On her tours the Queen usually gets to know the press quite well. She has a good memory for names. There *is* some informal contact, and in each foreign country she visits she will hold one cocktail party, mainly for the local press, but also to include the itinerant corps. It must all be kept absolutely off the record. For really 'good boys', there might even be jaunts on the Royal Yacht, or invitations to official receptions out of bounds to everyone else. This is again, of course, entirely off the record, but hopefully they enjoy the party.

No one would deny that royal tours overseas are exhausting affairs. The only question the sceptic will ask is whether the exhaustion and effort put into their preparation and execution is in any proportion at all to the infinitesimal long-term benefits which might accrue.

Back home, the Queen never gives interviews. If she did, what would she talk about? What *could* she talk about? All her official statements are made under ministerial guidance. If she emerged as someone with views on this or that question it would be the beginning of the end. Prince Philip, on the other hand, is allowed to hold views and to tread on a few corns from time to time. His occasional 'honest' outburst has indeed won him a measure of popularity. He might give up to a dozen interviews a year, usually on subjects which interest him, like wild-life preservation or his own Award Scheme. But if you want an interview with him, he decides (a) does he wish to see you, (b) has he the time, and (c) will it be worth while? (In my own case, I failed on all three criteria.) If you seek an interview with Prince Charles or Princess Anne, they do everything except take your fingerprints; and questions must be submitted beforehand in writing – just to make sure that the interview is serious.

The only other way in which pressmen can catch the Royal Family off duty is when they are taking their recreations – usually with and on horses – at Ascot Race Week, at the Badminton Horse Trials jamboree, or at polo matches in Windsor Great Park.

At Badminton, in April 1973, Princess Anne grew highly irate with the press photographers, who appeared mainly interested in catching her in the saddle with her boy friend, Lieutenant Mark Phillips, as soon as it seemed that the sound of wedding bells was in the air. But even at these events, much care is taken to set up the 'proper' photos: mum watches daughter riding by. It's a hardy annual and the hour is fixed; then the press must leave. If, by accident, a photographer should catch a Royal in an embarrassing or unguarded moment, he will not be able to sell his prize to any British newspaper or magazine, though he might dispose of it to some scurrilous publication on the Continent. But then, if he is identified as the photographer, that will be the last time he gets the chance.

One man who has made himself the sworn enemy of the Palace by photographing Royals in off-guard moments is the well-known Mr Bellasario, mentioned earlier. He has been at it since 1960, and has made himself a fortune. It is not a very defensible or gentlemanly exercise, of course, but neither is it a criminal offence. Even so, Mr Bellasario must be a man of unusual tenacity and ruthlessness to have taken on this running battle. He has probably studied the Royal Family at closer (and more ruffled) quarters than any other photographer or journalist.

Every British mission abroad has instructions to cut out any Bellasario article about, or picture of, the Queen, for forwarding to the Foreign Office and thence to Buckingham Palace. Commander Colville himself originally cancelled Bellasario's press accreditation, and then wrote to all the magazines who had bought his pictures in the past to 'encourage' them not to employ 'this detestable young man'. The Queen has herself complained to the Press Council about Bellasario's pictures, most notably in 1964, when the council upheld her complaint. Photographs of the Queen water skiing, it said, had been obtained by trespass, though Bellasario still denies this is so. He contends, with ample justification, that the main concern of the Palace authorities is to ensure that, *at all times*, the image of the Royal Family is portrayed *as they want it to be*.

But the Press Office at Buckingham Palace asserts that it does not exist to present an 'image' of the Royal Family; that there is no 'exposure schedule' for the Queen; that, if there seems to be a risk of her losing 'magic' by too many public appearances, these are not cut down. No official polls are taken to test her popularity. If the Queen grows annoyed with the press – and it sometimes happens – she might have the offending paper phoned or the editor written to. In general, however, the Press Office is pleased with its relations with the media. The only thing that could really foul things up would be another series of articles by one of the Queen's personal servants. But they are, today, all sworn to secrecy.

The basic purpose of the Press Council, set up in 1953, is to deal with public complaints about press behaviour. The indications are that, so far as the Royal Family is concerned, complaints tend to be brought by the public more than by the Royal Household itself. In 1954, however, Commander Colville did complain to the Council about the publication by the *Sunday Pictorial* of the experiences of a valet who had been two years in the service of the Duke of Edinburgh. There were two main stories in the memoirs: the honeymoon of Princess Elizabeth and the Duke, and the trip to Kenya during which the Princess learnt she had become Queen. The *Pictorial* claimed that, since it had published extracts from a book, what it had printed was public knowledge anyway. They also argued that the stories were not derogatory, that there were no intimate confidences and that nothing had been said that was likely to cause distress. Colville replied by letter to say that, while it had long been the custom for royal servants to tell what the butler saw, this had recently been tightened up. The *Pictorial* was therefore aiding and abetting a breach of trust, and possibly a breach of contract. His letter was circulated by the Press Council to newspapers, with a request for its contents to be noted.

Also in 1954, the *Daily Mirror* proposed to conduct a poll among its readers as to whether Princess Margaret should be allowed to marry a handsome divorcee, Group Captain Peter Townsend, if she wished to. They were frowned on by the Press Council, but undeterred returned to the theme. 'For Pete's sake put him out of his misery,' growled the *Mirror*. Foul play, gasped the Press Council, even though there was much to be said for the *Mirror*'s point that the matter was of legitimate interest since it could potentially involve Church, State, Crown *and* Constitution. We didn't want another 1936, did we?

Then, in 1956, the former Deputy Controller of Supply to the Royal Family published in *Woman* magazine a series called 'I Shopped for the Royal Family'. The Palace, in its complaint, did not suggest that the articles contained anything offensive or even indiscreet. But, Colville reminded the Council, papers *had* been asked to respect the privacy of the Queen's home life. Mary Grieve, as editor of *Woman*, said there were many precedents for similar articles. She believed that readers were sincerely interested in the personal and domestic life of the Royal Family, and that such articles sustained affection for the Monarchy (and, no doubt, the circulation of *Woman*!). The object of the articles, she said, had been to show, in a broad way, how the ways of the Royal Household had been adapted to the nation's changed life. She wanted to know whether Commander Colville was complaining only about particular passages, or whether he supported a complete ban on any information given to the press about the personal activities of the Royal Family. She added that the author had never given any undertaking not to write about his experiences. She felt that a ruling which sought to raise a fence around the Sovereign would not be in the lasting interests of the Monarchy. Colville replied that *all* articles about the Queen, no matter what they contained, infringed her privacy.

By then relations between the Palace and the press had grown so bad that a complaint was relayed by the Press Council to the Palace that the Palace Press Office neither gave nor understood the news that the papers wanted, nor gave the necessary guidance on what was, or was not, likely to become news. At this point Colville approached the Press Council to see what might be done to improve matters. Three proposals emerged: (1) That the quality and supply of news from the Palace should be improved. (2) That newspapers should refrain from tempting royal servants to breach their contracts by offering them large sums of money for their reminiscences. And (3) that royal news should at all times be handled with discretion.

Serious attempts were thus made to strike a balance between the legitimate need of the Royal Family to enjoy some degree of privacy, and the equally legitimate commercial need of the press to feed the people with abundant royal tittle-tattle.

But problems have kept cropping up in the least expected ways. In 1965, for example, when Princess Margaret was delivering an address to Royal Air Force personnel in Germany, seven words were deleted from the official script released to the press. These had referred to the number of German planes shot down during the Battle of Britain, and the Princess did not say them. 'Margaret Censored' screamed a *Daily Express* headline. The *Daily Sketch* said the cut had been made to avoid hurting German feelings. So Margaret's Press Secretary asked the Press Council if reporting the written part of a speech omitted in delivery, or comment on an unofficially supplied brief or script, was in accord with journalistic ethics. On this the Council was split, having three views. The first view was that, if the deleted part was confidential, then the press should have been specifically told so. The second was that the Palace should have given an official on-the-record explanation of the deletions. And the third was that it should be accepted journalistic practice to ignore such deletions. On balance, the council felt that the deletion should not have been reported without the speaker's express permission.

Complaints against that most respected of newspapers, the Sunday *Observer*, have further underlined the problem. A year or two before the Duke of Windsor died, he came to London for an eye operation and the *Observer* published a harsh cartoon by Trog. This showed the Duke in dark glasses being pushed in a wheel-chair, and his Duchess saying to him, 'And what she doesn't seem to realize is that without me she wouldn't have been Queen.' The more than three decades of social ostracism meted out to the Duke and his wife by the Royal Family had, quite rightly, been regarded as a discreditable and hidebound episode by many people not normally over-critical of the Monarchy. The editor of the *Observer* said the connection between the Queen and the Duchess was a proper point to make. But, if some people thought the Duke's illness was being satirized, he regretted that impression. The Press Council still held the cartoon to be offensive and distasteful.

Later the *Observer* was in trouble again over another Trog creation. This one showed Labour's Prime Minister, Harold Wilson, kissing the Queen's hand on the eve of his departure to meet Ian Smith, the Rhodesian rebel against the Crown. The caption showed the Queen saying, 'Don't feel you have to fly back each day to report, Prime Minister.' It seemed good stuff at the time. Yet one reader complained that it showed discourtesy to the Queen, and did no service to the Prime Minister at a time of crisis, by implying that substantial checks on the governing party in this country are tiresome and laughable. 'Cartoons of royalty and monarchs have been published in this country for the past 200 years without diminution of the Royal Family's prestige. Certainly no unfriendliness was intended by Trog,' commented the *Observer*. The joke was more on Wilson than on the Queen – on his well-known love of consultation and kissing the Monarch's hand. The Press Council rejected the complaint.

When, in 1964, the Queen had her last baby, the *Daily Express* obtained photographs of the Queen in bed with the new Prince shortly after his birth. They had already been published in France, and the American magazine *Life* had bought them. They were appearing throughout the Commonwealth. The *Express*, in publishing them, argued that the pictures had been shown to the Palace and commented that, since they had already been published in other countries, the British people should not be denied the same privilege. 'The Queen would have preferred that these photographs . . . of so personal a nature had not been published,' said the Press Council: for that reason they were 'unable to approve of further publication'. But the *Express* had a commercial scoop on a scale with which questions of taste could not be allowed to interfere. Further pictures were published the next day – plus a leading article on the subject. Individual complainants were answered by Mr Derek Marks, the newspaper's editor. He had had no specific request from the Palace *not* to publish the pictures. Indeed, in his view they were 'of a most seemly nature and could be calculated only to show the Queen and the Royal Family in a most favourable light.' It was confirmed by the Queen's Press Secretary, Mr Heseltine, that the Queen had made no direct request for the pictures not to be published. But, he said, 'Her Majesty trusts . . . that it will not be allowed to form a precedent for the future publication of private photographs, either of her own family or of those of any of her people.'

The end of the episode was that the Press Council found that Mr Marks had acted properly in notifying the Palace of his possession of the pictures, and that if the Queen had directly requested that they should not be published, it would have been wrong of the *Express* to have done so. In the circumstances, the Editor 'had not exercised his discretion improperly' (note the cautious double negative). So, the complaints were rejected – on the understanding that no such thing would ever happen again.

The *Sunday Express* had not been so lucky in 1966. The newspaper, through Mr Robin Douglas Home, had written to Prince Philip's secretary asking if the Prince could be interviewed by him on the role of the Monarchy in present-day Britain. The *Sunday Express* and Prince Philip have never been the greatest of friends, and the request was refused – on the grounds that 'the difficulties attaching to giving an exclusive interview on this subject were too great'. Then the oddest thing happened: the *Sunday Times* gleefully announced that the Prince had already given it an exclusive interview on that very subject. The *Express* criticized the Duke for giving preferential treatment to a paper which had his brother-in-law, Lord Snowdon, on its staff.

Colville, as the Queen's Press Secretary, complained that that could be called dishonest journalism. The Press Council rapped the *Express* as having no ground for complaint against the Duke.

So relationships between the Palace and the media have not been all plain sailing, even if, on the whole, the media does co-operate fully in propping up the institution of the Monarchy and if the journalists who deal with them (not normally a breed noted for sensitivity or respect for privacy in adversity when news is in the air) are a conforming and house-trained gaggle.

The BBC has actually had a senior staff member acting as liaison officer with the Palace since 1930, though it has never been a full-time job. There is no record of how the liaison began or from whom the initiative came. The liaison officer consults with all the Royal Households, but not directly with any individual member of the Family – that would never do. The BBC states that it tries to cover all royal occasions 'responsibly and appropriately': telescopic lenses and zoom microphones are banned. The BBC would clearly never appoint to such a delicate post a known republican or anti-monarchist – nor even a Roman Catholic. He must obviously be a 'safe establishment man'.

The biggest and most professional public relations job ever achieved in defence of the Monarchy was the well-known BBC television film that showed how the Royal Family are really just like you and me. This film, the official press hand-out said, was in response to world-wide requests following the announcement that Prince Charles would be invested as Prince of Wales in 1969. Like Lenin and Dr Goebbels, though many years later, the Royals had realized the hypnotic propaganda value of the screened moving image.

The film as it turned out was a large-scale commercial, lasting 105 minutes with a gestation period of eleven months: seventy-five days' shooting; 125,000 feet of film in 172 different locations. 'The Queen and her family were filmed in unrehearsed conversation both on and off duty throughout the year . . . The Queen saw the completed film; no cuts were made or asked for,' ran the press guff. But the job had already been done for her: 105 minutes had been skilfully selected from 43 hours of film. It is a safe bet that an anti-monarchist film editor, let loose with the same raw material, could have wrested from it a far less complimentary image.

But the illusion was complete: the film was top billing all over the world, especially in Canada and Australia. The Common wealth actually saw the British Queen feeding a carrot to her horse; watched the family have a barbecue; listened to their mundane conversation at the dining table; and saw them gathered around their TV set, evidently enjoying the cultural delights of an American slap-dash comedy show. The Monarchy came over like a well-tried washing powder, washing whiter than white. It was the real defender of our liberties and, while it remained, tyranny and dictatorship would be kept at bay. (No mention, of course, of how the monarchies in Germany and Greece – both producers of British royalty – managed to keep tyranny at bay during the present century.)

At first, ugly rumours went about that the Royal Family was insisting on all profits made from the film coming back to them. Later (much later), in reply to a direct inquiry, the Palace assured me that profits were going to charity.

The Royal Film is regarded in Palace circles as having been a great watershed – the greatest public relations *coup* of the reign. That may be a mistaken view. A hundred years ago, Walter Bagehot feared that the exposure of the Monarchy to a Select Committee would destroy its magic. Its doctored exposure to the TV cameras may, in the long run, prove to have been a fatal error of judgement. The film protested too much, and sought to convince the public too much. Its underlying theme – of how much the Royal Family is just like any other family in the land – is, in fact, a theme challenged in the whole of this book. At the end, readers can make up their minds for themselves about the truth or falsehood of the film's implicit claim.

We have therefore seen some of the ways in which the Monarchy in Britain today is approaching the problem of survival, short of making themselves the subject of a Grade I Preservation Order. But the times are changing. Recently, when Princess Anne's engagement to her soldier friend was announced, she was asked what plans they had for a family, who had proposed to whom, did they make love in a horsebox? A bit earlier, somebody got himself sacked from the weekly *Spectator* for wondering whether Anne was on the Pill. None of this had been referred to the Press Council.

The press is growing bolder. The new generation of journalists (as opposed to the eternal gossip columnists) is more likely to demand a strictly realistic approach to facts as they are and less likely to cooperate with the humbug of hidebound protocol. It will be interesting to see how the Royal Family manages to continue the process of coming to terms with the media over the next few years. They are certainly aware that their survival depends in large measure on a successful outcome to this adjustment.

2. THE PRICE OF MONARCHY

THE ORIGINS OF THE CIVIL LIST

It is over 200 years since the British people were first cursed and exploited by the German Hanoverians – a profligate, corrupt bunch of monarchs hedged about by German camp-followers and the all-powerful British aristocracy. The story of these inefficient, grasping foreigners is known in some detail. 'The time is not very distant,' wrote Tom Paine, rather over-optimistically, in *The Rights of Man* (1792), 'when England will laugh at itself for sending to Holland, Hanover, Zell or Brunswick for men, at the expense of a million a year, who understood neither her language, nor her interest, and whose capacities would scarcely have fitted them for the office of parish constable.'

The sordid details need not detain us. George III had died in 1820, after years of mental confusion and raving brought on by his curious illness. George IV wasn't any better a king. The political repression, corruption, ineptitude and cruelty which had driven the American Colonies to revolt continued as before. The Parliament of the day, unrepresentative of anything but wealth and privilege, granted the wretched new king an increased state income of half a million pounds – representing many tens of millions in modern money. No questions asked, no witnesses examined, no documents produced. More than that, the income from the Crown Lands – the so-called private property of the King surrendered in 1760 by George III – was left to the uncontrolled use of Ministers, for parliamentary corruption, war, the perpetration of injustice and the suppression of the mob. The Royal Household itself was described as 'a great nursery of indolence, parasites, and courtiers'.

The modern Civil List is assumed to have begun in 1760; but the first Civil List Act had been passed in 1697, and grants for the support of the Crown have been made by Parliament since the Restoration. In 1689 Parliament had voted an annual sum of £600,000 to William and Mary for the running of the civil government. The Civil List thus began as a payment to each king on his accession for the running of the whole apparatus of civil government. In those days a king *ruled and reigned.* George II had talked his Parliament into giving him £800,000 a year. And if the cost of government didn't reach the figure, he pocketed the difference – to enormous profit. A highly developed acquisitive instinct seems to be the outstanding characteristic of royalty down the ages.

Throughout the eighteenth century the Civil List was a source of great controversy. The income of innumerable politicians, public figures and tradesmen depended on it; and they waxed fat. Mr Edmund Burke, the arch-priest of late eighteenth-century Toryism, was one of the greatest critics of royal extravagance and corruption. He managed to get an Act passed in 1782 to curb it; but he himself had netted £87,000 between 1795 and 1830. As royal debts mounted, so the demand for closer scrutiny grew. And it was in this context that a 'bargain' was struck with the 1760 Civil List. The Crown was to be relieved of the entire cost of running the Government in return for surrendering the revenues of the Crown Lands. An annual sum, to be fixed at the start of each reign, was to be made meanwhile for running the Royal Family business. It does not seem such a good bargain today, when income from the Crown Lands is less than £5 million a year and the cost of government runs into thousands of millions.

In 1777, the Civil List was increased to £900,000 a year, but debts continued to mount and politicians to criticize. No wonder. In 1816 a financial statement was presented to Parliament. It was a revelation. The details were set out in the *Black Book* of 1831. It is sufficient here to enumerate a few of the handouts: the King's Master of the Hawks, £1,372 10s., the Chancellor of the Garter, £570 5s., the Groom of the Stole, £2,000, the Constable of Dover Castle, £4,100, the Lord Almoner for Alms, £1,119, and the Chairman of the Westminster Sessions, for dinners, £214 3s. Miscellaneous Lords and Ladies came on the pension payroll: the Dowager Duchess of Newcastle £1,000 a year, Lady Augusta

Murray £1,200, the Earl of Rochford £1,000 – to mention only a few. Pensions were excluded from Queen Victoria's Civil List of £385,000 a year. But the monarch could (and can) pay some pensions to her favourites. Victoria's Albert, the shrewd if high-minded German Prince Consort, managed to make some economies in the Royal Household. These, together with her income, enabled Victoria to pay £200,000 for the attractive house of Osborne, on the Isle of Wight, while Albert paid £300,000 for the Sandringham estate, which he purchased on behalf of his son, the Prince of Wales. Balmoral, in Scotland, had also been bought in 1852. The combined acreage of Sandringham and Balmoral was (and is) 47,000 acres – a bit more than a pair of pleasant private royal houses and gardens.

As royal wills are not published, no one knows how wealthy Queen Victoria was when she died. It is, of course, improper to inquire into such matters. Money only becomes disreputable when a working man is trying to get his share of the cake. However, Edward VII's Civil List was £470,000 a year, of which his Privy Purse, or private salary, was £110,000. Edward was 60 by the time he came to the throne. Having been Prince of Wales for half a century, he must have amassed a huge fortune from the revenues of the Duchy of Cornwall. The story of the duchies, however, belongs in the next chapter. Edward VII trailed behind him a good-humoured if shallow record of extravagance, vulgarity and dissipation. When he died Lord Esher said of him, 'He had an instinct for statecraft . . . He had one supreme gift, and that was his unerring judgement of men and women.' Especially women.

The Civil List figure was to remain unchanged, at £470,000 a year, until 1936. It was then, on the face of it, reduced to £410,000. This had been made possible in part by George V's temperamental austerity and his economies, largely during the First World War. Excessive entertaining was out, and the King wished for the money saved to go to the Exchequer.

The Civil List figure was held at £410,000 throughout the reign of George VI. His death, in 1952, ushered in the reign of the present Queen, the 'New Elizabethan Age'.

THE CORONATION AND THE 1952 CIVIL LIST

The Coronation of Elizabeth II on 2 June 1953 in Westminster

Abbey may justly be ranked among the century's greatest-full-colour spectaculars. On that day, 'this country and the Commonwealth were not far from the Kingdom of Heaven', said the Archbishop of Canterbury. John Masefield, as Poet Laureate, chimed in with 'Prayer for a Beginning Reign';

> Grant, KING OF KINGS, All-Merciful, All-Knowing,
> That in Her reign Her people may advance
> In all fair knowledge of starry sowing
> In all arts that rejoice
> In beauty of sound of instrument and voice,
> In colour and form that leave the soul befriended
> In ancient joy, our Land's inheritance,
> In thought, the quest for guidance never-ended
> For Light of THINE to make our living splendid
> In service to the Queen who guides our going.

You would never guess from Masefield's lines, heavy as dumplings, that he had once been a sensitive, talented versifier. Perhaps this threadbare bilge was more symbolic of the occasion than he would have cared to admit.

The fact remained that, after the sacrifices of the war years and the grey desperation of their struggle for recovery from near bankruptcy, the British people could, for a glorious moment, soak themselves in a fairyland of romantic delusion. For one day they could forget such cruel realities as food rationing, while the aristocracy, dukes and archbishops beckoned them back to medieval grandeur. To some it undoubtedly seemed a profound spiritual experience. And there it was, all on the telly for the very first time.

But while the Archbishop of Canterbury might say that the nation 'was at Holy Communion', others were out for the quick buck. One Greek Street auction for tickets, said to give access to a flat which overlooked the entrance to Westminster Abbey, saw four sold for £591. In fact the flat was a hundred yards distant. Then there was a row over families who were being evicted from furnished accommodation by landlords who wanted to relet to foreign visitors. One hotel in Kensington charged 5 guineas a head a night for a room shared by eight. The Duke of Wellington received substantial rent for the use of Apsley House. The Government declined to say how much they and Thomas Cook, the travel agents, had paid to rent his garden so that seats could be erected there, but it was reputed to be £6,000. Yet, only six years before, £50,000 of public money had been used to repair bomb damage to Apsley House *and* to provide the Duke with a rent-free flat while the work was done.

There were other problems. Even with velveteen instead of real velvet, and rabbit skin instead of ermine, the cost of a peer's robes would come to £145, plus £100 tax. A *velvet* robe, with rabbit trimmings, would cost £200, plus £130 tax. And the *real thing* would set a peer back £750, plus £500 tax. The aristocracy had fallen on evil, harsh days. Bad (blue) blood was caused by restrictions on access for the Lords of the Realm to see the ceremony in Westminster Abbey. A ballot would be unfair, don't you see? So peers under 21 were kept out.

A ballot was, however, thought appropriate for London's schoolchildren, and one in ten, or 33,000 of them, saw the procession. However, in 1953 children were so much fatter than at the previous coronation that, in fact, 7,000 fewer seats were available.

Then, plans to roast oxen were hampered when no chef could be found willing to take the responsibility of ruining several thousand people's meat rations at one go. And details of the Coronation Service were held up a little when nobody could decide whether the Duke of Edinburgh or the Archbishop of Canterbury should be first to pay homage to the Queen. There was no precedent. The Duke won. On the positive side, British medal manufacturers supplied a million Coronation souvenir medals to the colonies. I wonder what became of them (the medals, I mean)?

Lancashire textile firms weren't so lucky. The Queen's head could be reproduced on headsquares, but not, absolutely *not*, on hankies! Codes of conduct passed down similarly forbade the use of the Duke of Edinburgh's face on ice-cream wrappers or in any advertisement. A picture on a chocolate box was acceptable – so long as the manufacturer's name appeared only on the inside. And it could be used for a 'good-quality calendar'. Failure to comply was not a criminal offence, but it would be a breach of good taste. The uninhibited Japanese reaped rich harvests.

The usual crop of spoilsports was also in evidence. The borough surveyor of Twickenham sent a circular to householders to say that bunting was illegal – and he quoted Section 25 of the Public Health Act of 1925 and the Road Traffic Act of 1930. The Labour-controlled borough of Barking in the East End of London, uninspired and unimpressed by the fact that £825 was being paid for a Wedgwood dinner service for use at the Coronation dinner, declined to spend any money at all on Coronation celebrations. Several prominent Labour politicians had a bit of a moan. 'Why should we have all this neurotic outburst?' asked Barbara Castle. 'I hope it is the last Coronation of this kind this country will ever see, utterly unrepresentative as it is of the Britain and the Commonwealth of the ordinary people.'

And John Freeman, later British Ambassador to India and then to the United States, said, 'I disapprove of the ceremony of establishing the Head of the State in which we all have a share, and using it as an occasion for the glorification of every kind of anti-socialist belief, and every myth that can be found anywhere in our history. It is possible to have a constitutional monarch without this waste of money and ballyhoo.' David Low's cartoon in the *Manchester Guardian* was more brutally to the point. 'The Morning After', it was called; with a £100 million price-tag and a tattered book of *Fairy Princess Tales*.

But the show went on. Six distinguished British composers had been commissioned to write special music for the Coronation service. Seventy musicians were drawn from the nation's best orchestras, and a 400-voice choir shook the Abbey rafters. Outside there were 15,000 policemen on duty, and 29,000 troops – though troops on duty during the Coronation ceremony and its rehearsals had to be quartered in disused air-raid shelters under the House of Commons since there was no room for them elsewhere.

The new reign was off to a sparkling start. The only problem left was how to meet the bill.

THE 1952 CIVIL LIST

Michael Foot, the only Member of Parliament still in the House of Commons to have sat on the 1952 Committee, remembers how Winston Churchill, as Prime Minister and Chairman of the Civil List Committee, exerted a powerful influence. Churchill, as an arch-monarchist, desperately hoped to see the royal cash problem disposed of without unseemly rancour and with all speed. He did not want the reign of the young Queen to be launched with any sordid wrangle over money. By and large he had his way.

One or two of the Labour Members on the Committee murmured hesitating dissent. But nothing ever came of it. Labour's Leader, Clem Attlee, was as royalist as Churchill. No evidence of the Committee's proceedings was recorded or published, though there was little enough of it. Nobody attempted to produce a minority report. Some Labour MPs attempted a few amendments to the Report, both in Committee and in the Commons debate, but all were heavily defeated. The leading mouthpieces of the radical left, Michael Foot himself, an eloquent and brilliant debater, and Aneurin Bevan, the finest Welsh orator since Lloyd George, stayed strangely silent. Perhaps the Monarchy was felt to be a petty irrelevance, a meaningless bauble scarcely worth wasting one's breath on.

The debates in the Commons went their predictable way. The 1952 settlement gave the Queen £475,000 a year, which included £70,000 to take care of post-war inflation, and another £25,000 for those members of the Royal Family not specifically provided for otherwise. There was also an item of £13,200 for 'Royal bounty and alms'. So, when Her Majesty 'gave generously' to charity, she was in fact dipping into the arbitrary sum under this heading.

The former salary provision of £110,000 was, however, cut to £60,000. But this was done for two reasons. First, a separate annuity of £40,000 was made to Prince Philip out of the Consolidated Fund, whereas, in the previous reign, the personal financial needs of both the King and Queen had been provided out of the Privy Purse. Secondly, the Queen voluntarily accepted a 'cut' in salary of £17,000 a year – a ploy to be repeated even more strikingly in 1971. There was also the fact that the wages of all industrial workers employed on the upkeep of the Royal Palaces were transferred to the responsibility of the new Ministry of Works. (The wages bill of £25,000 a year in 1952 has subsequently grown to well over £2 million.)

Other annuities ran as follows: to the Queen Mother £70,000, to the Duke of Gloucester £35,000, and to Princess Margaret £15,000. The figures were purely arbitrary. Nobody knew how they were arrived at, and so nobody could challenge them.

We will come to Prince Charles shortly. Meanwhile the Queen's other (and as yet unborn) children were not forgotten. Younger sons would receive £10,000 a year at the age of 21, increasing to £25,000 on marriage. Daughters would get £6,000 a year at 21, and £15,000 when they wed. The rest of the family had to depend on the largesse of the Queen and how she thought fit to dole out the £25,000 a year granted to her by Parliament for the purpose. The upper limit on Civil List pensions, which has stood at £2,500 since 1937, was raised to £5,000. At that time the basic old-age pension was still under £100 a year!

Prince Charles was by then 4 years old, and already Duke of Cornwall. No separate financial provision was made, for was he not the 'private owner' of the Duchy of Cornwall, consisting of vast estates and property in London and South-West England? Charles would receive one ninth of the net revenues of the Duchy until he was 18, to provide 'partly for his maintenance and education and partly for the accumulation of a moderate capital sum for him on attaining his majority', the balance to go to the Exchequer. Then, between 18 and 21, he would have £30,000 a year from Duchy revenues. At 21 he would take the lot. So, between 1953 and 1970, the young prince accumulated his 'moderate capital sum' – about half a million pounds, entirely tax free. And was that all? No, not quite. A solemn provision of £30,000 a year was made for the four-year-old Prince Charles's hypothetical widow.

Not even this last absurdity could draw the fire of the official Labour Opposition. There were, it is true, a few rude Labour men from Scotland who wanted to cut the pay of the delightful Queen Mother and the idle Princess Margaret and who wondered what on earth Prince Philip would *do* with his £40,000 and thought it might at least be reduced by £10,000. But they got nowhere. Even Prince Charles's widow's pension escaped unscathed. When it came to the vote, most Labour MPs, including Aneurin Bevan, Michael Foot and Tom Driberg, had gone into the Tory lobby: the 'radical left' had paraded like chocolate soldiers. The only *official* Labour amendment had sought to provide for ten-yearly reviews of the Civil List, and that was turned down. It would be unseemly to seem to be looking too closely and too often into questions of royal expenditure. The contract was for a whole reign, and provision *had* been made for inflation, purred that smoothest of Chancellors, R. A. Butler. The House yawned, and went home.

THE CIVIL LIST OF 1972

The deliberations that produced the 1972 Civil List were the only ones in which I was ever closely involved, so I hope readers will be patient if some aspects of this story take on a personal note.

By the late 1960s, with the Wilson administration still in power, rumbles of discontent over the state of the royal finances began to be heard in Parliament. The £70,000 a year provided in

1952 as a hedge against inflation had served its purpose well enough during the early years of the reign, and as figures released later showed, the whole amount had not been needed in that early period. Up to 1961 a surplus was built up. But then it was steadily whittled away. Much ill-informed comment began to appear in the press on the Royal Family's wealth and tax position.

"My husband and I . . ."

On 21 December 1968, *The Economist*, never less than an authoritative, respectable high-Tory weekly, ran an article which said: 'The Royal fortunes at the time of the 1760 "bargain" yielded £6,000 a year. It's now worth millions of pounds' – the presumption being that the State was making a handsome *profit* out of the Monarch. 'Prince Charles pays tax,' the journal continued. 'As a result, out of his extra £175,000 a year [then the net revenue of the Duchy of Cornwall], *only* about £15,000 will actually be available for spending.' There was no factual basis for this statement, as we will see later (p. 86). However, to be fair to *The Economist*, the article did go on to say about the prospect of new inquiry that 'the ensuing debate would be better informed if the size of the Sovereign's tax-free fortune were known'. It was a sanguine hope. Things finally came to the boil early in November 1969 when Prince Philip announced during an American television interview that Britain's Monarchy would be 'in the red' by 1970. He then made some flippant remarks about having to sell a polo pony or two, and being forced to move to a smaller house. In jest, of course. But the effect was like lighting a bush fire. Press articles poured from Fleet Street and sold like hot cakes. Motions and counter-motions appeared in the House of Commons Order Paper.

On 11 November, Mr Wilson felt the time had come to make a statement in the House of Commons. He disclosed that, in 1968–9, discussions had been going on between Treasury officials and the Queen's advisers, as a result of which 'the Government informed the Queen's advisers that a new Select Committee would be appointed at the beginning of the next Parliament'. 'There is no need,' said the Prime Minister, 'for earlier action.' He did not mention that there *had* been earlier action. Several items of expenditure previously borne by the Royal Household had already been transferred to other Government Departments, including the costs of royal tours overseas and the costs of rail travel on royal functions within the UK.

Prince Philip's outburst over his family penury on American television looked like an attempt to put the political screws on these discussions. But, rather to my surprise, in answer to a direct question, Prince Philip has said he knew nothing about them (see page 238 of the Appendices).

The Tory Opposition forthwith pressed for the *immediate* appointment of the proposed Select Committee. 'Has the Prime Minister a soul?' pleaded Sir Arthur Vere Harvey (later rewarded with a peerage). But Wilson resisted. If the royal difficulties became intolerable they could be resolved by recourse to funds'. No Member pressed him on what these might be. When he reviewed Richard Crossman's *Inside View* for the *New Statesman* on 5 May 1972, Harold Wilson wrote, 'Tories can afford reverence and idolatry. A reforming party cannot. Ours fortunately never tries.' It is not easy to recognize Wilson's own record in this statement – certainly not in his relationship with the Palace and its denizens. But the relationship between Labour leaders and Royalty is a subject which deserves (and has been given) its own chapter.

The election of that summer was won by the Conservatives. The pay claim from the Queen arrived at the House of Commons in due course on 19 May 1971. Called 'Her Majesty's most Gracious Message', and 'signed by Her Majesty's own hand', it was read to the House by Mr Speaker ('all Members of the House being uncovered'):

> Her Majesty requests that consideration should be given by the House of Commons to the provision for Her Civil List made by Parliament in the first year of Her reign. Her Majesty regrets that developments in the intervening years have made that provision inadequate for the maintenance of that standard of service to Her people to which She believes they wish Her and Her family to adhere, and has commanded that the Papers necessary for a full consideration of the subject shall be laid before the House.
>
> Her Majesty desires also that consideration be given to improving the provisions made for HRH The Duke of Edinburgh, and other members of Her family, and the provision made in the first year of Her father's reign for HM Queen Elizabeth the Queen Mother and HRH The Duchess of Gloucester; and that provision be made now for HRH The Duchess of Gloucester and any future wife of a younger son of Her Majesty in the event of any of them surviving her husband.
>
> Her Majesty, being anxious to limit the burden that any new provision will impose on Her people at this time, is content to forgo the provision made by Parliament for Her Privy Purse.
>
> In commending these several matters to her faithful Commons, Her Majesty relies on their attachment to Her person and family to adopt such measures as may be suitable for the occasion.

The tone was fulsome and bold, but the attachment of the Commons to 'Her person and family' is not so secure as her advisers would like to think. A debate on the motion to set up a Select Committee took place on the next day, the 20th, even though Harold Wilson had made clear his hopes that there would be no debate, and that, if there was, no proposed committee members would take part.

A suggestion from John Grant, the Labour Member for East Islington, that the Committee might meet in public 'in view of the fog which surrounds the Royal finances'; and another from the blunt left-wing trade-unionist Norman Atkinson that the Committee should be able to subpoena witnesses – including the Queen! – evoked little response from the half-empty benches. The subject was one big bore for the parliamentary rank-and-file. So the Commons passed to the composition of the Committee.

Immediately the Commons debated this as proposed in the original Motion. Behind the scenes, each party had already nominated its members. The Tories were selected partly on a regional basis – one from Scotland, one from Wales, another from Northern Ireland – and partly by a mixture of parliamentary experience and 'greenness'. (Two Tory members had entered the House only in the 1970 election.) But all the Tories had one thing in common: as ardent pro-royalists they had made up their minds. The Queen was to receive whatever she asked for. Labour Members had been selected by the Parliamentary Committee – the misnamed Shadow Cabinet. Some individual Members, like myself, had made it known privately to the Committee that they wished to serve. In the event, Labour's was a formidable team: Mr Wilson, ex-Prime Minister; Mr Roy Jenkins, ex-Chancellor of the Exchequer; Mr Charles Pannell, ex-Minister of Public Building and Works; Mr Douglas Houghton, ex-Chancellor of the Duchy of Lancaster and Chairman of the Parliamentary Labour Party; Mr Joel Barnett, a skilled accountant; Miss Joan Lestor, a former Junior Minister and member of the Labour Party's National Executive Committee; and W. W. Hamilton, not unknown for his anti-monarchism.

In the debate on the composition, mine was the only name to be challenged. Mr Hamilton was biased, it was said. He could not be trusted with confidential information. But the critic was a lone voice, and the Committee was appointed with little rancour. Press suggestions that I had been included on the Committee by Mr Wilson to keep my mouth shut were untrue smears. He could not, and did not, make the selection. The appointment was made unanimously by the Labour Party's Parliamentary Committee.

The Committee Sits – in Private

The Select Committee lost no time in getting to work; Mr Barber, the Conservative Chancellor of the Exchequer, was elected Chairman, and forthwith two Memoranda were circulated: one from the Chancellor himself and one from the Palace. From these Memoranda it became obvious that the Tories had already decided to concede the royal claims in full. They were spelt out in detail in the Chancellor's Memo. That the ultimate figures differed by not one penny from the figures put before us at the outset was a clear indication that they had been agreed with the Palace months in advance. The function of the Select Committee was thus to put a coat of democratic whitewash over a process that was anything but democratic: a meaningless if sometimes vitriolic charade.

I had put forward my own propositions: (a) that the Committee's meetings should be held in public; (b) that all evidence taken orally should be recorded and published; (c) that the Committee should take evidence from persons or organizations critical of the Monarchy; (d) that visits by Committee members might be arranged to establishments used by and for Royalty and paid for out of public funds, e.g. the Royal Yacht *Britannia*, Buckingham Palace, Windsor, grace and favour residences, etc.; and (e) that evidence should be called for about the private wealth accumulated by the Royal Family as a result of the very lucrative tax concessions which they had enjoyed over the years; and especially the value of such concessions since 1952. Needless to say, none of my proposals was welcomed. The idea that we might actually visit royal establishments encountered amused derision. 'Count me out,' said Mr Wilson, 'I've no desire to go swanning around at public expense.' Well, I would have paid his taxi fare to Buckingham Palace, or have driven him down to Windsor. But then, against some muttered dissension from the Tory Members, the Committee came round to accepting that all oral evidence ought to be recorded by a shorthand writer, suitably vetted on security grounds. That, in itself, was a revolutionary change, but there the revolution stopped for the time being. Mr St John-Stevas was horrified that the Committee might report all it heard to the House. Ensuing debates, he argued would be too well informed, probably acrimonious, and thus damaging to the Monarchy. Mr St John-Stevas still clung anxiously to the proposition of his hero Bagehot that once you let a Select Committee get to work on the Monarchy the magic would evaporate.

A further point that troubled the Labour Members on the Committee was that they felt we should know a lot more about the private wealth of the Queen. When the subject came up, it was as if we had started telling dirty jokes in church. 'Try and find out,' challenged Mr Barber, 'and see what answers you get.' One more matter ruffled some feathers. Mr Barber was desperate to have done with the whole sordid problem as quickly as possible. He suggested three meetings a week, each lasting an hour and a half. Douglas Houghton exploded. 'We are all busy people,' he roared. 'We need time to read all the papers, to prepare our questions . . . and anyway, why all the rush?' We settled for two meetings a week. And our first witnesses would be Lord Cobbold, the Lord Chamberlain, and Lord Tryon, the Keeper of the Privy Purse and Treasurer to the Queen. They duly presented themselves on 21 June 1971, accompanied by a third Palace functionary, Mr Russell D. Wood, Deputy Treasurer to the Queen. All special pleaders with impeccable Establishment pedigrees (Eton and the Brigade of Guards, etc.). All dressed like prosperous undertakers up from Bournemouth. All staunch defenders of and beneficiaries from the *status quo*.

They were greatly apprehensive. It must have been daunting for them to be facing, for the first time in their sheltered lives, a bunch of tough, rough and rude politicians, at least one or two of whom were likely to hurl hostile questions. Lord Cobbold launched immediately into a long, carefully prepared, and written statement, obviously instructed to present at the earliest opportunity some partial truth about the Queen's private fortune. Various estimates had been made, said his Lordship, in books, magazines and newspapers. These had ranged between £2 million, suggested by Sir Richard Colville in a letter to *The Times*, to over £100 million. In view of recent publicity, said Cobbold, the Queen had instructed him to make certain comments to the Committee on her behalf. Her Majesty had been much concerned by the astronomical figures bandied about in some quarters suggesting that the value of her private funds now ran from £50 million to £100 million or more. She felt that these ideas could only arise from confusion about the status of the Royal Collections, which were in no sense at her personal disposal. She therefore wished Lord Cobbold to assure the Committee that such suggestions were wildly exaggerated. Her Majesty also wished him to state that the income from her private funds had been used in some part to assist in meeting the expenses of other members of the Royal Family: 'owing to the progress of inflation, they have, in many cases, heavily outrun the Annuities granted by Parliament to cover such expenses at the beginning of the Reign'.

It was hardly a *precise* statement of fact. How 'wildly exaggerated' were those estimates of the Queen's private fortune? Did she have £5,000,000 tucked away? Or £20,000,000? Maybe only £40,000,000? Was she really finding it hard to make ends meet? Did she *really* believe that the so-called exaggerated estimates were due to misunderstandings and 'confusion' about the status of the Royal Collections of art objects, stamps and Crown Jewels? Anyone interested enough to make an estimate in the first place is likely to know about the 'inalienable character' of those treasures.

So why did the Queen *instruct* Lord Cobbold to make such a meaningless statement? Mr Roy Jenkins, not well known for extreme republican views, put it differently. He conceded that Cobbold's statement 'gives us some degree of information'. In fact it did nothing of the kind. But, Jenkins went on, 'what we are concerned about is not the information given to us but the case we are going to be able to present to the House as a whole and to the public . . . I wonder,' he said, 'whether by going as far as that but by not being a little more precise there is not a possible danger of getting the worst of both worlds and approaching precision without really achieving it?'

Precision had not been approached in *any* sense. The Cobbold top bracket of £50 million to £100 million was designed to deflect alarm and anger while revealing nothing. The Queen knows, and we know, that she *is* one of the richest women in the world, with wealth accumulated because no Sovereign has paid death duties since they were introduced in 1894. Nor is the Queen's private fortune subject to any direct tax. On a private fortune of a mere £10 million, they would be poor investment advisers who could not get a 10 per cent annual return. Despite pressure for more detail, Lord Cobbold, on the Queen's instructions, declined to say more.

Who had advised Her Majesty to handle the matter in this insensitive ham-fisted way? Was it her Private Secretary, Sir Michael Adeane? Or, perhaps, the Chancellor of the Exchequer himself? It seems inconceivable that she could have acted on her own, without advice. Her attitude represented a constitutional outrage. Beneath the smooth and smiling veneer, the machinations revealed a shrewd, calculating business woman. But the Parliament of 1972 was not, in general, hostile to the Queen's secretiveness. Not even the radical Left cared too much. A hundred years before, when republicanism in Britain was in its hey-day, there would have been a full-blown crisis. The fact that Elizabeth Windsor was able to pull the wool over the eyes of a parliamentary committee with hardly any fuss showed the real strength of the Monarchy at that moment. Perhaps the duty of the Select Committee should have been to press much harder. But then the Leader of the Labour Party played no part whatever in the crucial exchanges. Indeed, he absented himself from them for 90 per cent of the time and served only in very much of a part-time capacity. The proceedings were a painful embarrassment for him. He contributed little of any consequence either to the cross-examination of witnesses or to any of the discussions on the various reports. Radicalism from the Labour side, such as it was, came not from Wilson but from Jenkins and Houghton – and even they were often strangely muted. Harold Wilson showed himself to be a firm ally of the Tory and Royal Establishment throughout the battle over the royal cash.

Meanwhile, the Select Committee got down to some questioning on the details provided in the financial Memorandum from the Palace. *In toto*, the Royals were £240,000 in the red by 1970. This was mostly due to salary and wage increases within the Royal Household since 1952. That bill had shot up by 167 per cent since the beginning of the reign. The Memorandum certainly contained some fascinating minutiae. Some expenses had gone up by about 80 per cent. The Royal Wine Cellar bill was £3,254 in 1952, and over £12,000 in 1970. The laundry bill had increased from £4,542 in 1952 to £7,267 in 1970. Purchase of horses, forrage, farriery, etc., had risen from £4,441 to £11,508, and 'ecclesiastical expenditure' from £1,877 to £5,770. There was even the cost of Royal Garden Parties: £5,998 in 1952, £24,402 in 1970. Oh, and the Game Account of the Yeomen had been £3,266 twenty years before. Now it was £10,297. What was it? We never found out. We were too pushed for time. For a footnote, spending on the Royal Library had been £8 in 1952. In 1972 it was *minus* £1,209! Members of our Royal Family are not, alas, renowned for their cultural tastes, attention to literature or intellectual pursuits. Perhaps their lack of imaginative endowment is the secret of their staying power.

But Norman St John-Stevas, the Conservative MP for Chelmsford, could hardly wait to put his searching questions. Norman is a witty, intelligent, articulate fellow, as television viewers and radio listeners will know. His unabashed, royal-blue Toryism and hankering after an old-fashioned Roman Catholicism reveal a soul that would have been at its happiest in those patrician, élitist days when Victoria was still on the Throne. For the moment, he was concerned about expenditure on choir-boys! And preaching fees! And the Royal Gardens! He was satisfied on all those crucial points. The Royal Gardens grow royal mushrooms and flowers – and make a little (tax-free) royal profit on the side.

After this, the questions of Mr Joel Barnett seemed pleasantly abrasive. He came immediately to a much more substantial point, which he hammered at throughout the Committee's proceedings and in the subsequent debates in the Commons. How, he asked, is the distinction made between public and private royal expenditure? A difficult question. For example, the Queen buys all her own clothes out of her own pocket. But every hat, every dress, every shoe, is a matter of great public attention and comment. Even her military uniforms, as Mr Wilson was quick to spot, are paid for out of the Privy Purse. So, she is a woman much put upon. Might she even be subsidizing us? A novel concept. But nobody had worked out any figures – or how she managed to keep going. Nobody, in fact, seemed to know much. Nobody even knew who appointed the Swan Keeper. 'I think it is nearly hereditary,' was the nearest we got to it. So the hereditary principle doesn't stop at the Monarchy or the Lords.

Miss Joan Lestor, a red-headed left-winger, wanted to know *why* the Queen had agreed to work for nothing. I had whispered the question in Joan's ear – why was she willing to give up her £60,000 a year pocket-money? My suggestion as a good trade-unionist that she be paid the rate for the job had no support. However, in the event it transpired the Queen was not going to work for nothing. Why should she? She expected the revenues from her 'private' estate, the Duchy of Lancaster, to increase. She was already receiving £300,000 a year tax-free from that one source.

Meanwhile, there was the £25,000 a year being given to members of the Royal Family not on the official payroll. Of this, £15,000 had gone to the Duchess of Kent until her death in 1968. Her daughter, Princess Alexandra, had received £1,500 from 1955, raised to £4,000 in 1965 and to £10,000 by 1969. The Duke of Kent's share rose from £2,500 in 1961 to £10,000 by 1970. There had been no payrise for Princess Alice in all that time, and she continued to receive the booby-prize of £2,000.

Apart from that, Princess Margaret, never one to conceal her feeling that the world owes her a living, was still enjoying her £15,000. But it was evidently not going as far as it used to in paying for clothes, hair-do's and mixing in London society's top set. The Queen Mother still had her £70,000, and the late Duke of

Gloucester his £35,000 – or £100 a day! – while he lay a permanent invalid.

But, said Lord Cobbold, it was 'absolutely clear' that all these royal people were out of pocket. As the Committee did not have access to any of their accounts, we never knew how much they were out of pocket, or what other means they had at their disposal.

The Committee continued to read and hear evidence – including that of Sir Basil Smallpiece, a captain of industry called in to examine the Palace administration, who assured us it was an efficient, streamlined outfit. In due course, Mr Barber, as Chairman, intimated his wish that our work should be completed before the summer recess so that a Bill could be introduced in the autumn. There were four options before us:

1. That the 1952 Civil List be updated, using the same data and adding a much bigger contingency sum than the £95,000 of 1952.
2. That *all* Royal Expenditure be transferred to Departmental Votes, implying regular questioning and debates in the House (a terrifying prospect).
3. Proposals made by Mr John Boyd-Carpenter, which would link the Civil List Cash with the income from the Crown Estate.
4. A compromise arrangement, by which a fixed sum would be paid out of the Consolidated Fund, and 'topped-up' annually by a Supplementary Estimate presented to the House.

Many hours of wrangling lay ahead.

The great advantage of an up-dated Civil List was its simplicity. All that had to be done was to provide figures showing the extent of inflation over twenty years, and its likely projected effect over the next twenty or thirty years – or however long the present reign might continue. The 1952 figures could be increased in proportion, and the £95,000 contingency figure of 1952 increased very substantially to offset future inflation. But the great disadvantage was that that latter figure would need to be so large that the idea could run into strong public opposition.

The idea for transferring to other Government Departmental votes expenditure hitherto carried by Classes II and III of the existing Civil List, that is to say, the salaries or expenses of Her Majesty's Household, came from Douglas Houghton. It was the only scheme proposed which cut across party lines. It had, and still has, a lot of advantages, seeming to be in accord with popular opinion on the nature of modern monarchy and its place in a constitutional democracy. And it ensured that *each year* proper and adequate financial provision could be made for the Crown as a recognized Department of State. But there was one insurmountable objection. *The Monarch herself didn't like it.* The Royal Household, said Lord Cobbold (Q.180), is 'a family administration . . . the employees from top to bottom think of themselves as Her Majesty's servants and Her Majesty certainly thinks of them as her servants'. Except that the taxpayer pays their wages. Moreover, if a Crown Department were set up, its expenditure would be subject to annual parliamentary scrutiny – and what was it that Bagehot said a hundred years ago? Something about the magic of the Crown disappearing if the exposure became too strong? Continual parliamentary accountability, persistent and perhaps hostile questioning and debate! The very idea had St John-Stevas and Boyd-Carpenter in a swoon. Boyd-Carpenter's own solution was, basically, to fix the total amount provided for the Civil List as a predetermined percentage of the net revenues accruing from the Crown Estates. Since Crown Estate net revenue had more than kept up with the rate of inflation over the previous twenty years (£880,000 in 1952, £3,200,000 in 1965), and was likely to do so for the foreseeable future, to fix a Civil List as a percentage of that Crown Estate net revenue would provide the Crown with a built-in protection against the erosive effects of inflation; and it would avoid the trouble of the Monarchy having to come crown in hand to the House of Commons periodically to ask for more cash. But Lord Cobbold had not been enthusiastic. The net revenue from the Crown Estate was unpredictable and varied from year to year. Annual income for the Civil List would therefore vary also, making budgeting extremely difficult.

In fact, whatever the difficulties, the whole argument was based on a misconception of what the Crown Estate is and who it belongs to. (See following chapter, pages 70–75.) Even so, Lord Perth, the First Crown Estate Commissioner and Chairman, produced a Memorandum based on principles similar to those propounded by Mr John Boyd-Carpenter. The process of Crown Estate income keeping up with inflation was likely to accelerate, since the Crown Estate Commissioners had been changing their policies on rent increases for urban properties – away from fixed increases over fairly long periods to one of much more regular increases more closely related to rack rents, or current market rates. So, concluded Lord Perth, if the Civil List were to be related to the net Crown Estate revenues, the Crown would be on to a good thing – as would the Exchequer. Yet the basic purpose was plain and understandable: to give the Crown a built-in hedge against inflation, take its finances away from the prying eyes of Parliament, and, at the same time, create the impression that the Monarchy costs the taxpayer nothing, or very little.

Boyd-Carpenter defended his viewpoint with vigour and eloquence. He had always been a forceful and attractive debater in the Commons, much feared and respected by top civil servants as a fierce watchdog guarding against any slackness in the control of public expenditure. But, when it comes to the Crown, you can clearly carry the question of public accountability, and public debate, too far. Some dark, impenetrable recesses, into which no one may peer, must remain. The myth that the Exchequer makes a profit from the Crown was busily cultivated: that the Exchequer obtains far more from the Crown Estate than it forks out on the Civil List. The historical origin of the Crown Estate, he implied, was irrelevant. His idea was not an innovation. The Prince of Wales, after all, had always been entitled to the *whole* of the net revenues of the Duchy of Cornwall. If the one was defensible, why not the other? The Exchequer could either let the Crown keep all the Crown Estate revenues, then make a periodic deduction; or else take 50 per cent and give the rest to the Monarch. The advantages of the scheme, in Boyd-Carpenter's eyes, were enormously attractive. It was a gold-bottomed guarantee against inflation, and, just as important, no money would have to be voted by Parliament; there would, therefore, be no more squalid Civil List Select Committees – and thus no debates in the House of Commons.

In fact, however, the Boyd-Carpenter proposal provoked acid discussion, though Mr Jeremy Thorpe, as the lone Liberal on the committee, backed it. 'We are discussing fiddling little sums of money,' he said. 'The annual cost of the Monarchy is the same as that of the British Embassy in Paris.' He clearly hadn't done much homework. Mr Jenkins struck a discordant but realistic note when he foresaw great difficulties in the Boyd-Carpenter proposals. It was a fallacy to pretend that the Crown Estates belonged to the Queen as private property. Secondly, the proposals would mean there would be less parliamentary control over royal expenditure than there had been in over 200 years. And thirdly, no one, not even the Queen, should be protected automatically from the consequences of inflation. He hit several nails on the head, and trod on a lot of toes – in particular those of St John-Stevas, who wanted, above all things, to avoid the 'indignity of constant recourse by the Crown to Parliament for money'.

By now the Chancellor was growing anxious about the time-table. Summer holidays were coming fast. Mr Whitelaw had undertaken to table a Motion in the House to enable the Committee to sit during the Summer Recess – possibly in the second half of September, to prepare at least a draft report. But, at the 2 August meeting, the Chancellor said that, after investigation, he had found the many commitments of committee members, and not least his own, would make it impossible to find any date in the summer recess at all convenient. He therefore hoped to produce, himself, a draft report some time during the recess. Members could then study it and be ready to discuss, amend or accept it after the House returned in October.

Before we broke for the recess, Mr Barber indicated first that both the Palace and the Leader of the House had accepted the view that a simple up-dating of the 1952 provisions involved such dangers as to make it unacceptable. Secondly, that an *annual* voting of the sums required had been rejected by the Palace on the grounds that that would give them no assurance of continuing adequate provision – and, even then, not without acrimonious debate that could be damaging to the institution. And thirdly, that after *months* of discussion between the Government and the Palace the fourth alternative had been agreed on: to pay fixed minimum sums annually out of the Exchequer, 'topped up' at the discretion of the Government. *This proposition had the great advantage of not being subject to detailed scrutiny by Parliament.*

Mr Barber's draft report was circulated to Members of the Select Committee in September 1971. It contained, as the original Message from the Queen had sought, important innovations. First, it broke a contract, namely, that a Civil List – any Civil List – should be made for an entire reign. Queen Victoria had reigned from 1837 to 1901 and there had been no extra Civil List in all those years. No provision had been made for any children Queen Victoria might have – and she had nine – though a series of Acts granted annuities to be paid out of the Consolidated Fund to the princes and princesses on the occasion of their coming of age and/or marriage. But the introduction of each Bill had not been preceded by the setting up of a Select Committee.

In the meantime, I was advised that it was 'procedurally impossible for a dissenting minority report to a Select Committee report to be produced. Members of the Committee may register their opposition to the whole or part of the Chairman's draft report by proposing amendments, which are published in the proceedings of the Committee.' That seemed quite unacceptable. The Chairman's draft report was so riddled with questionable features, and contained so many figures based on flimsy evidence, that a minority Report seemed the only alternative solution. I sought the advice of a Senior Clerk of the House, and he assured me that such a course *was* possible. My own Report was drafted, and in late September 1971 I took it to the Committee Clerks, who kindly checked that facts, figures and dates were accurate, though, of course, the opinions expressed were my own responsibility. The Clerks did suggest, very gently, that I might reconsider and tone down my last paragraph, especially a phrase about 'the Gracious Message of May 19, 1971' representing 'the most insensitive and brazen pay claim made in the last 200 years' (p. xlvii). Equally gently, I rejected the Clerks' advice, and my Minority Report was duly published with only minor amendment to the original version.

On 18 October 1971, a letter was sent to committee members indicating that the Chancellor, as committee chairman, had suggested that the form of the final Report be discussed informally in the light of the two draft Reports (his and mine), and that this should take place at a deliberate meeting to be held on 8 November. The Clerks' letter ended, 'Members may like to be reminded of the procedure when more than one draft Report is offered for formal consideration. A formal decision is taken, by vote if necessary, on which one of the Reports is to be considered. This having been done, only one Report is considered "paragraph by paragraph", with the opportunity for amendment to be offered and debated.'

As the Committee got down to the business again, Douglas Houghton gave notice that he, too, would be producing a Minority Report, together with a chart indicating the possible structure of his proposed Crown Department or Commission.

The question that my own Report be considered in preference to the Chancellor's was defeated by 9 votes to 3. All the Conservative Members and, of course, Mr Jeremy Thorpe (shades of David Lloyd George!) voted together. Most Labour Members abstained – as they did on almost all my own subsequent amendments to the Chancellor's Report. On the vote as to whether we should discuss the Houghton proposals, the margin of difference was one vote only. It might even have gone the other way had not the Queen made known her hostility. It is certainly to be hoped that some future Labour Government will have the courage to take the whole problem by the scruff of the neck once again and ensure that the feudalistic, aristocratic odour emanating from the Monarchy is finally eradicated, and that, so long as the institution lasts, expenditure on it is subject to far more public accountability.

Over the last seventy years, various items of royal expenditure have been transferred to other Government Departments, including all repair work and maintenance on the Royal Palaces. Over the last twenty years in particular, the process has continued. The cost of rail travel on royal functions within the UK was £28,000 in 1966–7, spent mainly on the Royal Train. In 1971–2 the comparable figure was £36,000, paid by the Ministry of Transport. When foreign Heads of State visit Britain, their hospitality is paid for by the Government, though part of it used to be paid for out of the Queen's Civil List – (in 1971–2 about £40,000 out of £169,000). Today she pays nothing, except perhaps for the odd day or so's entertainment at the Royal Palaces. In all, between 1952 and 1968, a million pounds was transferred in this way to the taxpayers. It was effectively as much of an *increase* in the royal finances as if a million pounds was being given outright – except that those who paid knew nothing about it.

Pensions to retired Royal Household staff are also paid separately by the Treasury, and amounted to £300,000 in 1970, as compared with £100,000 in 1953. The Royal Yacht and the Queen's Flight were costing £1,789,000 a year by 1971–2. The maintenance of palaces, and grace and favour residences came to £974,000. Stationery and office equipment was costing £46,000, and ceremonial and equerry attendance £71,000. Postal and telephone services cost £52,000. In all, close on £3 million was being paid for on Departmental Votes. Adding the Civil List provision and annuities brought the total to just over £3½ million, a figure only £55,000 more than the Exchequer was receiving from the Crown Estate in 1970 – a point that had been avidly seized on by the pro-monarchists.

When the Select Committee published its Report on 22 November 1971, it was clearly intent on doing three things: first, to give a substantial lift to everybody on the royal pay-roll; secondly, to make absolutely sure there would be no more prying Select Committees of nosey MPs; and finally, that by reviews at not more than ten-yearly intervals, no undue royal financial anxieties would occur in the future.

The Main Provisions

The Queen's £475,000 of 1952 was to become £980,000 as from 1 January 1972. Should that prove inadequate within ten years, it would be increased simply by Government Order. No oral or written evidence would be available to Parliament. A one-and-a-half-hour debate would suffice. Annuitants were to receive generous uplifts, varying according to the degree of 'hardship' suffered over the years. The Queen Mother was to receive £95,000 – an increase of £25,000 a year, or £500 extra a week, or £260 a day (Saturdays and Sundays included!).

The Duke of Edinburgh's £40,000 would go to £65,000 – an increase of 62·5 per cent. Princess Margaret's increase would be £20,000 a year – not quite as much as mummy, but an increase of 133 per cent. (No one knew why, except that it was presumed that her £15,000 had been far too low!) Princess Anne's £6,000, from 18, was to go up to £15,000 – a 150 per cent increase. By her marriage in November 1973, Princess Anne came in for a further increase to £35,000 a year, and thus achieved an increase of nearly 500 per cent in less than two years – at a time when the Government was appealing for wage restraint from workers earning less than £1,000 a year! (And she had a £200,000 honeymoon on the Royal Yacht thrown in.) The pension for Prince Charles's hypothetical widow was to be upped to £60,000. The younger Princes (Andrew in 1978 and Edward in 1982) may now expect £20,000 a year at their majority, or the same as a Prime Minister. Marriage will bring them into the £50,000 a year bracket. The Duke of Gloucester had the smallest increase, from £35,000 to £45,000, but then his circumstances made a productivity increase unlikely. However, the Queen did make a special plea for the Duchess of Gloucester, and any future wife of a younger son of the Duchess, should she become a widow. The Committee agreed that a pension of £20,000 a year be recommended for each prospective widow. (This was a greedily novel concept never before tried out.) Lastly, the Queen was to receive £60,000 a year to disburse as she wished among relations not specifically provided for.

Public Reaction

Press comment on the proposals was vast and varied, and certainly much better informed than it had ever been before on the subject of the royal finances (no thanks to the Tory committee members). A number of newspapers had even begun searching out public opinion before the Committee was set up. In November 1969, the *Daily Mirror* had wondered whether Prince Charles would be the first old-age pensioner to be crowned king, 'or, more to the point, should he be?' It suggested that the 'heir should automatically succeed at 35' and that modern Monarchs should retire at sixty. A subsequent *Mirror* Public Opinion Poll found 40 per cent in favour of the Queen's early retirement, and 49 per cent against. Among the young, 53 per cent were *for* early retirement, 41 per cent against. Six months later, the *Mirror* commissioned another poll among the young about their attitude to the Monarchy, and 2,000 in the 15 to 19 age-group were interviewed. Of these, 48 per cent thought the Royal Family played a useful role in twentieth-century Britain; 43 per cent thought otherwise. No less than 42 per cent thought that none of the Royal Family was in touch with everyday life, and an even higher proportion thought of them as *not* an ordinary family. In June 1971, a further *Mirror* poll showed a majority *against* an increase in financial provision for the Royal Family, with women more opposed than men. Within the 16 to 24 age-group, 26 per cent supported a financial *cut*, and 36 per cent were against the Monarchy altogether. The Select Committee had paid no attention to these portents of disenchantment with the Monarchy and all its works – coming even before the Committee had produced its recommendations.

The *Daily Mirror* is read by millions of ordinary working people, a 3 to 1 majority of whom felt that 'the Queen already has enough – or too much'. As one reader in Manchester wrote:

> If we cannot afford free milk for our kiddies, we can't afford any increase to a very wealthy family. There must be no Royal rise while we also have 7½ million folk on the poverty line in this country.

A £10 winning letter came from Dr S. Desmond Risley of Upper Beeding, Sussex:

> I am a doctor and retired from practice in 1966. In 1930 I was awarded the OBE for bravery during an earthquake in India.
>
> I have seen the world and have seen the suffering in it. It makes me sad to see the pensioners, men who have built up the Empire, living on meagre pensions. Give them more, and the Queen no more. I admire the Queen but I feel she has enough.

Not the letter of any long-haired revolutionary militant, but one from a mild old gentleman in peaceful Sussex. On 3 December 1971, the highly 'respectable' *Financial Times* put the case almost as bluntly:

> This is not a good time for anyone to recommend a large increase in the amount paid to the Queen. The report of the Parliamentary Select Committee on the Civil List, which yesterday recommended an increase of some 106 per cent, to nearly £1 million a year, is unfortunate not only in its timing but also in the adequacy of the information that it has laid before the public. *The Committee has not made any serious attempt to find out all the relevant facts about Her Majesty's private income* [my italics] and it has resorted to the practice of 'sidelining' to censor from its own pages such bits of evidence as it is officially thought right to conceal . . . The Queen herself works hard . . . She is an excellent and popular constitutional monarch. The costs of maintaining her position must assuredly have risen . . . since 1952 . . .
>
> But it is awkward to suggest that what many ordinary people will think of as her 'salary' . . . should be more than doubled, at a time when the Government is urging wage restraint on the rest of the population, and the number of people out of work is approaching a million . . . The report from the Select Committee on the Civil List has failed to make out such a *cast-iron* case for any increases.

Then, the *Financial Times*, normally so Establishment-minded, continued scathingly:

> The Committee has rejected a number of proposals for the future arrangements of the payment of Royal costs that might increase the degree of public scrutiny over the accounts. It has, indeed, chosen to *reduce* the amount of information that might be available in later years by providing for simple Treasury orders for future increases. Some of the related increases proposed are hard to justify, but these are side-issues compared to the central question.
>
> This is, *how much is the Queen's private income?* . . .

Does the Queen read the *Financial Times*? Probably not. But surely such a long, blunt editorial from such a pro-monarchist journal must have been drawn to her attention by her Private Secretary.

On Sunday, 5 December, the *Observer* was as cutting and critical:

> The finances of the monarchy are complex and confusing, and the report of the Committee on the Civil List has done nothing to simplify or clarify them. The 'million a year monarchy' is misleading because it does not include, for instance, expenditure on the royal yacht – which is getting on for a million a year in itself, or on the maintenance of royal palaces and residences, which take another million. On the other hand, to describe the Civil List review as a 'pay claim', as Mr William Hamilton, Labour's popular republican, has done, is equally misleading. It is more in the nature of an enquiry into the expenses of the Queen's public office.
>
> At a time when there is heavy unemployment and when wage increases are being restricted as far as possible, there is obviously bound to be some public criticism of the doubling of the Civil List annual payment . . . Some of this criticism might be lessened if people realized how long both our royal and our political leaders have gone without any increase at all. But more could have been avoided altogether if the Civil List Committee had accepted proposals put forward by Mr Douglas Houghton for turning the working aspects of the monarchy into a public department open to continuous parliamentary scrutiny.
>
> . . . The advantages of this proposal would not only be a proper amount of public accountability: the immensely arduous work that the Queen and her family put in will be protection enough against most cheap or unfair criticisms. It would also, by widening knowledge of how the monarchy works, actually increase the Queen's own privacy. As it is, no one can easily tell when she is on or off duty, nor who is paying for what out of which fund – the Consolidated Fund, the Civil List, the Privy Purse or her own apparently unknowable private fortune . . .
>
> This is an issue basic to democracy; it is much more important than whether Princess Margaret's 177 official engagements in 1970 really rated £15,000 (tax free) . . .

The Times of 3 December 1971 was more demure and circumspect – like a virgin not quite sure whether she should make the break:

The difficulty about determining the correct level of expenditure on the Royal Household at any particular time is that this is not an institution to which the techniques of cost-benefit analysis can be applied. There is no precise objective measurement of the proper level of expenditure. What the British people do know is that they have a monarch who is both popular and hard-working, and a Royal Family whose general style of life and performance of their public duties commands wide approval, and that there is no widespread popular demand either for more lavish display or for the comparative austerities of a bicycling monarchy.

Inflation, *The Times* tip-toed on, had made it 'all the more necessary to make more adequate provision for periodic reviews in the future. It ought not to be quite such a traumatic process as it has been this time . . . But the proposed review at least once every ten years . . . should provide for sufficiently frequent adjustments without continual public haggling over the Royal finances.' After all, 'a single retirement pension' had risen 'by more than three times' what it had been in 1952. Top people read *The Times*, says the advert. Top people write it, too. The pension in 1952 was thirty bob a week.

The *Sun* newspaper was far more earthy. Its poll on 3 December showed four out of five opposed to the increases. One letter from a Tooting, London, reader said: 'The Queen undoubtedly does a boring job to the best of her ability. But can we still afford the useless trappings maintained on public money?' Another from Oldham, Lancs: 'Royalty's way of life is a dream world of make-believe and extravagant luxury. It is too costly.' And, from Dursley, Glos: 'Royalty should be phased out. The Queen's title is just something from the past – a fairy-tale fantasy.' 'Let the Queen give back to the people some of the private Royal lolly,' said the *Scottish Daily Record* on its front page. While the weekly *New Statesman* for 10 December carried a harsh front-page cartoon showing a tattered, hag-worn Queen, a down-at-heel Philip at her side, begging for 'Supplementary Benefits'. The leading article, written by the journal's then editor, Richard Crossman, who had quite recently been one of Her Majesty's most distinguished and intellectual Ministers, growled, 'No doubt it was sheer bad luck for Mr Heath that the Opposition chose to raise the plight of the aged poor just before the decision on the Civil List was due to be announced. The inevitable comparison brutally reveals the chasm which divides the hard-fisted means test to which pensioners are subjected before they can receive supplementary benefit and the laxity with which royalty is permitted to supplement its income while refusing to reveal the size of its private fortune . . . In the interests of the Monarchy itself, the opposition of the Palace to full disclosure and public accounting should be overcome as soon as possible . . . It is clearly intolerable that the elected representatives of the people should be denied the essential facts . . . '

'The Monarchy, contrary to all Bagehot's predictions,' wrote Peter Jenkins in the *Guardian* on 7 December, had 'once more survived the pokings about of a Select Committee', which 'had failed to establish' clear distinctions between the private and the public expenditure and functions of the Monarchy, and had failed to devise means 'for bringing a not inconsiderable item of public expenditure under proper public control and parliamentary scrutiny'. It had been quite wrong to ask Parliament 'to cater lavishly for the Royal Family as the Head of the Establishment and the font of so much British snobbism, mumbo-jumbo and traditionalist complacency'.

All this, and much more, showed how little unanimity there was among the people as to the merits of royal expenditure on the lavish scale proposed by the Select Committee – the more so since the figures were shown to be based on scanty, one-sided, confused evidence.

The Parliamentary Debates

The first Commons debate took place on 14 December 1971, three weeks after the publication of the Report. Mr Barber showed his pride over the records broken by the Committee: more meetings held, more evidence seen, more schemes considered and more witnesses interviewed than by any other Civil List Committee in this century. There were no misgivings about the worth of evidence taken only from royal acolytes, or the point of asking questions to which answers were already decided. Mr Barber was more concerned to demonstrate that the proposals were not really a royal pay increase at all, only a reasonable expenses allowance – and that no public money would be saved by the adoption of the official Opposition's alternative scheme. In any case, 'the *total* cost of all aspects of the Monarchy, including the

Vote-borne services, does not much exceed the cost of our Embassy in Washington'. (Perhaps it is time we took a good hard look at that Washington establishment!)

Douglas Houghton put the official Opposition point of view, basing it on his own proposals. 'I can say sincerely that we are out to help the people and the Monarchy towards a better understanding of the realities of running an important institution within our parliamentary system,' he said. 'I can say without any qualification that there is nothing personal against Her Majesty in what we are proposing . . . Her Majesty is held in great respect and deep affection by millions of Labour voters.' If there were no wildly enthusiastic cheers of assent from the Labour benches, it was partly because the House was three parts empty anyway.

Richard Crossman made an abrasive speech which referred to his *New Statesman* article, 'Royal Tax Avoiders', and would have had the Palace wincing that night were the Court authorities noted for sensitivity or response to changing moods of public opinion. The speeches from Boyd-Carpenter and St John-Stevas were predictable royal obeisances. My own speech, I am glad to say, encountered violent hostility from the Conservative benches. Besides pointing out the *reduction* in public accountability involved, I described how the Queen Mother's tax-free rise, from £70,000 a year to £95,000, represented a taxable annual income of over £1 million, for that is what would be needed to produce a net income of £100,000. When I went on to refer to Princess Margaret as 'this expensive kept woman', formerly kept by the taxpayer at £15,000 a year tax-free and now to receive £35,000 a year – it had Mr St John-Stevas in a state of apoplexy. He rose to quote against me the parliamentary bible of Erskine May: ' . . . "disrespectful use of Her Majesty's name would normally give offence outside of Parliament; and it is only consistent with decency, that a member of the legislature should not be permitted openly to use such language in his place in Parliament." Does not that rule, by analogy, apply to the former Queen of this country, and to the Queen's sister?'

But the Deputy Speaker allowed me to continue. She was watching order very carefully, she said. So I continued, pointing out that since he had been four years of age, and up to 1970, Prince Charles had amassed a tax-free fortune of nearly half a million pounds. That he would be a multi-millionaire in his own right if, and when, he came to the Throne. How hard it must be for anyone to understand how such wealth accumulation, wholly unearned, could help to unite the nation or in any way validate the claim that one of the greatest attributes of the Monarchy is its unifying influence on a politically and economically quarrelsome people.

So the debate petered out and eventually came to the vote. On the Houghton proposal, there were 300 Government votes against and 263 Opposition votes in favour. On the Government proposal, the 300 Tory ayes stayed in the lobby, but all except twenty-nine Labour Members abstained. (A pusillanimous party, choked and leaden with its wish for respectability. Harold Wilson is the only Labour Leader this century who *never* opened his mouth during a Civil List debate.)

When the Civil List Bill came before the House on 21 December, it was much the same story, with variations on earlier comment. The only Member to come out as a 'copper-bottomed republican' was Jack Dormond, who represented a radically minded Durham constituency. So far as he was concerned 'the whole of the Royal Establishment, from the Queen downwards, could go tomorrow, lock, stock and barrel'. (No Palace invitations for Mr Dormond.) As for me, I was suitably terrified when Norman St John-Stevas warned me that I could be sent to the Tower for the kind of remarks I was making. The Opposition vote did reach forty-five, but still included none of Labour's ex-Cabinet Ministers, apart from the mischievous Dick Crossman.

Unfortunately, as soon as the Bill was in Committee Stage and I had tabled a myriad of amendments, I was struck down by pneumonia early in January. 'Not for nothing,' said Douglas Houghton to me later, 'is Her Majesty described as "Defender of the Faith".' I received a heartening telegram from my friend John Grant, the Member for Islington East: FRIENDS AT WESTMINSTER AND BUCKINGHAM PALACE WISH YOU A SPEEDY RECOVERY STOP WISH YOU WERE HERE. The Palace prelate Norman St John-Stevas used similarly felicitous language when he remarked: 'I fear that, in part, I may have been responsible. For some time I have been praying against him, and I fear I may have overdone it. So we now have a debate which I do not suppose one could call Hamlet without the prince because that might cause offence, but certainly Hamlet without the ghost.' It's hard to harbour bitterness in the House of Commons, unless the iron has really entered your soul. The system is as corrupting in that sense as the Monarchy itself. They're all such 'nice' people . . . well, nearly all.

For the overall Civil List provision, there were forty Labour votes to 173 on the other side. (Thus only a third of the 630

MPs had been interested enough even to turn up.) Even on the annuities, against which there was known widespread hostility, only thirty-four Labour Members bothered to vote against, to 148 for the Conservatives (or, little more than a quarter of the total membership). And so it was all over. The cash was in the royal till – all £980,000 a year of it. A gracious snook had been cocked at the Commons.

In the meantime, one ex-amateur boxer had challenged me to fight for the Queen's honour. Anonymous threats of assassination arrived almost daily in my postbag. I had to employ an extra temporary assistant to open, read and analyse my mail, which came from all over the world – from Canada to the Philippine Islands, from Caithness to Cornwall. In no other crisis of the last twenty years, nuclear weapons, German rearmament, Suez or, in the 1960s, the Common Market, did I receive a minute fraction of the letters I had over the royal issue.

The *Daily Mirror* of 16 December 1971 had run a front-page open letter to the 'Dear Queen':

> Dear Queen,
>
> Don't be too upset. Of course, Willie Hamilton, that well-known maverick and Scottish MP, was very rude to your sister, Princess Margaret.
>
> To call her 'this expensive kept woman' was going too far. All that can be said in his favour is that he had the right to say it.
>
> After all, as Mr Hamilton had to admit, Princess Margaret had three or four public engagements a week last year – and she is, of course, married to that brilliant photographer, Anthony Armstong-Jones.
>
> Indeed, the highest mountain in Wales is named after him.
>
> And Wild, Wild, Willie was also guilty of a little *lèse-majesté* towards Queen Elizabeth, the Queen Mother.
>
> For Willie to call her Princess Margaret's 'old mum' was being a bit familiar . . .
>
> As a constitutional monarch, Your Majesty, you are in the unfortunate (or fortunate) position of being unable to lay down the law – unlike your predecessor, the First Elizabeth. She would have clapped Wee Willie into the Bloody Tower.
>
> But you have a fair point when you say: 'If I am Sovereign, why shouldn't I be Sovereign of my own household?'
>
> All right. Loyalty is loyalty. Affection is affection. But facts are facts.

> For every ONE reader of the *Daily Mirror* who wrote to this newspaper approving the new financial arrangements EIGHT were AGAINST.
>
> And a high proportion of those eight were pensioners.
>
> This doesn't mean that *Mirror* readers want a republic: perish the thought!
>
> When they were asked their views (the same citizens) 9 out of 10 were in favour of the monarchy in the United Kingdom.
>
> BUT [it went on] is it right that you should get the 'extra' [cash] and keep secret the size of your private fortune? AND be free of all tax?

Rough water

Never had any Civil List proposals had a rougher ride. Labour Party leaders had, in fact said to me privately, and even in the private committee discussions, things they did not choose to say in public. Some Tory MPs had expressed to me private support of my opinions – though not, of course, in the language I had chosen. The front page of the *Daily Mail* of 15 December 1971 had described my speech as 'the bitterest attack ever made on the Royal Family in Parliament [which] rocked the Commons last night'. But on the same day a *Guardian* editorial commented, 'to say that the Queen's private income is irrelevant . . . is altogether too deferential . . . There is a need for more openness and clarity . . . A constitutional monarchy needs to be democratic in form as well as in good intent.'

The *Financial Times* anticipated some of the questions to which the Select Committee had to try to find answers when, on 3 June 1971, it said, 'It [the Select Committee] should ascertain from the Inland Revenue whether the Queen actually pays income and surtax on her private income, at the full rate. If so, it should in all reason be left private. *If not, details of the private holdings, and the tax relief thereon, should be ascertained and published, the relevant income to be taken into account in assessing the total resources available to the monarchy.*' This was precisely the point made by Labour Members of the Select Committee and rejected by both the Government and the Palace. Even *The Times* had followed a similar line of reasoning.

There was thus a wide spectrum of respectable opinion demanding more disclosure of the real extent of the Queen's private fortune. The demands, and speculations, were nothing new. In the debates of a century ago – in 1872 and in 1889 – there had been similar demands. It was known that Queen Victoria had accumulated savings from her Civil List; especially after she was widowed and went into virtual seclusion. In 1871 a pamphlet written by the historian George Trevelyan asked, 'What Does She Do With It?' On 19 March 1872, Sir Charles Dilke, the Liberal MP for Chelsea, moved for an inquiry into the royal fortune. He was howled down, even though Gladstone was Prime Minister and no love was lost between him and Queen Victoria. 'The whole notion [of a vast private fortune] is utterly visionary and groundless.' But then Gladstone went on to say that he had no information on the matter! And Dilke found only three supporters.

By 1889 the House had become less deferential. Asked to give an extra £36,000 a year for the children of the rakish Prince of Wales – the future Edward VII – MPs pointed out that he already had an income of £113,500 plus Marlborough House and Sandringham (bought after his coming of age out of £600,000 accumulated from the Duchy of Cornwall revenues).

By then a Select Committee had extracted the fact that the Queen had, over fifty years, saved £824,000 on her Civil List. In 1852 she had also been left £250,000 in some old gentleman's will. How much had Victoria invested? Nobody knew. Sam Storey, the then MP for Sunderland, estimated the Queen's investments to be worth £3 million. 'Absolutely untrue!' shouted the Leader of the House, Mr W. H. Smith. But how did *he* know? As Lady Longford says in her biography of Queen Victoria, even that quarter of a million left to the Queen by the old man must be worth many millions today.

In fact, 116 Liberals voted *against* Edward's £36,000 – a far much higher vote than was cast by Labour Members on several occasions in 1972. The *Reynolds's News* of Victoria's day was as brutal as Dick Crossman's *New Statesman* a 100 years later: 'Every one of her subjects has a vested interest in the contents of Queen Victoria's Brobdingnagian stocking.' We *still* have a right to know. The information is still withheld. Until it is forthcoming, there can only be continuing speculation and suspicion.

The True Wealth and Taxability of the Royal Family

Before we move on to take a closer look at some other sources of royal finance – the Duchies of Lancaster and Cornwall – and the revenues and origin of the Crown Estate, it may help to keep everything in perspective if we summarize the situation on these two issues so absolutely central to the whole debate over the controversial 1972 Civil List.

There is no doubt that the Establishment worked hard to screen the Royal Family's private wealth from Parliament and the people. And, of course, they succeeded. We are left only with guesstimates, and despite Lord Cobbold's assertions to the Select Committee, it is hard to imagine that, with her private estates at Sandringham and Balmoral, her tax-free income from the misnamed 'private' Duchy of Lancaster, and the other enormous private collections of jewellery, furniture, antiques and hard cash acquired by inheritance, gifts or purchase, the Queen is worth less than £100 million. It is probably much more. She may not know exactly herself.

The accumulation of the private fortune may be said to have begun in earnest with Prince Albert well over a 100 years ago. Albert was careful with his cash to the point of meanness. Between 1840 and 1860 he raised the income of the Duchy of Cornwall from £16,000 to £60,000 a year. He didn't spend the profits but stacked them away for his son Edward. He cut spending to the bone. The wine cellars were put under lock and key. The royal candle-ends were closely guarded from pilferage by the ill-paid staff. When, in 1852, the old miser left Queen Victoria a quarter of a million, she grabbed it with both hands, though she had never met the man. After the death of her beloved Albert, Victoria's love turned to an obsessive accumulation of possessions and wealth. She became a lonely, hoarding recluse. Her voluminous writings – royal vapourings straight from the horse's mouth – sold like hot cakes. Gifts poured in from all corners of the Empire – gold, diamonds, exquisite wood carvings and furniture – while sugar was strictly rationed to the staff at Windsor and newspapers were cut into squares for use in the loos. When she died, Victoria left an estate worth £4 million with no tax paid.

Royal tight-fistedness seems catching. It was practised with equal avidity by George V and Queen Mary. Not a drop of wine was wasted, nor anything relinquished. Reputedly, Queen Mary left the present Queen a fabulous collection of antiques with gold and silverware.

The private estate at Balmoral was bought by Prince Albert in the 1840s for about £31,000. Today, the Scottish estate covers 80,000 acres. No valuation has ever been made public, but it cannot be worth less than £20 million – and, with the rapidly increasing development of North Sea Oil resources and the consequent enormous demand for land in the Aberdeenshire area, it could well be worth £50 million by the early 1980s. Similarly, Albert bought Sandringham, in Norfolk, for £220,000 on behalf of his son, the Prince of Wales, later Edward VII. It sounds like chickenfeed today, when its houses and 20,000 acres must be valued at not less than £10 million, and probably far higher. Edward VII poured £1 million into Sandringham over sixty years ago. And, in 1973, the present Queen, showing a similar streak of business acumen, decided to put in another quarter of a million. At the same time, she applied for house improvement grants of £1,000 a cottage from the small Freebridge Lynn Rural District Council. How many such grants have been obtained over the years we can never know. We can only be certain that these were, in effect, extracted from poor rural workers by a lady sitting on her own goldmine.

In his evidence to the Select Committee, Lord Cobbold specifically mentioned the fact that the Queen and Prince Philip 'obviously own a considerable amount of furniture, pictures, jewellery, etc., in their own right'. Too true. The private collection has nothing to do with the Crown Jewels, which are *public* property, or, as Lord Cobbold said, inalienable. And, over generations, the Monarchy's private Aladdin's cave of gold, diamonds, pearls, rubies, emeralds, and sapphires has multiplied with presents from every quarter of the globe, from every Empire and Commonwealth country, from every visiting or visited Head of State, and from private individuals. The Queen's wedding gifts alone, twenty-six years ago, were valued at not less than half a million pounds, including a 2,000-year-old necklace given by ex-King Farouk of Egypt, and ninety-six rubies set in gold from the impoverished people of Burma. It is all soaring in value daily, as is the income from the Duchy of Lancaster.

It is impossible to take Lord Cobbold's assertions, that estimates of the Queen's private fortune had been 'wildly exaggerated', in any way seriously. It is more probable that they are almost all wildly *conservative*.

One of the myths most carefully fostered by the pro-monarchist establishment is that the Queen and the Royal Family pay their taxes just like any other citizens. Readers of this chapter will have realized by now that this is a gross distortion of the facts. Even so, we can see the myth perpetuated in many authoritative sources. Norman St John-Stevas, for instance, in a contribution to a book called *The Monarchy and Its Future* (1969) wrote, 'It is sometimes thought that the Queen is not liable to pay income tax, but this is not the case . . . Other members of the Royal Family pay tax in the normal way.' Likewise Andrew Duncan, in *The Reality of Monarchy* (1970), stated that, 'Prince Philip is only allowed between 50 and 60 per cent (as tax-free expenses) by the Inland Revenue.' Then, that most ardent of royalists, Sir Charles Petrie, in *The Modern British Monarchy* (1961), has said that Queen Elizabeth II's 'private estates, and any income she may derive from private investments, are subject to the ordinary rates and taxes which her subjects have to pay'. There was even a Central Office of Information pamphlet, *The Monarchy in Britain*, first published in 1969, which stated that the Queen pays income tax arising from her private estates but not on the Civil List, and that, '*all* other members of the Royal Family pay income tax and death duties'.

A later (1971) version of the booklet corrected some figures, but even the most up-to-date version of this official Government pamphlet persists in asserting that, 'The Queen . . . does [pay tax] on income arising from her private estates.' And that, 'All other members of the Royal Family pay income tax and death duties.'

Did Mr Duncan get his information straight from the horse's mouth – from Prince Philip himself? There is no Royal who is not allowed 100 per cent of his or her annuity as tax-allowable expenses, except for Prince Philip. He was on the 80 per cent figure between 1952 and 1972. So the Prince's memory was playing tricks if he gave this information to Mr Duncan.

As for the statement in the COI booklet that the Queen pays tax on income from her private estates, the Memo, from the Treasury to the Select Committee (Appendix 12), stated in Para. 4: 'The Queen is not liable to assessment to income tax or surtax, and is entitled to claim repayment of any income tax suffered at source (e.g. on company dividends). She is not liable to capital gains tax.' In his evidence to the Select Committee, Sir Douglas Allen, the Permanent Secretary to the Treasury, explained (Q.320) that the Queen pays *rates* on her private estates at Sandringham and Balmoral. And Mr J. P. Strudwick, Assistant Secretary at the Board of Inland Revenue, stated (Q.325), 'We have been advised that it [the Crown Private Estate Act] does not refer to farming profits' and that it 'no longer has any application in the inland revenue field'. So the pamphlet is inaccurate on that count. *The only tax which the Queen pays on her private estates is local rates*. It is true to say that she did pay Selective Employment Tax, and that she voluntarily agreed to pay betterment charges under the Land Commission, though both are now abolished. She does pay all indirect taxes, including Customs and Excise duty. When she comes back from abroad she declares what she has bought, just like the rest of us (as Mr Wilson, in particular, was at pains to establish), and is 'prepared' to pay duty (*if* the Customs decide to ask for it!)

The second point quoted from the pamphlet is equally misleading. Members of the Royal Family who do not receive annuities, but who receive grants under Class V of the 1952 Civil List, e.g. Princess Alexandra, the Duke and Duchess of Kent, etc., do *not* pay tax on such grants. To that extent, the COI is again wrong. *These are considered to be tax-free 'gifts' from the Queen.* It is inaccurate, also, to say that all other members of the Royal Family pay income tax and death duties. The Prince of Wales's substantial unearned income from the Duchy of Cornwall is wholly tax free, and if he died prematurely his accumulated estate would not be subject to death duty.

No wonder confusion exists in the public mind as to the tax liabilities of the Crown. Whether such confusion has been deliberately created is a matter for cynical conjecture. For this reason, the evidence given by Treasury and Inland Revenue officials on the taxation position of individual members of the Royal Family was probably the most crucial evidence ever heard by any Civil List Committee. It was not evidence that could have been given without the consent of the Queen. So why did she consent so readily to 'open the books' on personal taxation matters while she declined to deviate one iota from her position of non-disclosure in respect of her private wealth? Did she feel, a little belatedly, that she had been too rigid in one direction and should therefore be more flexible in another? Or did she calculate that total revelation in the one direction might be less damaging than, or deflect attention from, the other? We can only guess at the motivations, but, whatever they were, the Treasury and Inland Revenue evidence did much, if not all, to clear up misunderstandings on the tax position.

However, the *Financial Times* leader of 3 December 1971, already quoted from, summarized the problems that this left unsolved as follows:

> A Treasury memorandum printed as an appendix to yesterday's report confirms that this [the Queen's private] income, however much it may be, is not liable to income tax or surtax

or capital gains tax; Her Majesty is, indeed, entitled to claim repayment on income tax suffered at source, such as on company dividends. None of her property is liable to estate duty. Now it is true that the Queen has used moneys from her own private resources, as well as contributions from the Privy Purse, to offset the rising cost of official expenses of other members of the Royal Family – a cost that can fairly be said to be a burden that the public should bear. But what is not known, and what cannot be properly ascertained from the committee's report, is how much of these amounts the public is in fact contributing in the form of tax reliefs. Tax is not paid as a form of Treasury-supported income; it is in a direct sense a 'salary' to Her Majesty . . . *Without the facts* [my italics] there can be no basis for an assessment that the general run of people would see to be fair . . .

The total wealth of the British Royal Family remains a closed book – one of the most closely guarded secrets of modern times. They resolutely refuse to divulge the real figure. Their investments are clandestine, and no investment is ever made in the name of the Queen herself.

The royal fortunes have been built up partly by the skill of highly professional investment advisers – but mainly by unique tax concessions, granted by Parliament to no other citizen of this country. The fact remains that the annual sums the country pays to the Monarchy are completely free from parliamentary scrutiny. No questions may be asked, beyond such matters as the gleaming expensive swan, the Royal Yacht *Britannia* (expense and maintenance of which is borne by the Ministry of Defence), and the Royal Palaces. The Royal Family's refusal to disclose its personal fortune, and its equally strong determination to hang on to its uniquely privileged tax position, must lay it increasingly open to the charge of voracious grasping on a monumental scale. One day the people will demand the truth about the unacceptable face of royal capitalism, and, should they get it, it is hard to imagine the institution surviving the process.

3. THE CROWN ESTATE, THE DUCHIES AND OTHER MATTERS

The Crown Estate

As we have seen, enthusiastic monarchists often indulge in the fantasy that Britain actually makes a profit out of its Royal Family. This sleight-of-hand is achieved by comparing the revenue accruing to the State from the Crown Estate with the sums paid for the Civil List, and drawing the conclusion that the State gets a very good bargain. Sir Charles Petrie, the distinguished monarchical expert and writer, can write provocatively, even critically, about our modern Monarchy. But in his book *The Modern British Monarchy* he figured the equation as follows: £641,000 was the total (in 1960) paid out on the Civil List and annuities, from which must be deducted the £80,000 which the Exchequer collected from the Duchy of Cornwall, leaving a net total of £561,000. Receipts from the Crown Estate in that year were £3,200,051, so the country was 'making a profit out of the monarchy of nearly a million pounds a year' (after the Crown Estate Commissioners had deducted a further £1·6 million as expenses).

Yet, as Kingsley Martin pointed out in *The Crown and the Establishment*, it is a 'legal fiction' that the crown lands, in central London and elsewhere, 'belong' to the Monarchy, or that they are 'voluntarily' surrendered to the Exchequer at the beginning of each reign in return for the Civil List provisions. It is a confusion that has been deliberately created and maintained, so let us look at the facts.

William the Conqueror, once he had subdued the opposition in 1066, was, literally, monarch of all he surveyed. At the Norman Conquest, as long before and long after, a king acquired most of his wealth and cash from confiscated land. Possession equalled power, and the ability to reward followers meant that power could be maintained. So William handed out parcels of *his* land as *he* thought fit, though, naturally, the Crown kept vast tracts back for itself. Subsequently the enormous Crown estates were gradually dissipated by William's successors. Kings being sovereigns in the true sense, they could do what they liked. From the reign of William II in the late eleventh century, down to that of William III, 600 years later, the so-called 'private' royal lands were continually sold off or given away.

In the early seventeenth century, possibly the most uncouth, objectionable and unhygienic of the Stuart line of kings, James I, descended on England like a Scottish plague. He lost no time in granting vast estates to his Scottish camp followers while showering knighthoods on all and sundry. Soon after his accession, a plot to throw off the English yoke in Ulster was discovered. James took the plotters' land and two million acres fell to the English crown. Thus, by 1608, did Ulster belong to King James to be dispersed among Scottish and English settlers. Then, to protect them, he sold baronetcies at £1,080 a go, raising enough money to keep an army. One large estate was given to James's friends in London: hence modern Londonderry – and the living bitterness of twentieth-century Ireland.

It was much the same story in the Scottish Highlands, where obnoxious ruffians like Argyll and Huntley were given full powers to colonize the Highlands and maintain good order among the wild clan chiefs. James was also set on restoring bishops to Scotland, and his problem was not in finding bishops, but in finding the cash to pay them. The Scottish nobles had seized the Church lands at the Reformation; they were holding on to their loot; they still do.

But, by now, Parliament was flexing its muscles, seeking to place limitations on the Crown's freedom of action. The King didn't like it, so he got by without a Parliament altogether from 1610 to 1614; until his need for money compelled him to call a new House. And that was soon dismissed. James was determined to be an absolute monarch, and the ensuing struggle of despotism *versus* constitutional monarchy would not end until 1688.

Charles I succeeded his father in 1625, and he, too, tried to raise money without going to Parliament, and by similar dubious means: selling off land, recourse to forced loans, and so on. Worse was to follow with the Catholic James II, who came to the throne in 1685 with great personal power and the people favourably disposed. He was granted a big income for life. Parliament seemed ready to give him anything he wanted. But his Catholicism, and his determination to make it the national faith, expedited his downfall, though not before his second wife had given birth to a son. A happy event in normal circumstances; not now. There were doubts as to whether the Queen had had a baby at all; suspicions that it was a sinister Jesuit trick to keep off the throne James's Protestant daughter Mary, who had married the Dutch Prince of Orange. The King found himself alone, isolated, friendless, except for Catholic sycophants. William of Orange was invited to sail and deliver the country 'from popery and slavery'. On 23 December 1688 the wretched James fled to France, and so ended one of the most evil-smelling chapters in British history. The country was well rid of him. But, in effect, he had *abdicated.* The throne was *vacant.* The job must be filled *by Parliament,* the succession decided *by Parliament.* So the Crown came under parliamentary control; and, it followed, the so-called Crown Lands were at Parliament's disposal.

The Bill of Rights of 1689 provided for the succession. It declared what the King could and could not do. It stated specifically that the Monarch had no right to violate the fundamental laws of the land. From then on, the King was virtually *under contract* to the nation – almost, if not quite. William III gave or sold Crown Lands to those who had helped him on to the throne. Parliament could have stopped him had it been so minded. It was not, and the net revenue of the lands was reduced to some £6,000 by the end of William's reign. The King had been induced to grant nearly the whole of the estates to his supporters in Parliament. In this way a single family, the Portlands, came by five-sixths of the entire county of Denbigh. No king, up to and including William III, had been able to resist the greed of those rapacious courtiers who were to become the ancestors of the great landed gentry of the nineteenth century and would survive as hangovers into the twentieth. Parliament was not yet the complete master, nor the Monarch yet the perfect servant.

The continuous alienation of the Crown Lands, however, became the subject of successive protests and proceedings in Parliament, and on Queen Anne's accession in 1702 the first Crown Lands Act was passed. This restrained the Crown from alienating any part of the property, and it was this Act which asserted the supremacy of Parliament in deciding how the revenues of the Crown Lands should be disposed. Similar Acts were passed in 1714 and 1727 on the respective accessions of George I and George II.

We saw in Chapter 2 how the Civil List developed out of an annual sum granted at the beginning of each reign to cover the running of the civil government. The original Civil List Act of 1697 had granted £700,000 a year. This was expected to pay the salaries and pensions of ministers, judges and other public servants; also the expenses of the whole Royal Family, the upkeep of the Royal Palaces, various pensions to public servants and the cost of the secret service. Variations on this theme continued throughout the first half of the eighteenth century, until eventually the 'bargain' of 1760 was struck. Then the Crown was relieved of all charges for the running of the government machine, in return for which it 'gave up' any claim to the revenues of the Crown Lands (except that of the two Duchies), receiving instead a fixed annual Civil List for the duration of the reign.

The Crown Lands Act of 1760 provided that the land revenues should be carried to a general fund and applied to certain specific purposes, one of them being the support of the Crown's Civil List. But a later Act of 1787 transferred all the 'hereditary revenues' to the Consolidated Fund, i.e. to the Government.Thus is the charade of the Crown 'voluntarily' surrendering the revenues of its private lands at the beginning of each reign in return for a fixed Civil List – to last for the duration of the reign – calculated to deceive. The nurturing of myths about the 'hereditary rights' of the Royal Family to revenues from lands which are so patently public property – which have, since 1786, been publicly controlled and publicly developed by Commissioners appointed by the Chancellor of the Exchequer and answerable to Parliament – is beyond the credulity of any rational mind.

The Crown Estate began with plunder – by William the Conqueror – extended by the confiscation of monastery estates in the reign of Henry VIII. The greed, perfidy, corruption and extravagance of successive Monarchs had made the estate virtually bankrupt by the end of the seventeenth century. By 1760 the Crown had been glad to be rid of the burden of paying the cost of Government in return for a guaranteed annual income. That is substantially the position as it is today.

But, as has been generally admitted in recent years, there remains a remarkable lack of knowledge about the Crown Estate. There have been at least seventeen Acts of Parliament dealing with the Crown Lands. All the previous legislation relating to the Crown lands was consolidated in the 1961 Crown Estate Act, which defined the duties of the Estate Commissioners. The powers conferred on them in managing the Estate are 'the powers of an absolute owner, subject only to certain restrictions designed for the protection of the reversionary interest of the Heir Apparent'. But, as Mr W. A. Wood, the Second Crown Estate Commissioner, admitted in his evidence to the 1971 Select Committee (Q.462), the Estate is, in effect, *a public estate*.

Virtually all of its most valuable assets lie in the heart of London, including Regent's Park Estate, most of Regent Street, Carlton House Terrace, property goldmines in Mayfair, Piccadilly and Whitehall, not to mention properties at Ascot, Windsor and in the Home Counties. It includes everything and anything from shops, flats and houses to factories and mills. Over 60 per cent of the gross revenue comes from this urban ownership. Agricultural land (about 150,000 acres) produces about 20 per cent of the Estate's total income. This land is spread over large estates in Scotland – much of it wild moorland (excellent grouse shooting for top people) – and rich arable and pasture land in England. Then miscellaneous revenue comes from mineral royalties, forestry, salmon fishing in Scottish rivers and the sale of sand and gravel from the foreshore all round the British coasts. There are also large investments in government securities.

In 1956, the capital value of the estate was reckoned to be *at least* £50 million, which would indicate that its value today must be well in excess of £150 million. But, as was pointed out in 1956 in a parliamentary debate, the net return on £50 million being obtained by the Crown Estate Commissioners was a bare £1 million. This was compared with the net return Church Estate Commissioners were getting on landed properties valued at about £15 million: £2,125,000. The *gross* receipts on the Crown Estates in 1970 were still only between £6 million and £7 million.

The value of the estate has been enhanced over the years by public investment, and a rapid urbanization which has escalated the price of land in central London to millions of pounds an acre. It has also been enhanced by the fact that no estate duty is payable, since it is property belonging to a corporate body, an institution; and estate duty is not payable by institutions. That this enormous public estate, with its vast potential, and containing many buildings and areas of supreme national interest, should consistently yield so little to the public Exchequer would seem to indicate that the whole basis of its management is long overdue for reassessment. But that problem lies outside the scope of the present book.

In the meantime, anyone who suggests that Piccadilly, Leicester Square and Regent Street, or the shingle and sand on our beaches, or the bed of the White Cart Water in Paisley, are the personal property of the Sovereign, is asking us to believe in fairies.

The Duchy of Cornwall

A royal charter of 13 March 1337 created the eldest son of the then reigning monarch, Edward III, to be Duke of Cornwall. It was a new rank in the English peerage.

Edward III was then 24, having succeeded at the age of 14. His reign was one of bloody wars, first with Scotland and then with France, and the King needed money to finance his war games. This meant going to Parliament, and they had begun to ask awkward questions. Indeed, in 1340 a parliamentary committee was to be set up to inquire into how the last cash hand-out had been spent. No doubt it was with such difficulties in mind that the King decided it might be prudent to make separate, private provision for his eldest son. The charter provided the new duke and his heirs (the first-born son of the monarch) in perpetuity with vast estates in Cornwall and Devon – property subsequently extended into Somerset, Dorset, Gloucestershire, Wiltshire, the Isles of Scilly, and, last but by no means least, Kennington in South London. The original estate had been 'acquired' from the Earls of Cornwall, whose holding dated back to the plunder of William the Conqueror.

Over the years, lands and properties were bought, sold and exchanged, until the present size of the estate is 128,930 acres, organized into 'manors' of 100 to 4,000 acres, varying from tenant farms on Dartmoor to the flower farms of the Scilly Isles. The main London property is the Manor of Kennington: only 45 acres and largely residential, but with some commercial and office property, plus the valuable Oval Cricket Ground. In 1970, the country rents were about £300,000. The Kennington rents were just over £300,000 in the same year.

Charles Philip Arthur George Windsor, born on 14 November 1948, came into this lucrative property at the age of four in 1952 for the quite fortuitous reason that he was the first-born son of his mother, who had happened to become Queen, and because of a royal charter over 600 years old.

The accounts of the Duchy of Cornwall are presented annually to Parliament, but, unlike other parliamentary papers, they are not generally made available to MPs. Perhaps this is a part of the coyness of the Monarchy in revealing its true wealth. If so, it has been indefensibly connived in by successive Conservative and Labour governments. A Member can, however, obtain a copy if he makes a specific request (see Appendix B), though it is surprising how many Members do not even know that much.

As with all other land and properties in our hard-pressed economy, prices and rents are soaring. Kennington itself is a goldmine. A current valuation would not be under £30 million. Ten million pounds was the estimated valuation put on the Duchy's 50,000 acres of agricultural land. Therefore Prince Charles can draw on *known* personal property worth at the very least £40 million – a figure which will almost certainly have multiplied many times by the time he succeeds to the Throne, assuming another twenty years' reign for the Queen.

Between 1952 and 1970, the Duchy's total gross revenues were well over £9 million. Over that period, Prince Charles received a tax-free income of about half a million. In 1970 his net income from the Duchy was up to £105,000 – equivalent to a taxable income of about £900,000. When Prince Charles went into the Navy, it was announced that he would give his naval pay to a military charitable organization. This gesture had followed one of, apparently, even greater 'generosity', when it was publicized that he had voluntarily relinquished his right to half of his entitlement to the whole of the net revenues of the Duchy of Cornwall.

Such exercises in public relations are transparently designed to persuade the plebs that the Prince and his advisers are making financial sacrifices in the national interest. The total entitlement is, in fact, likely to become so fabulous as to constitute a major embarrassment. Should Prince Charles pick up his phone tomorrow to tell the Chancellor of the Exchequer that he now wished to take the whole of the revenues of the Duchy, there would be no need for Parliament to be informed; his tax-free annual income could be doubled from £100,000 plus to a quarter of a million *at a stroke*. One would consider it would need insensitivity on a medieval scale to do any such thing.

But then the Duchy of Cornwall *is* run like a feudal estate. Byelaw 29 of the Cornwall River Authority grants it the following immunity:

> Nothing in these Byelaws shall operate to prevent the removal of any substance on, in, or under (or the erection of any structure building or machinery or any cables, wire, or pipe on, over or under) lands belonging to his Majesty in right of his Crown by any person thereunto authorized by the Commissioners of Crown Lands or lands belonging to His Royal Highness the Duke of Cornwall or the Possessor of the Duchy of Cornwall for the time being by any person thereunto authorized by the Council of the said Duchy.

Well and good. But a constituent of Mr John Pardoe, the Liberal MP for North Cornwall, recently bought his farm from the Duchy. He had letters to show that the Duchy had sold it to him together with the right to take sand and gravel from the river bed which passes through the farm. But now he finds himself constricted by the River Authority's Byelaw 13:

> No person shall dredge or raise or take or cause or permit to be dredged or raised or taken any gravel sand ballast clay or other material from the bed or bank of the river except with the consent of the Board which consent may be given subject to conditions.

So the farmer must go cap in hand to the authority's board for consent to exercise his rights. While, a few yards along the same river bed, on the next farm, which the Duchy still owns, the landowner may continue to take as much sand and gravel as he likes, despite the no doubt good reasons behind Byelaw 13.

The same constituent of Mr Pardoe's drew attention to Appendix B of the *Guide to Agricultural Wages Structure in England and Wales*, entitled 'Workers' Questions and Answers'. No. 27 reads as follows:

> Q: I am a Crown employee. Could I obtain an Employer's Declaration?
>
> ANSWER: Yes. Although *a craft certificate has no effect while you remain in Crown employ*, it would be binding on a subsequent employer.

Why, in heaven's name, should it not be binding on the Crown?

In fact, the feudal aspects of the Duchy's administration have in recent years taken on a decided flavour of the ruthless ethics of a big-business empire. On 31 December 1971 letters went out from the Duchy of Cornwall Office in Kennington Lane advising tenants of proposed annual rent increases through to 1976. A number of the Duchy properties were tarted up – cheap carpeting of tenement corridors, and other decoration – to 'justify' substantial rent increases. The Duchy warned its tenants that these increased rents were 'considered to be less than the "fair rent" ' and informed them that, in future, rent must be paid monthly in advance.

The Duchy as a whole is in fact run from a headquarters office at 10 Buckingham Gate, London SW1. The curious may look up the Council members in a current *Whitaker's Almanack*.

Back in the Scilly Isles in 1961, on 29 September, the *Sunday Express* carried a story headed: 'Widow Thomas fights Duchy for Home':

> The Duchy of Cornwall has ordered Mrs Adeline Thomas, a 65-year-old window, to quit the 30-acre flower farm in the Isles of Scilly, which has been farmed by her family for more than 200 years . . . by ancient practice most of the Duchy land is let on a yearly tenancy and in many cases the farmers have built their own houses and farm buildings over the years. Such a farm is Salakie [Mrs Thomas's], with its 5-bedroomed farmhouse, with 6-ft thick walls.

This obscenity was carried out by the Duchy, in the name of the 12-year-old Prince Charles. Mrs Thomas, who still lives in Cornwall at the moment of writing, remembers the incident as 'feudal tyranny'. She wrote to me after her last visit to the Scilly Isles in summer 1972 to let me know that the 'old feudalism is still operating'.

There are forty-five Duchy cottages on St Martin's, many of which stand empty in the winter. These are holiday homes for rich mainland dwellers. Mrs Thomas did apply for one in which to spend her remaining years. In vain.

One other peculiarity of the Duchy of Cornwall deserves a mention. This is that when anyone dies intestate in the Duchy, and no relation can be traced, their estate passes direct into the hands of the Prince of Wales. Between 1952 and 1962 a sum of £43,820 was garnered by this means.

After Edward VIII abdicated in 1936, he went into exile and lived a life of opulence in Paris. How did he manage? Did he receive financial help from the Royal Family? We do not know.

But he had been Prince of Wales and Heir Apparent between 1910 and 1936. During those years the revenues of the Duchy of Cornwall, totalling over £3 million, accrued to him. So, as Duke of Windsor, he lived out his exile as a multi-millionaire.

For the year ending 31 December 1973, the total salaries bill for the Estate (London establishment only) was £35,625. Upkeep of the Duchy Offices came to nearly £30,000; and payments made to Prince Charles were £265,046. On the other side of the balance sheet, total receipts were £1,314,946: £59,929 was collected in dividends on securities, and the sales of wood, etc., brought in over £252,000; over £244,000 was spent on buying shares, and more than £240,000 made by selling or redeeming securities. And now mineral prospecting is going on in the Duchy on a substantial scale. The income from mineral royalties is likely to increase sharply over the next few years.

Prince Charles, in titular ownership of assets worth over £40 million *now*, in 1974, will inevitably be a millionaire several times over before he is 30. Yet, in the 1973 Civil List, Parliament had agreed to make a provision for his hypothetical widow of £60,000 a year! Thus is our Prince of Wales one of the richest absentee landowners in Britain. He has visited his properties in the Scilly Isles *only once* in the last decade (see page 241). The best-selling royal telly film contained a clip that showed Prince Charles and his mum 'sitting in' at a board meeting that purported to discuss the future development of the Oval Cricket Ground at Kennington. The fictionalizing process goes on creating its bland propaganda under a smooth public-relations umbrella.

The Duchy of Lancaster

When the 700th anniversary celebration dinner of the Duchy of Lancaster was held in Gray's Inn on 26 October 1965, one of the guest speakers was the Right Honourable Douglas Houghton, MP, Chancellor of the Duchy at the time. In his speech he tried to trace the institution back to its origin. It began in 1265 when Henry III granted to his second son, Edmund, the first part of what is, in Duchy circles, described with fastidious taste as 'the original inheritance'. But how, Mr Houghton asked, had Henry III acquired the estates in the first place? Had he stolen them? Or bought them? Or confiscated them? An acknowledged authority on these matters is Sir Robert Somerville, the former Chief Clerk to the Duchy. He described the King's 'transaction' as 'confiscation', the lands as 'forfeited lands': 'seized into the King's hands' from the Earl of Leicester. In other words, the Duchy was founded on the loot and booty of civil war: the property of Simon de Montfort and the Earl of Ferrers, forfeited after the defeat of those rebellious barons in 1265–6.

Simon de Montfort has been described as originator of our Mother of Parliaments. But not everyone is so generous in their assessment. Mr E. R. Wheeler, the present Clerk of the Duchy, described him as 'a bad man' in his evidence to the Select Committee of 1971–2. Yet this baronial warlord did establish that the law was above the king. And anyway, what of the king who purloined his land? Henry III's reign of fifty-six years has been dismissed by historians as one of incompetence and the misuse of power.

During the fifteenth century, the Duchy, like the Crown, changed hands in the Wars of the Roses. Later on, the Duchy profited from the dissolution of the monasteries, but in the seventeenth century first the Stuarts, and then William of Orange, disposed of large tracts of the Duchy to raise funds.

When, in 1760, George III gave up the other hereditary estates in return for a Civil List, the Duchy receivers were six years behindhand with their accounts. The previous year's profits had been £16 18s. 4d.

Why was the Duchy not surrendered in 1760 along with the other hereditary lands and revenues? The answer seems to go back to the reign of Henry IV. He had been Henry Bolingbroke, the son of John of Gaunt (himself the fourth son of Edward III). John of Gaunt was also the son-in-law of Duke Henry, who had been made the Duke of Lancaster in 1351. When Duke Henry died, John of Gaunt was created Duke, and held the Duchy until he died in 1398. So, when Henry Bolingbroke became Henry IV, he took immediate steps to make sure that the Duchy was administered separately from other Crown properties. Subsequent charters continued the arrangement, until it was finally approved by Parliament in the reign of Henry VII. It has never effectively been challenged. And the Duchy revenues have been a constant source of royal contentment ever since: a valuable source of ever-increasing tax-free revenue.

By 1838 the Duchy was yielding £5,000 net. By 1855 this had grown to £20,000, by 1872 to £40,000, by 1896 to £60,000, and by 1946 to £90,000. Total receipts, which in 1944 were £154,791, had risen to £779,076 by 1970, £940,000 by 1972 and £1,380,602 by 1972–3 (see Appendix B). It looks like an impressive record of shrewd management.

Properties owned by the Duchy may be found in Yorkshire, Staffordshire, Lancashire and other parts of the North-West of England. Until the passing of the 1938 Coal Act, the Duchy owned coal mines in Yorkshire, Staffordshire and even Glamorgan. It has the ownership of all of Lancashire's foreshores, including half the bed of the River Mersey from which sand is dredged and used in the production of glass. The total acreage now administered by the Duchy is about 52,000, over 20,000 of which is in Yorkshire. Though the greater part is agricultural and moorland, there's a fish-and-chip shop in Pickering in Yorks, warehouses, offices or residential leaseholds in London's Strand and the City, Aldershot, Bedford, Bristol, Kettering, Leeds, Leicester, Lewes and Northampton, and residential properties in Cockfosters, Middlesex, Hadley Wood, Herts, and Harrogate, Yorks. All told, the Duchy has property of one kind or another in no less than twelve counties. As a 'private' estate it is a mixed bag. But, as a 'private' estate, it also has a Cabinet Minister appointed to it who is described as the Chancellor of the Duchy of Lancaster. And, unlike any other 'private' estate in the country, it must by statute submit to the House of Commons annual audited accounts.

The office of Chancellor of the Duchy has existed for nearly 600 years, since 1399. For the last 200 years, the Chancellor has been a member of the Government, and usually a member of the Cabinet with other important but non-Departmental duties. Recently, former Chancellors of the Duchy have become Prime Ministers, as with Winston Churchill and Clement Attlee. Others became Chancellor of the Exchequer, like Iain Macleod.

The situation was complicated by the fact that the Duchy authorities also exercise judicial authority within their area; they were responsible for the administration of the Lancashire Chancery Court until the County Courts Act of 1971 became effective. Douglas Houghton used to allocate Friday as his 'Duchy Day' – spending a lot of time looking at recommendations for magistrates in the Duchy – many hundreds were needed, and it was important to keep a political balance; not to mention a religious balance, in an area that has a high proportion of Roman Catholics. One magistrate let it be known that he would not convict anybody exceeding the 70 m.p.h. speed limit on motorways.

Chairmen of Urban and Rural District Councils at that time

became magistrates automatically, by virtue of their office. It became an embarrassment to the Chancellor when some of these gentlemen proved to have had court convictions themselves. Happily, this automatic right has now gone.

There are also something like forty Church of England 'livings' within the patronage of the Duchy. The Chancellor might or might not take an active part in exercising this patronage. Hugh Dalton, who was Chancellor of the Duchy in 1947, recalled in his memoirs how a previous Chancellor had insisted on hearing at least one sermon, sometimes two, before deciding on whether or not an applicant was fit for a particular living. MPs who knew of discontented vicars in their constituencies would often approach the Duchy Chancellor with a view to a transfer! Such transfers could be, and sometimes were, arranged as the Chancellor could do so without the consent of the boss bishop! Retired naval padres often find their way into a living in the Duchy.

One of the most intriguing curiosities of the Duchy's accounts is the 'No Kin Account', which deals with the estates of persons who die intestate within the Duchy and who have no traceable kin. The account always has liquid assets available to it in case, after the lapse of an indefinite period, some relative should establish a legitimate claim.

Then there was the Bastardy Account: an account dealing with intestacy cases when the only next-of-kin was illegitimate. Recent legislation has happily enabled an illegitimate child to lay claim to a parent's estate. But, a few years ago, there was the interesting case of Miss E. F. Wilson (who has given me permission to cite her name and the details). Miss Wilson had cohabited with a Mr C. A. Doherty between June 1954 and May 1955. A child had been born in June 1955, and the association between Miss Wilson and Mr Doherty lasted until his death in August 1957. On 22 November 1954 Miss Wilson gave notice to the City of Liverpool Register Office that she intended to marry Mr Doherty, her address at the time being in Liverpool, and Doherty's in Warrington. But the marriage never took place. So, when Mr Doherty died intestate, the Duchy tried to trace relatives – with no success. Miss Wilson claimed that, as his common-law wife, she was entitled to the estate of £4,750. The Duchy, however, contested her claim – until, after many years and the help of a solicitor, the Duchy awarded Miss Wilson £250 in August 1970. At that point she wrote to me, and I made representations to the then Chancellor, the Right Honourable Geoffrey

Rippon, MP. To his credit, Mr Rippon investigated the case, and within two months a cheque for £2,000 had been sent to Miss Wilson. But despite repeated efforts, no further payment has ever been made to her. The Clerk to the Duchy, Mr Wheeler, came to the House of Commons to see me about the case – but said they remained adamant that Miss Wilson had had a fair deal. So the remainder of Mr Doherty's estate will go eventually into the Privy Purse – peanuts for the royal coffers.

Between 1952 and 1972, the Duchy netted, from intestacies alone, close on £1 million. The origin of the law on intestacy is summarized in *Halsbury's Laws of England*, and the process is today governed by the Administration of Estates Act 1925, Section 46 of which specifically states that, in the Duchies of Cornwall and Lancaster, intestate estates go direct to the Crown as *bona vacantia* – property which no one can claim. This goes back to the concepts of feudal tenure of land and the medieval common law: the theory that since all land is held of some lord, if the tenant dies without heirs it is only right that the lord should have back that which he gave to the tenant – because there is no one else left to perform the feudal services.

Provision for intestate estates, however, goes back to even earlier times. A statute of King Canute provided for the distribution of the property of an intestate amongst his wife and relations: 'If any one depart this life intestate . . . let the property be distributed very justly to the wife and children and relations, to every one according to the degree that belongs to him'; the lord was not to 'draw more from his property than his lawful heriot'. These quotations are taken from the judgement of the Judicial Committee of the Privy Council in the case of Dyke *v.* Walford 1846. This was an odd case, argued between the nominee of the crown *as* the crown and the nominee of the crown in right of her Duchy of Lancaster. The question was whether the personal property of an intestate bastard who died domiciled in the Duchy passed to the Queen as Queen of England or in right of her Duchy. The judgement found that the right of the Crown to property which has no other owner 'must have existed from the foundation of the monarchy'. The court also ruled that this right had been passed from the Crown to the Duchy under the terms of the charters which established the Duchy. The court accepted that 'the Duchy, and such rights as were originally granted with it, became vested in Her Majesty, by a title distinct from Her Crown'.

Be that as it may, let us now move on to take a more fundamental look at the Duchy of Lancaster's accounts, taking 1953 as our starting point. In that year total receipts came to £319,326 16s. 5d. Rents had yielded £125,000, dividends had paid £12,000, and £26,000 was derived from the proceeds of devolutions and forfeitures. Property tax of £47,000 was recovered *in full.* On the other hand, management expenses came to over £24,000 and maintenance expenses were £45,000. The cost of church stipends, donations and 'ceremonial officers' came to £4,000, and £2,000 went towards the Chancellor's salary. The Queen received £100,000. And £56,000 worth of 3½% War Stock was bought. There remained a balance in the bank of £75,000.

The accounts for the year ended 29 September 1972 told a very different story. Income had risen from £319,000 to £940,000. Rents – mostly farm rents – had increased to £404,552. Devolutions and forfeitures rose to over £127,000 in 1971, though they fell to £80,243 in 1972. Over £12,000 worth of income tax was recovered. The new balance in the bank stood at over £144,000. And, more important, the Queen was now taking £300,000 a year. In 1952–3 she had taken only £100,000. By 1958–9 this had increased to £120,000, by 1960–1 to £140,000, by 1961–2 to £160,000, by 1965–6 to £200,000, and by 1967–8 to £220,000. The next year it reached the ceiling of £300,000. The pattern of steadily increasing pressure on the Duchy for payments to the Privy Purse – to ward off that evil and embarrassing day when the Crown would have to approach Parliament for more money – became clear. After the Civil List increase of 1972 the Queen reduced her take to £260,000. But it was back to £295,000 in 1972–3. The greed appears to be constant.

The Duchy of Lancaster, while mainly comprising agricultural land, does have a big investment portfolio. The 1971 Accounts showed that in the previous two years over £1 million had been spent on the purchase of securities, and under £100,000 on the purchase of land. In 1972, £895,000 worth of securities were bought, and £750,000 worth sold. In the last two years alone (1972 and 1973), well over £2 million has been spent on buying shares. The Chancellor himself has exercised much influence in this switch of investment from land to shares. The Duchy doesn't speculate in land, but it can, and does, reclaim tax paid on dividends. The full list of share holdings is never disclosed; but the Chancellor can veto any investment. A Labour Chancellor, for example, might refuse to allow the Duchy to invest in South African shares, or Distillers Ltd, or in, say, the beer-brewing industry. The consequences of a major clash between a radical, left-wing Chancellor of the Duchy of Lancaster and the Duchy officials representing the Crown could be considerable. If the situation has never arisen, it is partly because there has never been a Chancellor sufficiently radical to upset the Duchy apple-cart, nor a Government sufficiently courageous to end the feudal nonsense involved.

The Duchies and the Taxman

The tax position of the Duchy revenues is said to be embodied in the Crown Private Estates Act 1862. The purpose of this act was to 'remove doubts concerning, and to amend the law relating to, the private Estates of Her Majesty, Her Heirs and Successors'. Section 8 provides that:

> The private estates of Her Majesty, her heirs or successors, shall be subject to all such taxes, rates, duties, assessments, and other impositions, parliamentary and parochial, as the same would have been subject to if the same had been the property of any subject of the realm; and all such rates, taxes, assessments and impositions shall, so long as such private estates shall be vested in Her Majesty, her heirs or successors or in any person or persons in trust for Her Majesty, her heirs or successors as aforesaid, be ascertained, rated, assessed or imposed thereon in the same manner and form in all respects as if the same estates were the absolute and beneficial estate of any of Her Majesty's subjects.

The purpose seemed clear and unequivocal. The Crown's 'private' estates were to be subject to the same taxes and rates as the private property of any other person in the realm. Therefore, since the Duchies are regarded as private royal estates, do they not come within Section 8 of the 1862 Act? They do not. In a letter of 23 March 1967, Mr James Callaghan, the Chancellor of the Exchequer, had this to say:

> The Crown Private Estates Act, 1862, provides that the same taxes shall be paid on those properties [Sandringham and Balmoral] as would be payable if they were in other ownership than that of the Crown. This Act is still in force *but there is no similar provision regarding any other property of the Crown or the Duchy of Lancaster* [my italics].

My own early attempts to obtain some information on the tax position of the Duchy of Cornwall some years ago ran into a brick wall. At my request, the impartial House of Commons Library research department made inquiries of the Duchy about estate duty payable: 'I spoke to the Duchy Solicitor who was rather cagey and not very forthcoming, but confirmed that the rule about estate duty on Crown Land also applied to the Duchy of Cornwall. He did, however, seem to imply that this was not the whole story, and suggested that if you wanted more information you should write to the Duchy Secretary' – then Sir Patrick Kingsley, KCVO. So I did.

'The question you raise is one we do not normally discuss with people who are not connected with the Duchy,' replied Sir Patrick. 'I much regret that I cannot satisfy your curiosity.' His training – educated at Eton, New College, Oxford, then in the Queen's Royal Regiment before becoming Secretary and Keeper of the Records of the Duchy of Cornwall in 1954 – fitted him well for telling such commoners as me to mind their own business. As the Commons Library researcher commented, '. . . it seems to be one of the things about which little is known and even less may be said'.

There was, however, some clarification in the evidence given to the 1971–2 Select Committee. No tax at all is paid on the net revenues of the Duchy of Cornwall, the reason being based on an opinion on this matter given by the Law Officers of the Crown in 1913. At that time the Duchy taxation question was raised in relation to mineral rights duty, and again in 1921. Mineral rights duty was one of the four duties on land values imposed by Lloyd George in 1910. This tax would have fallen heavily on the Duchy of Cornwall. The Treasury witnesses of 1971 were not too certain how things had happened; they 'guessed' that the Inland Revenue had asked the Duchy of Cornwall to make returns of its mineral royalties and then the Duchy officials asked whether they had to do so (Q.374). (The 1913 opinion was given on 18 August by Rufus D. Isaacs, John Simon and W. Finlay, and is printed in full in Appendix C.)

There was a reference to the 'peculiar title of the Prince of Wales to the Duchy of Cornwall' in paragraph 1. Mr Strudwick, as an Inland Revenue witness, gave the Select Committee an illuminating answer to the question as to what that peculiar title was: 'I am afraid I cannot say' (Q.357). It seemed strange, to say the least, coming from a witness who would undoubtedly have been fully briefed.

The 1921 legal opinion had related to other duties, particularly to income tax, and had said that 'the exemption in relation to the Duchy income is absolute'. In response to further questioning from Harold Wilson, Mr Strudwick indicated that, 'In 1921 we did put to the Law Officers the specific question of liability to income tax and the Law Officers of that time, who, I understand, were named Hewart and Pollock, confirmed completely the 1913 opinion and said it applied to income tax, *but again gave no reasons* [my italics]' (Q.407).

It was all, said Sir Douglas Allen, top dog at the Treasury, 'based on *principle*'. 'Principle' reared its head again when, on 9 February 1972, I asked Mr Barber, as Chancellor of the Exchequer, whether he would 'now review the opinion made by the Law Officers in 1913 and 1921 concerning the tax liability of the revenues of the Duchy of Cornwall'. The answer was a written and brusque, 'No, Sir.' So I asked the Chancellor to enlarge on his answer. He replied on 14 April: 'The Law Officers gave a firm opinion in 1921; nothing has happened since then affecting the constitutional principles involved to which I could point as a reason for seeking a further opinion, and I see no point in merely inviting the present Law Officers to review their predecessors' opinion.'

But *what were* the constitutional principles involved? Nobody has ever actually defined them. As Mr Wilson remarked in the Select Committee: '... The secret seems to have been buried with Sir Rufus Isaacs' (Q.409).

We can, however, say that, since the start of her reign in 1952, the tax-free income paid to the Queen from the Duchy of Lancaster alone has totalled £3 million. It may be remembered that in Mr Wilson's statement to the House of Commons in November 1969 he said that the Civil List finances would not be in the red until at least 1970 or 1971. In other words, the £475,000 of the Civil List was still adequate at the time to meet requirements. This does, however, conflict with evidence given to the Select Committee that the Queen had been devoting *part* of her Duchy income to the shortfall in Civil List provision. It is only possible to interpret such evidence as is available as meaning that almost all the money paid from the Duchy to the Privy Purse over the last twenty years has gone to augment the considerable royal fortune. Yet, when the Labour Government was operating its wage freeze in the mid 1960s, with a wage increase norm of 3½ per cent a year, the Duchy authorities applied to the Chancellor of the Duchy to increase their rents by 33⅓ per cent. Their application was rejected, but as soon as the wage freeze was abandoned, Duchy rents increased substantially. This had been a decision exclusively within the discretion of the Chancellor, acting on the advice of the Council of the Duchy. So much for all that nonsense about the Royal Family's income having been 'frozen' since the 1952 Civil List provision.

The whole question of the ownership of the Duchies of Cornwall and Lancaster has been revised and discussed inside and outside Parliament often enough over the years. Eighty years ago S. M. Davidson wrote in *The Book of Kings*:

> Before the Norman William landed in England there was hardly a manor or ecclesiastical benefice in the country that he had not by anticipation apportioned among himself and his followers. His own share, to be sure, was a handsome one, and though repeatedly confiscated and largely alienated, the crown lands were still of considerable value at the Revolution of 1688. If they ever did belong to the kings of England as individuals – that is to say, as private estates – they completely lost that character when James II fled to France. They then reverted to the nation, and parliament, as representing the nation, used them as it had a mind. The pretence that the Guelphs have some personal right to the duchies of Lancaster and Cornwall, from which they are permitted to draw large revenues, is as hollow as their more general claim to all crown lands. The crown lands are in the strictest sense national lands, and ought, for the sake of accuracy and clearness, to be always so designated. Any revenue accruing to royalty from such sources is contributed by the nation as surely as if it arose from the tax on tea or on tobacco. It is important to remember this, *as apologists of the monarchy have succeeded in breeding considerable confusion in the public mind on the subject* [my italics].

In Parliament, on 18 March 1872, Sir Charles Dilke said in a speech: 'There is not likely to be made today any attempt to contend that the Duchy of Cornwall is the private property of the Prince of Wales.' He went on to quote some words used by Lord Brougham in 1837: 'I should like to see the man, whether in the Ministerial or Opposition benches, gifted with the confidence which must be exhibited by him who would affirm that Cornwall and Lancaster are private and personal property, and not public funds vested in the Sovereign only as such; enjoyed by him as

Sovereign, and in right of the Crown alone; held as public property for the benefit of the State, and as a parcel of the National possessions.'

Dilke was to return to the problem in the 1910 debate. 'How,' he asked, 'did the property of John of Gaunt come into the possession of William III? The title to the Duchies is more absolutely Parliamentary than almost any other title in the country.' Dilke's principle is as sound and incontrovertible now as it was then. As soon as it has a mind to do so, Parliament can dispose of the Duchies as it thinks fit. The brutal fact is that the Royal Family, with the passive connivance of Parliament and people, has been able to cling to property acquired by devious and dubious methods over many preceding centuries. It is property that has escalated in value, largely by means of public investment – in roads, railways, drainage and the rest – and by invaluable tax exemptions for which no rational reason has ever been forthcoming.

It seems inconceivable that Parliament and the people will continue indefinitely to tolerate the monstrous, obscuring untruth about the 'hereditary revenues'. Meanwhile we may expect the monarchist establishment to continue to resist any clean, once-and-for-all definition of the status of the Duchies. Their best defence lies in a confusion of half-truths and uncertainties. It will hardly, however, satisfy those who feel that, if we must retain a Monarchy, it should at least be based on foundations of truth rather than fiction. We might start by renaming the Crown Estates the Public Estates, incorporating into them the Duchies of Lancaster and Cornwall, and running the whole on a professional basis, accountable to Parliament, with net revenues accruing to the Exchequer to be used in the public interest. Some of the revenue could well be set aside to pay a monarch or a Prince of Wales whatever might be considered the fair rate for the job. That would be one step along the road to more 'honest monarchy'.

The Grace and Favour Residences

The origin of grace and favour residences is as obscure as anything associated with the Monarchy. There is no account of them either in standard works of reference or in histories of the Royal Palaces. The first reference to grace and favour residences as such appears in the middle of the eighteenth century.

When George III came to the throne, money for the upkeep of the dignity of the Crown and the salaries of public servants was derived from the so-called hereditary revenues (Crown Lands) and certain taxes – principally the Excise and the Post Office. Income from these sources proved inadequate, and so, to clear the mounting debt, George III called on Parliament with the first version of national assistance being applied for by a British royal family. This led to the 1760 'bargain' and the 'surrendering' of the Crown Land revenues on the accession of each succeeding monarch. But one small part of these revenues and possessions has always been, and is still, kept in the Sovereign's hands. These are in the form of grace and favour residences, of which the majority are found at St James's Palace, Kensington Palace, Windsor Palace, and Hampton Court.

In 1776, Dr Samuel Johnson wrote to the Lord Chamberlain:

> Being wholly unknown to your lordship, I have only this apology to make for presuming to trouble you with a request – that a stranger's petition, if it cannot be easily granted, can be easily refused. Some of the apartments at Hampton Court are now vacant, in which I am encouraged to hope that, by application to your Lordship, I may obtain a residence. Such a grant would be considered by me a great favour, and I hope, to a man who has had the honour of vindicating His Majesty's Government, a retreat in one of his houses may not be improperly or unworthily allowed. I therefore request that your Lordship will be pleased to grant such rooms in Hampton Court as shall seem proper to Sam Johnson.

Dr Johnson's hopeful request was refused, but it showed that grace and favour residences in royal palaces were then allocated by the Crown on the advice of the Lord Chamberlain – very much as they are today on the advice of the Keeper of the Privy Purse.

W. H. Payne, in his *History of the Royal Residences* (1819), says of Hampton Court that the western court 'is divided into several suites of apartments occupied by private families, having possession from the Crown' and that 'the apartments on two sides of this [Clock] court are occupied by private persons; the suite on the third floor was appropriated to the uses of the late Prince of Orange'.

On the accession of William IV in 1830, the Civil List was reduced by Parliament and, among other things, the repair and maintenance of royal palaces and gardens were transferred to the annual Parliamentary Votes. In about 1877, the whole question of grace and favour residences was submitted to the Treasury and became the subject of a number of Treasury Letters (now in the Public Record Office). The position then decided still stands, namely, that the appropriate Minister (now the Department of the Environment) should be responsible for repair and maintenance of the structure and services, and for modernization, on change of occupation, at all grace and favour residences.

Tenants are responsible for their own internal maintenance costs and decoration. They also pay their own rates and fire insurance, and the cost of lighting, heating and water. But they pay no rent. Rent increases do not affect these highly privileged occupants.

Hampton Court Palace's last resident King was George II. Thereafter the Palace was gradually divided into a number of private apartments allotted by 'grace and favour'. In Queen Victoria's time it became the Queen's general custom to grant apartments to the widows or children of distinguished servants of the Crown and Nation. They are now customarily granted for life to widows of those who have served their country well, almost invariably the widows of military men. Occasionally residences have been granted to distinguished men themselves, as in the cases of Field Marshals Lord Wolsely and Lord Birdwood. But Hampton Court is now a superior kind of widows' home.

At Windsor Castle there are thirteen small houses in the Lower Ward which are allotted to retired officers of moderate means who have served with distinction in the Army. These are known as the Military Knights of Windsor. They date from 1348, and have their own quaint uniform, including a cocked hat with plume. They play a colourful role in all ceremonies of the Noble Order of the Garter, and attend Sunday-morning service in St George's Chapel at Windsor Castle. According to *Whitaker's Almanack 1974*, not one of the Military Knights holds a rank lower than major. Few of these gentlemen could claim to be of 'moderate means' as compared with many gallant ex-servicemen or their widows who are still eking out war pensions barely above subsistence level.

In 1964 I raised a question about the Military Knights of Windsor in the House of Commons, and my queries attracted some correspondence from residents in the town. Certain of these 'Knights' had sat as councillors on the Windsor Borough council. Naturally, they were Conservative – to a man. As such they had voted for the abolition of the local rate subsidy for council houses. They had actually taken part in the standard Tory propaganda about how wrong it is that taxpayers should subsidize 'well-off' council-house tenants!

In 1971 there were, in all, 121 grace and favour residences. These included eight at Buckingham Palace, twenty-seven at Hampton Court Palace, thirteen at Kensington Palace. Hyde Park accounts for one in the Ranger's Lodge. They are bestowed solely at the wish and whim of the Sovereign, mostly to members of the Royal Family, active and retired Court officials. Fifty-seven are occupied by Court staff, mainly office staff, domestic and other junior staff.

Senior retired Court officials are invariably allocated a posh grace and favour residence, acquire lucrative posts in the City business world, and live happily ever after while the taxpayer pays the rent. Sir Alan Lascelles, for instance, was the Queen's private secretary in the early 1950s. He retired some years ago, to live in a rent-free residence in Kensington Palace and be a director of the Midland Bank. Grace and favour residences give valuable rights, privileges and protection to those who can curry the royal favour. The taxpayer's only privilege is to foot the bills.

And the bills can be quite substantial. When Princess Margaret was given the tenancy of 10 Kensington Palace, £4,428 was spent on it in 1960 for 'redecoration and other services to prepare the accommodation for occupation by HRH Princess Margaret'. By 1962, a further £800 had been spent on the same young lady's house. But she was already planning a move to Apartment 1A, Kensington Palace. The initial contract for the work in 1962 had been for £65,000. The estimate had risen to £72,600 by 1965. To date the taxpayer has paid out about £80,000 on keeping Princess Margaret and her family in accommodation that is up to the standard she is accustomed to enjoy: enough to rehouse sixteen homeless families at current prices.

On 14 July 1964, I wrote to the Queen suggesting that, since *all* taxpayers paid for the maintenance and modernization of all grace and favour residences, and since they were allocated by her to people who had rendered service personal to her or to the nation, she might consider allocating houses to two retired Fife miners and their wives. I gave their names and addresses. Each husband had worked fifty years, risking his life daily, digging the coal that kept Buckingham Palace warm. The reply from Sir Michael Adeane, the Queen's Private Secretary, was courteous:

I am commanded by the Queen to thank you for your letter

of 14th July on the subject of the allocation of Grace and Favour Houses.

Yours sincerely,
Adeane.

I've heard nothing since. There must be a long waiting-list.

Such houses should be handed over to the appropriate local authority, so that they can be allocated according to genuine need.

The Royal Palaces

Since 1936 most of the costs of maintenance of the Royal Palaces have been a burden borne by the taxpayer through the Ministry of Works. Estimated costs of maintenance were transferred to the Exchequer in 1947, 1951 and 1952. In 1971–2 we set aside £385,887 for Buckingham Palace alone. This was to include over £35,000 for fuel, gas, electricity and water, and over £28,000 for the maintenance of furniture. At Windsor Castle the total was £377,584, fuel bills being over £45,000 and maintenance and operating costs £260,000. For Hampton Court Palace, the estimate was £265,766, for St James's Palace it was £197,802, and for Holyroodhouse in Edinburgh it was £101,104 – and Holyroodhouse is occupied by the Royal Family for less than two weeks in each year. All in all, we are having to spend over £2·5 million a year just to maintain the Monarchy in a string of palaces, quite apart from our involuntary subsidizing of the favoured *élite* lucky enough to be granted grace and favour residences.

The Royal Yacht

Since the Royal Yacht *Britannia* first entered service in 1954, she has cost the taxpayers of Britain over £12 million. She cost £2·25 million to build. Her first refit in late 1954 cost £67,000. Her eighth, in the autumn of 1969, cost £355,000. And her most recent, in June 1974, cost £1·75 million – or more, in 1954 terms, than the original cost of building her.

Annual running costs have escalated from over £29,000 in 1953–4 to over £750,000 in 1970–1. When *Britannia* is in service, the crew consists of twenty-one officers and 258 ratings. The weekly costs in 1967 were £7,700 in service, £5,500 in dock. Following repeated criticisms of this lame and expensive duck in House of Commons defence debates by the late Emrys Hughes, the republican MP for South Ayrshire, the Queen suggested that the yacht might engage in some exercises. That began to be done only in 1968. And the joke is still told how, in the event of war, *Britannia* could be converted into a hospital ship. Few would believe it, but since that was put forward to help to justify its being built in the first place, the fantasy must be sustained to justify its continued existence. Then, of course, as a trading nation with a great sea-faring tradition, what is more natural than that we should have a floating prestige symbol to sail the oceans of the world?

In fact, to take the five-year period from 1961 to 1966, we find that *Britannia* was in service for 337 days, or an average of only *sixty-seven* days a year. At least a proportion of these journeys were, quite simply, royal recreational jaunts. More and more people must surely be asking themselves whether, in these days of economic crisis, we can go on affording this incredibly expensive, gleaming toy for the sake of the odd royal honeymoon or getting the Queen Mother off on a Mediterranean trip every now and then. If the crew need to keep up their training, they could always take old-age pensioners on ten-day cruises or give infinite pleasure to retired pneumoconiotic miners and their wives.

A group of MPs were allowed to visit the yacht in Portsmouth Harbour in late 1971. You could eat your dinner off the deck, or off the engine-room floor. There is more gold braid about than in the rest of the British Navy. We were not allowed to see into the private State rooms, and were told that any drinks we wanted on board would have to be paid for. Quite right, too. Why should *we* drink at the taxpayers' expense? The very next day Princess Anne was having her twenty-first birthday party on board. Who paid for the drinks then?

The Queen's Flight

Originally established in 1936, the Queen's Flight consists of three light planes and two helicopters. The initial capital cost was £1·2 million and annual running costs are about £800,000. The machines are maintained, manned, and paid for by the Royal Air Force. Personnel, during 1971–2, consisted of twenty officers, 156 RAF other ranks, and four civilians. Certain Ministers of the

Crown, top military brass or other VIPs may use the Flight with the Queen's permission or at her invitation. Apart from that, the aircraft may be used almost at will by all members of the Royal Family – but only when travelling 'in pursuance of their Royal functions'. That, anyway, is the theory. In fact, Prince Philip has been known to use the helicopters to get to and from polo matches – at an expense (1971 rates) of £116 each flying-hour. The applause that greets his deft arrival from the air may one day grow sour if people start to count the cost.

The Royal Train

The twelve vehicles of the Royal Train are hardly used, yet they have to be paid for and maintained by British Railways, the cost being borne on the Vote of the Department of the Environment. It has not in the past been great by Royal standards: only £9,000 in 1965–6, but rising to over £33,000 in 1970–1. However, when the rolling stock does need to be replaced or substantially modified, it is the taxpayer who foots the bill. On 4 April 1974, the *Daily Express* reported that it had been found that the two day coaches of the Royal Train, built in the early 1940s for George VI, were 'no longer compatible with modern day-to-day operations'. The seats were hard and the '1930-style cocktail cabinet in the Prince's carriage' did not suit his 'up-to-the-minute technocrat image'. The replacements were to be the very best available, 'the ones being built for the high-speed train'.

> Made from steel, they come complete with air conditioning, temperature control and double glazing. The braking is better. Most important, so is the ride.
>
> To add to the royal couple's comfort, special furniture and fittings will be added. 'We'll get the list from the royal household, then we'll fit them at the Wolverton works,' says British Railways.

The cost? A 'regal £50,000 a piece'.

The Royal Train is probably the most immobile form of transport in Britain today that's still outside a museum. Little more needs to be said, except perhaps it should be going to one.

4. THE LABOUR PARTY AND THE CROWN

The first recorded reference to the Crown's Civil List by a leading Labour politician in the House of Commons was made by Keir Hardie on 11 March 1901, a few weeks after the death of Queen Victoria. During the debate, Sir M. Hicks Beach, the Chancellor of the Exchequer in Lord Salisbury's Conservative government of the day, had admitted to the House 'gross abuses on the Civil List in former days'. Hardie spoke to complain that the House would still not be allowed to investigate all the facts. He made a plea for 'the desirability of presenting to the nation an honest and straightforward statement of the cost of maintaining the Head of the State'. When it came to the selection of Members to serve on the Select Committee, Hardie moved an amendment to ensure 'that there should be one direct representative of the working classes on the Committee'. The amendment was defeated by 307 votes to 17. Hardie, as one of only two Labour MPs in that Parliament, must have been acutely aware of the cruel realities of the class war.

On 9 May the new Civil List was duly presented to the House by Hicks Beach. Economies *were* to be made. The salary of the Master of the Horse would be cut from £2,500 to £2,000 – and that of the Mastership of the Buckhounds would be abolished altogether, along with the Royal Hunt. Yet, despite this effort at public relations, a long critical speech was made by Mr Labouchere, the spiky Liberal MP for Northampton. He moved to reduce the total sum proposed from £470,000 to £415,000.

Hardie followed this with a curious speech that started by criticizing the cutting of the salary of the Treasurer of the Household from £900 to £700. He also criticized a similar cut in the salary of the Controller of the Household, and the reduction by £100 a year of allowances to the Lords-in-Waiting. (Two of them had even got the sack.) Even the salary of the Captain of the Gentlemen-at-Arms had been cut by £200 a year, Hardie observed. He couldn't understand 'such a cheese-paring policy . . . while at the same time an increase is being made in the amount voted to the King and his Royal Consort'. But he did make one relevant point: that at a time when workers had 'clamoured in vain for years to have their wages increased from 19 shillings to 24 shillings a week', it didn't seem right to vote more money for the King and Queen. A moderate speech from such a revolutionary as Hardie. His Labour colleague, John Burns, the Member for Battersea, reminded the House that, in the great British Empire, which was still in its hey-day and had been so much beloved of the late Queen, there were people in India 'living' on 30s. *a year*. Our glorious Empire!

When the Civil List Bill came before the House – sitting as a Committee – Hardie used much stronger language. He declared that 'as a believer in Republican principles', he could not 'see any use for a Royal Family'. It had become an anachronism. Court life was the centre of sycophancy, and led to an unhealthy state of public opinion. 'Everything the occupant of the throne did or left undone, said or left unsaid, is eulogized and glorified as being the highest wisdom.' But, he conceded, the working people were generally favourable to Royalty. In the event, he could muster only fifty-eight votes to support his point of view. A small vote by modern standards. But it was the *whole* of the then 'Lib-Lab' group in the Commons, the 'Lib-Lab' group being a coalition between Labour and the anti-imperialist Liberal wing.

The Third Reading of the 1901 Bill took place on 18 June after the Government had tried to get it 'on the nod' – that is, without debate – at midnight on the 11th. That trick had been thwarted by the vigilant Mr Caldwell, the Liberal MP for Mid-Lanarkshire, who made an objection to the Duke of Cornwall being entitled to the revenues of the Duchy of Cornwall. 'It is unfortunate,' said Mr Caldwell, 'that the Duke of Cornwall, or any member of the Royal Family, should be placed in the position of a landlord, because questions of non-payment of rent and eviction must necessarily arise.' He could not 'conceive any position more injurious to the Royal Family'. Times don't change.

Mr Labouchere took up the same point and the Chancellor replied sparsely on the principle of the hereditary revenues of the Crown: '. . . To deal with the hereditary estates of the Crown as if they were the estates of a private individual would be an error', he said. But the *revenues* from them remain the property of a private individual, the Duke of Cornwall, to use as he thought fit. Hardie then latched on to the same issue. Why hadn't the revenues of the Duchies of Cornwall and Lancaster been surrendered in 1760, along with the rest of the hereditary revenues? he asked. He got no answer in 1901, as a later committee would get no answer in 1972. So the last vote on Edward VII's Civil List came on 18 June, and the opposition mustered sixty votes.

The next Civil List debates came in 1910 with the accession of George V and were handled by the Liberal Chancellor of the Exchequer, Lloyd George. Lloyd George was probably the most fiery orator that Wales has produced. He was also possibly the most radical Welsh politician ever to have reached highest office. He loathed the Establishment, the obscene wealth of the rich and the privilege that went with it. First elected to Parliament in 1890 at the age of 27, he had early gone on record with fierce criticisms of royal finances. Later he curbed his tongue, but his private views on the Monarchy as an outdated and expensive bit of feudalism remained unchanged. Queen Victoria had, of course, detested him, and Edward VII had objected to his appointment as Chancellor in 1908.

By his 1909 Budget, Lloyd George had given great offence to the Crown, the Peerage and the landowners as he seared them with his lashing tongue. But, after the House of Lords rejected the Budget, the Liberals lost overall control of the Commons in the January 1910 general election. However, they remained the largest single party.

In the summer of 1910, Lloyd George paid a visit to Balmoral to stay with the new King and Queen. He was completely bowled over by their charm and kindness. When it came to his speech on the Civil List, he recalled that, in 1889, a precedent had been created to make financial provision for the sovereign's children, on marriage. The proposition was that each son of the new king – other than the Duke of Cornwall – should have £10,000 a year from the age of 21, plus another £15,000 on marriage. Lloyd George also reminded the House that the only tax paid by the Crown was income tax, and that only voluntarily, on the assumption that the tax was only temporary. As an assumption it dated back to 1842!

By 1910, the Labour group had thirty-nine MPs in the Commons and their Leader was G. N. Barnes, an ILP member and a former trade-union militant. Barnes launched into a long speech. The Duchies should be public property, he said. The House should compare 'the barbarous Poor Law' treatment of poor widows with the £70,000 a year being voted for Edward VII's widow, Queen Alexandra. We should not, he said, referring to the Earl of Chesterfield, then in the sinecure of Lord Steward, pay £2,000 a year for a 'decorative dude who plays golf and shows his fine figure in the West End of London'; and there were other 'kept men of the Government given fancy names', who were hangovers, relics of the old days of George III and Lord North. He compared the Civil List figures with the 15s. a week being paid to a Labour Exchange employee. And he also had a few sharp words to say about the then Prince of Wales – later to be Edward VIII. The revenues from the Duchy of Cornwall had been £43,000 in 1863. By 1910 these had grown to £92,000 – all being handed over to a 16-year-old strip of a boy.

Barnes then made a point that is as pertinent today. We should not, he stated, be paying a penny of public money to the royal children other than to the Heir Apparent and to royal widows. He recalled a speech that Charles James Fox had made in 1802. 'From the time Parliament exonerated the Crown from the expense of levying Fleets and Armies,' Fox had said, 'from that moment the *hereditary revenues became the property of the public* [my italics].' Oh, for a modern James Fox to be Prime Minister!

One other complaint by Barnes was over the inadequacy of the information given to the Select Committee. The only fact made public in 1910 was that the Committee had finished its entire business in under five hours. Few wage claims can have ever been settled more speedily: the parliamentary debate itself only lasted four hours. In the four votes registered, the Labour tally was 26, 21, 20 and 19 respectively. But what was lacking in quantity was made up for in quality. The roll of honour included names like Keir Hardie, Fred Jowett, Ramsay MacDonald, Jimmy Thomas, all radical spirits then, whatever some of them became later. We could have made no such comparable list in 1972. The Labour Party of today has grown far too respectable and respectful of the Establishment. 'Recipients of outdoor relief!' boomed Keir Hardie on the proposition to pay the royal offspring. And on the Welsh radical's conversion to the monarchical cause, the Labour MP John Burns growled that Lloyd George had had 'housemaid's knee ever since'.

Civil List debates are the only parliamentary occasions when the affairs of the Royal Family may be discussed in any detail. The story of the MacDonald era, however, is instructive in that it throws some light on other aspects of Labour's relationship with the Establishment and demonstrates how corrupting the parliamentary system can be. Things are little better today than they were forty years ago.

In 1906, thirty-nine Labour and ILP candidates were elected to the House of Commons. Their success was largely due to a deal made three years before by Ramsay MacDonald and the Liberal Chief Whip, Herbert Gladstone. The Scottish Labour Party had been started by Keir Hardie back in 1882, and eleven years later it linked up with Hardie's new Independent Labour Party (known as the ILP). While it had gained local council seats in Glasgow in the 1880s, it had no success in national elections until Hardie's election as MP for West Ham South in 1892. But the 1895 election turned out to be a total Labour failure, and that convinced Hardie that parliamentary representation could only be won by some kind of alliance with the Liberals. As Secretary of the ILP, MacDonald agreed. So, in 1903, agreement was reached, and the seeds of future schism within the Labour Party were sown. By 1906, the Labour Party was reckoned to be a growing political force, but the ILP group remained essentially more to the left, more Scottish, more parochial and, as it proved, less corruptible – with the exception of James Ramsay MacDonald. In 1905, MacDonald showed the direction he was taking when he published his *Socialism and Society*, a scenario for a gradual evolution from Liberalism – and a far cry from the revolutionary fervour of Clydeside. We need not dwell long on MacDonald's pathetic biography. It would be too unkind. It has been done often and at length elsewhere. Sufficient for the moment to demonstrate how the poor illegitimate lad from the Scottish Highlands came to the pinnacle of political power, only to be corrupted by his insatiable desire to be loved, admired and accepted by Establishment and aristocracy.

By 1922 two distinct schools of thought were well developed in the Labour Party. The first, represented by Jimmy Maxton and John Wheatley, was the no-compromise group spearheaded by the 'Red Clydesiders' who stayed true to the revolutionary spirit of Keir Hardie. The second was the 'respectable' group – those who were anxious to throw off the cloth-cap image, to behave like gentlemen. Some miners' MPs began to wear spats, and transport workers' MPs silk hats – the very hallmarks of the gentleman. Labour Party tactics during the early 1920s became designed to please Hampstead Garden Suburb, with only the occasional nod of acknowledgement towards Poplar or Glasgow or the places where Labour's support was deep and revolutionary. In February 1923, a motion moved by Philip Snowden in the Commons actually dared to mention 'Socialism'. MacDonald was highly displeased as Leader of the Opposition, and there was little further talk of 'Socialism'. Meanwhile, his trade union MPs soon turned weak at the knees as they were seduced by the bright lights of London and the easy club-life of the House of Commons.

Only Tom Johnston, another of the original militant 'Clydesiders', shattered this contemptible complacency. He protested against a multi-million-pound subsidy for the Sudan Cotton Corporation – after his party leaders had agreed to it – and implied that Asquith's son stood to gain financially from the deal. The House, and MacDonald, were deeply shocked by his breach of social etiquette.

Outside the suffocating atmosphere of that strange Chamber, social pressures were applied to the horny-handed sons of toil. Invitations to classy 'luncheons' began to be snapped up, as Tory MPs today collect directorships. Davie Kirkwood, yet another 'Clydesider', hadn't been at Westminster a fortnight before receiving from Lady Astor an invitation to a party at Cliveden, her fine house in the Thames Valley – at which Royalty would also attend! Kirkwood didn't trouble to reply.

But, very soon, class collaboration was being officially organized by the party machines. Labour MPs and their wives began to receive invitations to the Royal Garden Parties – through the official, weekly written instructions of the Party Whip. (It still goes on, and few think of not accepting.) There was the masterly idea of a bumper party – again at Lady Astor's. All the Labour MPs were to be invited – and the Prince of Wales was to be present! James Ramsay MacDonald would be there, too, of course. No sooner was the idea floated than Labour MPs holding semi-official positions in the Parliamentary Party were touting for acceptances like bees round a honey-pot. Hardly a voice of dissent was heard as the Parliamentary Labour Party set sail on the tranquil and debilitating waters of Westminster, all got up in spats, boiled shirts and top hats.

The Clydesiders, however, were deeply incensed by such insidious gnawings at the roots of their faith. One languid summer evening in 1923 James Maxton shook the House and his own Leader by getting himself suspended. The Conservative government had been on one of its economy campaigns – this time by cutting the allowance on poor babies' milk. Maxton referred to Sir Frederick Banbury, a big businessman and Tory diehard, as a murderer of children, and then declined to withdraw the remark when asked to do so by the Speaker. So he was chucked out of the House, which then got back to its nefarious business. But not for long. Within minutes, John Wheatley, Campbell Stephen and Geordie Buchanan had been suspended also. It was left to Emmanuel Shinwell to restore the quiet and bland serenity to which the Commons is traditionally accustomed, especially on warm summer evenings.

In the end, MacDonald ordered the four to apologize to Mr Speaker and the House. They still declined. Party discipline was invoked. But nothing came of it. The defeat of the minority Conservative government in January 1924, which led to MacDonald being invited to form a Labour Cabinet, intensified the rat race within the Parliamentary Labour Party. Leaders and would-be leaders scrambled for office like pigs grunting at the trough. MacDonald chose his Cabinet as most Cabinets are chosen: not so much on grounds of personal ability as on whether it would be safer to leave certain people *outside* or have them softened up *inside*.

Thus the 1924 Cabinet was one of the right, with most of the big trade unions having a usually safe and solid representative. The left was represented by John Wheatley, Fred Jowett and Josiah Wedgwood. George Lansbury was kept out because he had upset George V by saying he would like to deal with him as Cromwell had with Charles I.

Gracious ladies, alarmed by the advent of a Labour Government and fearing political rape, had their fears immediately allayed when James Ramsay MacDonald, the first Labour Prime Minister, turned out in full court dress for his first Court levee. Beatrice Webb recorded the comedy in her *Diaries, 1924–32* (1956). To begin with, Walsh, 'the ex-miner and present War Minister', was carried off by Haldane, 'to dine with him in order to instruct him how to behave with his Generals' and also 'to see whether he could fit him out with a frock-coat for Buckingham Palace the next day'. She then describes how her own husband, Sidney Webb, donned a frock-coat and tall hat he had bought in Japan in 1912. The Ministers were all drilled by Hankey, the King's Private Secretary, to behave like the proper Establishment figures they had now become: '. . . they were all laughing over Wheatley – the revolutionary – going down on both knees and actually kissing the King's hand; and C. P. Trevelyan was remarking that the King seemed quite incapable of saying two words to his new Ministers: he went through the ceremony like an automaton!'

So it was that Ramsay MacDonald and his motley crew heralded in the revolution, like circus clowns enjoying the paint, powder and ridiculous garb – all symbols of a society they had been elected to destroy.

Meanwhile, how did the Labour MPs' wives behave, and those of Labour Ministers? They formed the Half-Circle Club – so named because it catered only for the one sex. There Mrs Webb was to try to housetrain the wives of Labour MPs and Ministers to behave properly. Or, as Tom Johnston wrote in the radical journal *Glasgow Forward*, 'to see that Labour people were properly trained and taught to avoid eating with their knives and spitting on the carpet'. The real object, according to John Scanlon in his book *The Decline and Fall of the Labour Party* (1932), was to enable provincial MPs' wives to rise socially and be at ease with the 'best' people. Many leaders' wives were associated with the club, but some working men's wives found it was easier to relax with duchesses and countesses than with the upstart snobs who ran the Half-Circle.

Beatrice Webb's description of the club is a little less cynical. 'I am aiming,' she wrote, 'at bringing into the workaday Labour world an element of intellectual distinction. We have to remodel official society on the basis of simple hardworking life tempered by fastidiously chosen recreation and the good manners inherent in equality between man and man.' No revolutionary sentiment there. The Webbs were middle-class academics, as far from Clydeside in their thinking as London is from Peking.

In earlier party days, eve-of-session Labour receptions had been held in a common hall. There the humblest party member could pay his shilling or two and see, touch, and even perhaps talk with his leaders. But no longer. The 1924 eve-of-session reception was held at the Hyde Park Hotel. Tickets were issued only to those approved by the Half-Circle Club. The cloth-cap image had gone with the wind.

And while the Labour Hen Club was busy trying to smooth off the rough edges from Labour MPs' wives, something more had to be done about their men, sitting in the staid and dignified House of Commons. Most of the new Labour MPs had had a lot of local experience – in trade unions, local councils and the Co-operative Movement. They had mostly been soap-box orators and propagandists. But now they were thrust on to a national stage: the political cathedral of the Palace of Westminster. Rough and uncouth Labour MPs had to be trained to forget their soap-box, street-corner manners. They had to be taught how and when to bow when leaving and entering the Chamber of the House of Commons. They had to know how to address other MPs correctly. All MPs are honourable, but some are more honourable than others. Every MP is an 'Honourable Member', but others are 'Right Honourable', and still others are 'Honourable and Gallant', or, it might be, 'Honourable and Learned', or a combination of the lot. So a class in deportment was started. The instructor was Professor Lees-Smith. He wasn't even an MP, and never had been, but he had read it all up. The revolution could wait. Deportment was all.

Well, not quite all. Ministers dressed in knee breeches were good for many a press cartoon. Their wives gave daily press interviews. One who'd lived all her life among cotton mills told how she nearly swooned when she achieved her life's ambition – meeting the Queen. Another told of the thrill of having tea with a countess. Mrs J. R. Clymes wrote in the Labour *Daily Herald* that all Labour leaders' daughters should be presented at Court. Many were – and still are. The Royal Garden Party became *the* accepted thing in 1924. By 1931, it 'had become an essential part of the class struggle'.

No Labour Minister or under-Minister felt he could be seen at the House, unless in a tail-coat – except for John Wheatley, who was too busy grappling with the housing problem. When the second minority Labour Government came in in 1929, Wheatley, the one ministerial success of 1924, was dropped. He had committed the unforgivable sin of refusing to buy a top hat and court dress. W. W. Jowett, who had also refused to dress up in 1924, was likewise ignored. 'If there was to be unity in the Cabinet, all must not only think alike but dress alike.'

The Liberal Party collapsed in the 1929 election. When Baldwin resigned on 4 June, it cleared the way for another MacDonald-led minority Labour Government. The shape of things to come was crystal clear from its first Cabinet meeting. At least one earth-shaking decision had been made: that when Cabinet Ministers went to the Palace to collect their seals of office from the King, *all* must be dressed in morning-coats and silk top hats!

Sidney Webb accepted a peerage and, as Lord Passfield, became MacDonald's Colonial Secretary. Beatrice rationalized their decision to go to the Lords, but she did refuse to be addressed as Lady Passfield, thus helping, as she rather hopefully put it, 'to undermine the foundations of British snobbishness'. She grew quite bitchy about the social round of Ministers and their wives. Thus, on 4 October 1930, she described a Buckingham Palace dinner party for delegates from the Dominions: 'Mrs Lunn, the Under-Secretary's wife, had donned a conventional black satin, obviously bought for the occasion from the local Co-op. Ethel Snowden, with a paste tiara, and a cheap fashionable frock, was the intermediate link between us humble folk and the court circle.'

And what of MacDonald? He had fought the election on a manifesto, *Labour and the Nation*. Whatever its merits, it was immediately forgotten. Not surprisingly. Even in 1929, the Parliamentary Labour Party contained its share of mere adventurers, opportunists, careerists, aristocrats and social climbers, besides not a few genuine, simple, honest-to-God Socialist workers. But with such an amorphous mass, and with MacDonald at the helm, not even a nodding acquaintance with Socialism was possible.

MacDonald's obsession with gaining acceptance in the highest echelons of society is now a painfully well-known fact of history. Many Labour MPs, suddenly finding themselves with a fortune of a salary at £400 a year, were determined to stay on the gravy train, even if it meant supporting MacDonald in whatever he did or did not do. Relative comfort had killed compassion. While the unemployment figures soared to three million, MacDonald wined and dined with the Duke and Duchess of Sutherland, with the Marquis and Marchioness of Londonderry, and, between times, made speeches of silky eloquence.

By January 1931 he had Beatrice Webb singing his praises enthusiastically: 'what an artist the man is, how admirably he thinks and feels about external affairs . . . he has enormously increased his prestige'. Even as late as June 1931, the Government seemed to be in no danger. A record number of Labour MPs attended the Royal Garden Party – without even bothering to blame their presence there on their wives' insistence.

By 13 August the Labour Government was finished.

King George V returned to London from Balmoral on the 23 August with the financial crisis at its height and Conservative and Liberal leaders demanding savage cuts in unemployment benefit and taxes. One of the King's first acts was to instruct Sir Frederick Ponsonby, Keeper of the Privy Purse, to inform the Prime Minister that he, the King, had decided that, *while the emergency lasted*, the Civil List should be reduced by £50,000. His Majesty, wrote Sir Frederick, 'desires personally to participate in the movement for the reduction of national expenditure'. The Prince of Wales at the same time contributed £50,000 to the National Exchequer. Such meaningless, fruitless gestures could have brought little comfort to the millions on the dole whose means-tested pittances were forthwith cut by 10 per cent.

Without consultation, or even informing the rest of the Labour Cabinet, George V then appointed MacDonald to be Prime Minister of a National Government. The King's attitude in the 1931 crisis was very much what one would expect from a bewildered country gentleman of the old school: 'Come on now, chaps – let's all pull together to solve this crisis.' He probably did his best to be fair. He probably did not act in any overtly partisan way. But, whether or not that be true, he helped by his action to put the British Labour Party into the political wilderness for a generation.

It was a victory for the capitalist financiers of Britain and America. MacDonald, Thomas and Snowden became the greatest traitors the British Labour Movement has ever known – corrupted by the capitalist class society they had been elected to overthrow.

Clem Attlee and the Common Task

At the time when the 1935–6 Civil List Bill was on its way to becoming law, Clem Attlee had become Leader of the Labour Party, by default. A small, insignificant-looking man, from a middle-class background and with no great oratorical gifts, Attlee would later prove himself to be a tough, radical Prime Minister in the first post-war Labour Government of 1945–50.

On 7 May 1936, when the Bill was being given its Second Reading, he immediately moved an amendment that the revenues of the Duchies should be transferred to the Exchequer. By Attlee's standards, it was a lengthy speech. It lasted twelve minutes. He based his case on two propositions. First, that it was undesirable for any member of the Royal Family to have to rely on fluctuating revenues like those of the Duchies; and secondly, that the holding of these estates by the Crown might bring it into conflict with Parliament over questions like mining royalties. Attlee also foresaw the dread possibility that revenues from the Duchy of Cornwall might increase to such an extent that the Heir to the Throne could receive a greater income than the actual Monarch.

Attlee's speech was not that of any red-blooded revolutionary – it was scarcely pale pink. It had nothing of the former boldness of a Hardie or a Barnes. Had the Labour Party then come to terms with the Monarchy, or had the Monarchy learnt to live with the prospects of a future Labour Government? At all events, ninety-five votes were mustered for Labour's ploy. Less than half the House bothered to vote at all.

During a later debate on the financial resolution to the 1936 Bill, Mr Attlee went a little further – backward. Thus, on 24 May 1937, he said ' . . . there is no suggestion, in our opposition, of republicanism or of opposition to the Monarchy . . . we accept the Monarchy . . . I am prepared to rest myself on the dictum of the late John Wheatley, who said, "I would not raise a finger to turn a capitalist Monarchy into a capitalist Republic". ' And, Attlee went on to remind the House, the republican movement of the 1870s had not been a socialist movement at all, but one of 'bourgeois Radicals'. He did, however, complain of the 'fulsome adulation' of the Monarchy, 'the vulgar snobbery of a large section of the press, perpetually holding up the King or the Royal Family and giving the utmost vulgar publicity that they would give if they were selling some of their own goods' and 'enveloping the Royal Family with a continual round of obsequiousness'. It did the Monarchy no good at all. The Monarchy really would have to adapt itself to a society moving towards more equality and classlessness.

In all, there were seventeen minutes of what Winston Churchill called 'great mildness', 'studied moderation' and 'absolutely up-to-date modernity'. Churchill was likewise studious in the moderation of his attack on Attlee's pusillanimity. It was gentle ridicule of a speech that had been ridiculously gentle: a tame mouse of a speech, signifying nothing and riddled with dry rot.

That debate took place in the immediate aftermath of the abdication of Edward VIII. The episode is scarcely worth a mention here, except to observe that Attlee played his constitutional role of upholding the dignity of the Crown in its leading crisis of the twentieth century. Perhaps he was right to do so. As a young man at the time, I recall how massively indifferent the working people were to the whole episode. With the unemployed still counted in millions, the struggle for self-survival was more critical than the matrimonial, constitutional and regal rigmarole which so exercised the minds of the black-coated statesmen, civil servants and legal luminaries. Durham and Scottish miners were as much concerned with the Whitehall and Westminster goings on over Mrs Simpson and the King as were the Chinese. Now, however, the Coronation of George VI was imminent. Mr Pethick Lawrence, from the Labour Front Bench, grieved over the 'clothes barrier' between the Crown and the people. Many Peers, he complained, wouldn't be able to go to the Coronation because they could not afford £150 for the fancy dress. He touched lightly on the great discrepancies of wealth between the Royal Family and their undernourished subjects. He hoped that the young Princess Elizabeth would be able to mix 'with young men and young women of all classes in her adolescent life'. Alas, his hopes for the young princess were not to be realized. She was virtually closeted away from the common herd throughout her youth, and gives every appearance of being as far apart from them in her middle age.

But, on the last lap of the 1937 royal cash debate, the Opposition mustered 123 opposing votes to 199 for the government. Radicalism on royalty was not yet dead, even if the flame was spluttering.

Ten years on, and the first Labour Government with real power was in control. Mr Attlee was its Prime Minister, and Sir Stafford Cripps its severe, austere, brilliant Chancellor of the Exchequer. Both, in their salad days of opposition, had made, if not blood-curdling republican noises, at least critical comments over the pomp and circumstance surrounding the throne. 'All bunk and bunting', was the endearing phrase Cripps had used.

But now, on 17 December 1947 – in times when he and the Labour Government were rightly keeping a tight rein on public expenditure; when food rationing was still very much with us; when we were still only two years from the end of the war which had nearly bankrupted us – the same abstemious, revolutionary, left-wing Sir Stafford was proposing that, from the date of the royal marriage: (1) Princess Elizabeth should receive £40,000 a year. (2) Her Prince should get £10,000 a year. And (3) the widower's pension should be £25,000 a year. No Conservative Chancellor could have treated the young Royals more royally. The basic old age pension was then 26s. a week.

But the Government's magnanimity – and insensitivity – didn't stop there. Nine-tenths of Princess Elizabeth's £40,000 was to be tax free, as was four-fifths of the Duke's £10,000. Cripps's 'bunk and bunting' jibe was chucked in the dustbin of history. Now, he said, it was desirable 'to make adequate financial provision for the proper and dignified discharge' of all the functions and duties burdening the royal backs. The lack of power *may* corrupt. Complete power corrupts completely. The voters who had elected a Labour Government with such a huge majority in 1945 did *not* vote to maintain such immoral, vulgar and unnecessary extravagance.

Mr Attlee summed up with his usual brevity. The Royal Family, he said, led 'simple lives' and were 'approachable people', hard working and with 'no excess of luxury'. No one could have accused Attlee of being less acrobatic than Cripps. We had travelled a long, long way since 1935.

Only Arthur Greenwood took a passing glance at the republican case on that occasion. If he hadn't been a British citizen, he said, he would have been an *active* republican. As it was, he was 'a convinced constitutional monarchist'. And he did not want the debate to 'descend to the level of an unseemly brawl about money'. Some of Greenwood's colleagues were unkind enough to remind him, and Cripps and Attlee, of what they had said in 1937. But politicians are hardly notable for their consistency – and the sweet fruits of office can lead men through strange manoeuvrings of conscience and conviction.

By 1952 the Tories were back in power and the new Queen and her camp-followers had to be provided for. A proposal to establish another Select Committee was made by R. A. Butler, the smoothest Chancellor in the business. A little desultory criticism came from the Labour benches that no Scottish Labour MP was on the Committee. The republican spirit was still alive among the old-guard ILP survivors; and in the person of Emrys Hughes, the Welshman who represented South Ayrshire and who had married Keir Hardie's daughter. Mr Attlee, however, excused the omission of a Labour Scot from the Committee on the grounds that the thing had been rushed on him. The point wasn't pressed. Mr Butler meanwhile soothed the House to sleep with his version of the speech traditionally made by Chancellors on every similar occasion since 1902. There was the increase in the royal work load; the changed but continuing relationship with the Commonwealth; the need to relieve the Monarch 'of any financial anxiety'. Had not the cost of living trebled since the beginning of the century? Striking royal economies had been made; the Household was run on the most economic basis; almost frugal, you might say. Moreover, the Queen had voluntarily agreed to a cut of £17,000 in her salary; it was called an abatement – and the House 'Hear, hear'd' the sacrificial gesture. The £30,000 a year pension was provided for the widow of the Duke of Cornwall, who was then unmarried; which was natural, since he was only four years old. But, as Mr Butler said, in such matters 'one has to look a certain way ahead'. One new provision would give royal daughters £15,000 a year on marriage, the same pittance going to Princess Margaret.

Mr Attlee, still Labour's pilot, made two proposals. First, that there should be ten-yearly reviews of the Crown's finances. And secondly, that large sums provided for a child like Prince Charles and his prospective widow were unnecessary. But he thought it 'a great mistake to make government too dull'; that we mustn't let the devil get all the best tunes – which, we gathered, had been the reason for the downfall of the Weimar Republic in Germany. Attlee knew all about dull government. He hadn't much to learn, either, about making spurious speeches on royal finances.

John Parker, Labour MP for Dagenham, had the temerity to remark that the Royal Family's large private fortune should be taken into account when the Civil List sums were being prepared. The House was as deaf to such comments then as it has been since. On 9 July, Hugh Gaitskell, soon to become Labour's new leader, wound up the debate with a half-hour of excruciating middle-class deference interspersed with an occasional, apologetic criticism.

Mr Butler's task had been made easy. The figures, he assured the House, had been cut to the bone. 'The whole position of the horses has been examined. The number has been reduced from 86 to 35.' The Duke of Edinburgh *did* need a special staff and a special fund, though Mr Butler wasn't quite sure why. 'I have not got the answer in my head,' he said. Butler was like that. Too clever by half. Which is why he became the best Tory Prime Minister Britain never had.

Attlee's ten-yearly review proposal attracted 211 votes and was only narrowly defeated. But a proposal to cut the overall sum from £475,000 to £250,000 won only twenty-five supporters. Through the Government's monarchical lobby that night went Nye Bevan, Michael Foot, Clem Attlee, Hugh Gaitskell, and other notable 'left-wing' Labour radicals. The Labour Party in Parliament had proved itself to be the alternative Establishment. The Crown could sleep easily.

The fifty years from 1902 to 1952 had seen two Labour minority governments and, from 1945 to 1950, a remarkable revolutionary post-war government. The country had been ready, eager and determined to change society – in the most fundamental ways. The Crown was regarded as, at worst, an irrelevance and relatively inexpensive, and, at best, as a fairy on a Christmas tree – pretty but powerless, and giving pleasure to tourists and our own toiling masses.

In many respects, the post-war Government did not let the people down. Great and lasting measures of social and economic reform were carried through and are now woven into the permanent social and industrial fabric of the nation. But the republican fervour of a 100 years before had become no more of a threat to the Monarchy than a Christmas cracker in Parliament. The abdication of Edward VIII in 1936 had been a seven-day wonder, thanks to the cooperation of the Labour Opposition with the Baldwin establishment, the Church, the press and, let it be admitted, the overwhelming support or indifference of the British people, not to mention the impeccable behaviour of the abdicating king and his bride-to-be.

Seldom has a monarch succeeded to the throne so unprepared and ill-fitted for the job as George VI. He had the nervous disability of a stammer, which didn't help. Internally, the country was bitterly divided by class and politics. Externally, the cancerous growths of Nazism and Fascism were driving the world remorselessly towards war – aided and abetted by Britain's policies of appeasement.

In such gathering storms the Monarchy had little part to play. The Government, the Labour Party and the nation had vastly more important problems and challenges on their hands. When war came, it created a wonderful if fearful uniting force for the British people. And it helped to consolidate the foundations on which our constitution is based.

After other crowned heads had toppled like skittles in a bowling alley, our Monarchy survived because, in military terms at least, we won that war. It could not have lasted otherwise. The Monarchy's very insignificance had helped to ensure its survival.

Harold Wilson meets the Queen

The insoluble problem of the post-war era has been inflation, but the 1952 Civil List settlement had foreseen the problem. It had made a contingency provision of £95,000 a year, of which £70,000 was to be set aside to meet rising costs and prices. That £70,000, with a bit of judicious juggling, did actually keep the royal finances out of the red until 1971.

Through the earlier parts of this chapter we have seen how the attitudes of Labour Party leaders to the Monarchy changed and developed from Keir Hardie to Attlee and Gaitskell. We therefore now come to see how things were with a Labour Party led by Harold Wilson.

When Wilson became Leader of the Party in February 1963, it was regarded as a victory for the left over the right wing. He had challenged Gaitskell for the leadership in 1961. He had associated with Aneurin Bevan in resigning from the Labour Government in 1951. Almost everybody regarded Harold Wilson as being on the left, as well as one of the shrewdest political manipulators in the business.

The Labour Party won the 1964 election by a whisker. Its victory was in no small measure due to the scores of speeches that Wilson made in the months leading up to the election – about the white-hot technological revolution that had to be harnessed for the common weal; about the need to rid ourselves of the privileged class society with which we had been saddled for far too long. Inspiring stuff, and it did the trick, if only just.

When Wilson went along to the Palace to be sworn in, he took with him the whole family – wife, two sons and father – two carloads, in fact, including his Private Secretary, Marcia Williams. She later remarked that it must have been 'the most unusual and unorthodox swearing in of a Prime Minister for many a year'. It certainly showed a well-developed sense of the theatrical effect, and if Harold Wilson had been pressed into dressing up as Ramsay MacDonald had done, he would not have hesitated.

A Prime Minister's weekly Tuesday-evening audiences with the Queen usually last no more than an hour, according to personal information kindly given to me by Sir Alec Douglas-Home. Three or four important issues of the day may be lightly touched upon. On one occasion Harold Wilson kept Marcia Williams and his Principal Private Secretary waiting even longer than usual. Perhaps he had felt the time had come to discuss current economic problems in some depth, or to explain to the Queen in detail the difficulties then being faced by the mass of her people. He certainly might have talked to her on such subjects with great authority. But not a bit of it. The riveting subject had been the new riding habit the Queen had ordered for the Trooping the Colour. It sounds a far cry from the white-hot technological revolution.

Wilson is nothing if not a political realist – 'pragmatism' became a fashionable term during his first premiership. So did opportunism and gimmicry. When it suited his purpose, he never shrank from using the Monarchy for his own political ends. He himself records how, on 11 October 1965, he sought an audience with the Queen at Balmoral to discuss Rhodesia. It was pure coincidence, of course, that the Balmoral visit happened just at the start of the Tory Party's Conference in Brighton. Balmoral, not Brighton, stole the headlines. Harold, not Heath, attracted the limelight. Naturally, nothing came of the visit. But it had served a purpose, albeit a fleeting one.

The Queen was again to be used over the Rhodesian issue. On 25 October 1965, Mr Wilson himself flew to that country, 'bearing letters from the Queen to the Governor and to Mr Smith'. The letters were in all probability drafted by Wilson himself. Perfectly constitutional, and absolutely proper. Mr Smith had to be seen to be in rebellion against the Crown. The Queen was the catspaw. And in the long run it made not a scrap of difference to what was going to happen anyway.

The fact is that, when it came to it, Wilson's attitude to the Monarchy was at least as sycophantic as that of any other Prime Minister in this century. No doubt he would explain his subservience as being no more than realistic. He knows, or thinks he knows, that this style of deference goes down well with the British people, themselves class conscious and ever willing to pull a forelock to their 'betters'. He's certainly had less to say, one way or the other, on the subject of the Monarchy than any other Labour Leader.

At the outset of Wilson's term of office, the Government decided to take possession of the Palace of Westminster from the Queen. Since 1133, the Houses of Parliament had been run by an appointee of the Crown – as if they were still a Royal Palace. Henry I had appointed one Aubrey de Vere to be Lord Great Chamberlain. The Office was to be hereditary to Aubrey's heirs. Its subsequent history became a story of unsavoury, mind-boggling complexity. On occasion the office reverted to the Crown whenever the current holder committed treason or some such crime. The office was reacquired by the de Veres during the reign of Henry VII, when John de Vere, 13th Earl of Oxford, filled the position. All later problems stemmed from the fact that the 14th Earl died without issue in 1526, leaving no single heir general. So the office was granted to the 15th Earl of Oxford, *for life only*. On his death in 1540, it passed to Thomas Cromwell, and after that to various other noblemen. The office was recaptured by the Earls of Oxford during the reign of Elizabeth I. But, in 1625, the 18th Earl died, leaving as heir male a second cousin, and as heirs general three sisters of the 17th Earl. There were several other rival claimants to the office, but it went to the cousin, Robert Bertie, Lord Willoughby of Evesby.

By Charles II's accession at the Restoration there were four claimants to the office, but it stayed in the Bertie family until 1779, when Robert Bertie, the 4th Duke of Ancaster and Kestwen, died without issue. The claimants then became:

1. Lady Willoughby of Evesby, with her husband, Mr Burrall.
2. The Duke of Ancaster, with his uncle, Lord Robert Bertie.
3. Lord Percy (later 2nd Duke of Northumberland) as senior co-heir of Lady Latimer, eldest sister of the 14th Earl of Oxford.
4. The Dowager Duchess of Atholl, as heir general of the Countess of Derby, eldest sister of the half-blood of the 18th Earl of Oxford!

A pretty kettle of fish.

In 1781 it was decided that the office be vested in the two sisters of the late Duke and their representatives. So, nearly 650 years after this great office had been granted by Henry I to Aubrey de Vere and his heirs, it was, according to Geoffrey White in an article in *The Complete Peerage*, 'split up between two ladies who were not his heirs and were not even entitled to quarter the Vere arms'. It had been an 'amazing opinion' on the part of the judges.

The struggle couldn't end there. It was reopened in 1901 with claims over who was to officiate at the Coronation of Edward VII. By then, dating from the split of the office in 1781, the *de facto* joint holders of the office were the Earl of Ancaster and Earl Carrington (later Marquess of Lincoln) as descendants of one of the 1781 sisters, and the Marquess of Cholmondley as descendant of the other.

Other claimants also came forward, but the Crown opposed all claims, arguing that the office had reverted to the Crown at the death of the 14th Earl of Oxford in 1526. So the question was referred to a House of Lords Committee. Their ruling was, according to White, 'incomprehensible'. They ruled in favour of the *status quo*, and the three joint holders were left in possession.

The astonishing thing is that it still went on exactly as before until 1964, when the new Labour Government decided the time had come to shed this piece of historical nonsense. The dismantling was to be undertaken by the newly appointed Minister of Public Building and Works, Charles Pannell, a bluff Cockney-born engineer with a great sense of constitutional propriety, personal determination, integrity and courtesy.

The moment Pannell went along to the Queen to tell her that the Palace at Westminster was going to be nationalized and taken under 'workers' control', he ran into considerable opposition. Not from the Queen herself, who was charming and graceful about it, but from the Court Establishment as it closed ranks with all those who felt that ancient privileges were being threatened.

The two families principally involved were still the Earls of Ancaster and the Marquesses of Cholmondley, still ready to fight to the death to keep it that way. They took the sinecure in turn. It had been the Cholmondleys' turn when Queen Elizabeth II came to the throne. The 5th Marquess had twice been Lord Great Chamberlain – once in Edward VII's reign, and again for the period 1952–66 when (at the age of 83 – perhaps that is the retiring age for the office!) he was succeeded by his son, the 6th Marquess.

But what can this great office entail that it should be fought over so strenuously for so long by noble families, and when none of the present holders has what could be defined as a true title?

Centuries ago, the Lord Great Chamberlain was described as 'an officer of great antiquity and honour, being ranked sixth great officer of the Crown'. A big part of his job comes at a Coronation. He then dresses the King, carries his coif, sword and gloves, the gold sword and scabbards to be offered to the Monarch, and the royal robe and crown. He also undresses the King and waits on him at dinner, having for his fee the King's bed and all the furniture in his chamber, the night apparel and the silver basin wherein the Monarch washes, and the towels. When a queen is crowned, the more delicate of these duties are delegated to a lady of her choice.

Until 1964 the Lord Great Chamberlain had ruled the roost throughout the Palace of Westminster. While the House of Commons was actually sitting, between 2.30 p.m. on a Monday and 4.30 p.m. on a Friday, the Speaker reigned supreme. But, outside those hours, the Lord Great Chamberlain took lordly control. He could, and did on occasion, prevent MPs from entering the House on a Saturday or a Sunday. Once he actually stopped Mrs Marcia Williams from going to Harold Wilson's office when he was Leader of the Opposition.

But now Charlie Pannell had joined battle to sweep away the medieval set-up. And he won – so far as the House of Commons was concerned. In the Lords, the opposition, notably from Labour peers, proved too entrenched. There the 6th Marquess of Cholmondley remains active in looking after the fixtures and fittings to this day. But in the Commons his writ has ceased to run.

The point of this lengthy anecdote is that if the abolition of the rule of the Lord Great Chamberlain in the Commons was achieved, the credit belongs to Pannell alone. He had had to fight his own battle. Once it was won, it was a different story, and Wilson announced the victory in the Commons with no word of praise for the man who had done the hard graft. The important thing was that the Prime Minister avoided the need to enter into a conflict of opinion with the Monarch, and even with her more reactionary cohorts. That, you may say, is politics – more's the pity!

Much of the nepotism and feudalism within the Palace of Westminster has been eliminated in these last ten years. (It's not a decade since a Member whose daughter was being married within the precincts of the Palace could only get permission for photographs to be taken on condition that they appeared exclusively in the *Tatler* and *Field* society magazines!) But too much still remains. And it will not be ended under any future Premiership of Harold Wilson. It is not so much that he is afraid of the Establishment. He is part of it.

As we have seen in earlier chapters, Wilson has been diligent in keeping silent when it comes to a controversy involving the Monarchy. His presence on the Select Committee set up after the 1970 election was a painful embarrassment to him. He absented himself more often than not and contributed nothing of any consequence to cross-examination or discussion. Similarly, out of all the Civil List debates since the formation of the Labour Party seventy years ago, he is the only Labour Leader who has never opened his mouth.

Maybe Wilson's judgements on these matters are sound. To gain power, a political party, above all its Leader, needs to plan strategies which will exploit to the full its political advantages within the system in which it operates. The ideological fervour which inspired such early pioneers of the Labour Movement as Keir Hardie may be outdated or may have to be compromised if power is to be held and maintained.

Wilson is nothing like Hardie, whom the King declared *persona non grata* at the Royal Garden Party. Neither is he like MacDonald, who, after becoming Prime Minister of the National Government in 1929, delightedly told Philip Snowden, 'Tomorrow every Duchess in London will be wanting to kiss me' – a pleasing thought for one who had for so long ached to be invited inside. Wilson and the Labour Party want and need power. In Britain, a radical party inevitably faces a largely hostile press and a people innately conservative; and also instinctively monarchist. The Labour Party must therefore be seen to be moderate, be seen as basically, if not too enthusiastically, pro-monarchist. Openly denouncing the Monarchy could be political suicide.

Meanwhile the experience of political power in the post-war years has whetted cravings for respectability. The corrupting, suffocating influence of the cloisters of Parliament has done its work. Fierce, fiery Clydesiders like Davie Kirkwood and Manny Shinwell turn into *Lord* Kirkwood and *Lord* Shinwell. Mr Wilson will end his political career as the Earl of Huyton. The ability of the British ruling class to absorb and contain its enemies is a well-known continuing fact.

But there are other considerations to explain Labour's attitude to the Monarchy. Equally important is the view that the Queen and all she stands for is an irrelevance. That the Monarchy is no longer a burning issue – not even for the far left of the Party. The Monarchy is therefore tolerated by the left since it's seen to be not only powerless, but irrelevant to the problems of the people. Inequalities in society, including both class structure and status differentiation, stem from the capitalist system. In that broad context, the symbol of the Monarchy becomes a triviality, a dubious joke. Yet there are already signs that, in the future, the left is likely to adopt a more critical attitude than it has done in the recent past.

Harold Wilson would probably agree with the sentiment expressed by Keir Hardie when he said:

> In this country loyalty to the Queen is used by the profitmongers to blind the eyes of the people; in America loyalty to the flag serves the same purpose. Law and order, by which the commoners are kept quiet whilst they are being fleeced by their masters, must have a symbol, and anything will serve. Therefore, until the system of wealth and production be changed, it is not worth exchanging a king for a president. The robbery of the poor would go on equally under the one as the

other. The king [queen] fraud will disappear when the exploitation of the people draws to a close.

Be that as it may, I can personally attest that Labour Party leaders say things in private about the Royal Family that they would never say in public. Some conform more enthusiastically than others. Richard Crossman once vowed he would never dress up in the ridiculous garb specified for the State Opening of Parliament. When it came to it, he did, albeit under protest. Nothing is as insidious as the venomous charm of the Court and its officials.

It is a fact that, never in its whole existence, has the Labour Party debated the Monarchy at any Annual Conference. In 1955 the Walton Constituency Labour Party submitted a resolution to the Conference in favour of abolishing the Monarchy. It caused a fierce row in the local party – and, of course, was stifled.

Perhaps George Bernard Shaw was right when he wrote, 'The snobbery that surrounds Monarchy is the price we pay for its political convenience.'

5. THE MONARCHY AND THE CLASS STRUCTURE

'There are men and classes of men that stand above the common herd' – Robert Louis Stevenson, *Underwoods*, Dedication

One of the perennial justifications for the continued existence of the Monarchy is the claim that it stands above the hurly-burly of party strife and partisan interest in society at large as much as in Parliament. The Monarchy, it is said, is a neutral, detached institution – the cement of the nation, by which all classes and conditions of Britain's citizens may be united in a patriotic bond. But the fact that the Monarchy is the cornerstone of the Establishment in Britain is very different from saying that its presence operates without bias in favour of the people at all levels of society. Is there any reality at all in the idea of the Monarchy being an impartial influence uniting Britain's peculiarly class-ridden society? Certainly not.

Virtually every foreign visitor to Britain is struck by our economic and social caste system. Though the dividing lines may be less sharply drawn than they were a 100 years ago, it is still all-pervasive. There is even a hymn about it in the Established Church's hymnal:

The rich man in his castle,
The poor man at his gate:

God made the high and lowly
And ordered their estate.

Every man is expected to know his station. His class is 'divinely' ordained, like the Monarchy itself. But, for a class system to work, there has to be a two-way process of cooperation. People must look up to those who expect to be looked up to, and be happy to be looked down upon. You can see the point perhaps for a feudal society, with its system of mutual service and protection. In a complex, modern democratic society it seems a remote and pathetic harking back to a long-lost age.

'A man . . . is only a king,' Karl Marx wrote, 'because other people behave as his subjects. Yet they for their part believe themselves to be his subjects because he is king.'

Tradition, and reverence for tradition, all too often makes the heart master of the head.

By 1844, when Frederick Engels was writing about the situation as he saw it in Britain, the Monarchy had already lost much of its political power. Yet the 'tyranny of property' was still the aristocracy's key to rule, and the Monarchy remained the keystone to the artistocracy. The Monarchy gave the ruthless power of the aristocrats an illusion of respectability. As Engels felt compelled to observe:

> The British Constitution is an inverted pyramid; the apex is at the same time the base. And the less significant the monarchic element has become in reality, the more significance has it acquired for the Englishman. Nowhere . . . is this non-ruling personification worshipped more than in England. The English journals surpass the German by far in slavish servility. This disgusting cult of the king as such, the worship of a completely emasculated and meaningless notion, not even a notion, but the mere *word* 'king', is the consummation of monarchy, just as the worship of the mere *word* 'god' is the consummation of religion, even if both words are meaningless. In both cases, the main thing is to see to it that the main thing, namely, man, who is at the back of both of these words, should not come under discussion.

But Engels was a foreigner and an intellectual. We could hardly expect him to understand the vital importance that tradition plays in British society, well-screened against the bracing winds of rationalism. The average Britisher still loves to seize the opportunity of acting out a need to put on a show of deference. Even the elected, sovereign House of Commons takes no umbrage at being made to stand, like suppliant intruders, at the Bar of the House of Lords while the threadbare feudal pageant of the State Opening of Parliament is performed – the principal actress being the Queen herself, surrounded by her family and a mothballed aristocracy largely clad for the day in hired costumes of rabbit or ermine. That is the custom, the way it is always done, the harmless tradition, and everyone goes home happy. The British Constitution, no less than the Monarchy, would hardly survive another day if it were based on rationality, reality or logic.

There is a revealing sentence in Walter Bagehot's *The English Constitution* where he writes 'the poorer and more ignorant classes – those who would most feel excitement, who would most be misled by excitement – *really believe that the Queen governs*' (my italics). Thus Bagehot and his Tory ilk have seen the Monarchy as a piece of constitutional machinery for deceiving the ignorant, for keeping them deferential and reverential. Even today, a 100 years on, poor simple folk, and some not so poor or so simple, will still write to the Queen direct after all attempts to move a Government Minister have failed, in the misplaced belief that she could somehow have the ultimate word.

Marx, Engels and Bagehot were all writing before working people in Britain had the vote or were represented in Parliament, before they had the benefits of free education or were organized in trade unions. Progressive social legislation in the nineteenth century was pushed through Parliament by outside pressure, helped by the tenacity and enlightenment of a few MPs – some of them aristocrats, but strong individualists who acknowledged the force of moral indignation and were cast in the philanthropic mould. Any gains that were made were almost invariably made against the wishes of the Crown. Never in British history has the Monarchy stood out firmly for the rights and freedom of the individual. On the contrary, it and the aristocracy have survived only because they have instinctively sensed when to make a concession or compromise to the socially dispossessed, whether by granting the vote, providing free education or passing trade-union or factory legislation.

Down the ages, by virtue of upbringing, education and friendships, the Monarchy is both conservative and Conservative. The conservatism of Queen Victoria is well documented. She had a real horror and contempt for the great mass of 'her' people: and a mortal fear of anyone who looked remotely as if he was trying to represent them: 'No one is more truly Liberal in her heart than the Queen, but she always deprecated the great tendency of the present [Liberal] Government to encourage instead of checking the stream of destructive democracy which has become so alarming. This it is that, she must say justly, alarms the House of Lords and all moderate people.'

In Victoria's vocabulary 'moderate' invariably meant conservative, if not downright reactionary. Her 'moderation' on education was notorious. In her *Journal*, for 30 July 1886, she wrote of it as 'rendering the working classes unfitted for good servants and labourers'. She spoke with equal incomprehension and intolerance of 'the mad, wicked folly of "Women's Rights", with all its attendant horrors, on which her feeble sex was bent'.

In our present age, we see the Monarchy trying, sometimes with an air of defensive rearguard desperation, to keep in tune with the times. Examples will be found in other chapters of this book. Meanwhile they would like it to be thought that attempts to 'democratize' the institution have been sincere and effective. Unfortunately for this image, the unvarnished, unromanticized facts tell a different story.

The close, continuing alliance between the Monarchy and the English upper classes is amply illustrated in the pages of *The British Imperial Calendar* for 1973. The Royal Households, including the Queen's and the Queen Mother's, are riddled with the woodworm of the aristocracy: a freemasonry of titled and decorated Dukes and Duchesses, Admirals and Marchionesses, Lords and Ladies – with every letter of the alphabet after their names and every titular honour before them.

And even as the Royal Households are crammed with acolytes of the upper crust, so are the hobbies and pastimes of Royals and their associates those of the upper classes. The annual rituals include Royal Week at Ascot, where tycoons and Tories in top-hats, their wives in the most absurdly lavish dreams that the dress and hat designers can devise, blow themselves out on smoked salmon and champagne, basking in the reflected glory of Her Majesty's presence. (The Ascot Office at St James's Palace, run by Lieutenant-Colonel the Marquess of Abergavenny, sees to it that nobody gets into the Royal Enclosure who doesn't pass strict tests of social acceptability.) Then, for Prince Philip and the Royal Yacht, there's an aquatic equivalent in Cowes Regatta Week. These are at least as much social as sporting occasions. Together with the Badminton Horse Trials, the huntin', shootin' and fishin' in Scotland in the autumn, the polo at Windsor Great Park with assorted industrialists and other worshippers of Mammon, they help to associate the Royal Family closely, intimately and exclusively with *one* class, *one* political party, and an economic system that has always operated against the interests of the more deprived of Her Majesty's humble subjects.

When it came to schooling, Prince Charles was sent to a rugged equivalent of Eton – the bleak but pricey Gordonstoun in Scotland, where cold showers and rock-climbing were presumed to do more for character building than decadent straw boaters and smooth green playing-fields. But it is unlikely that he met at Gordonstoun the sons of coalminers, or even of schoolteachers – not at fees of over £800 a year. Princess Anne was similarly sent to a posh, single-sex school. It was an opportunity her mother never had – as far as it went.

Like all the children of other members of the Royal Family, the Queen's younger children, Princes Andrew and Edward, have been placed in the same private education sector. This is, of course, to operate freedom of parental choice, but it is a freedom denied to a vast majority of British families, many of whom are having to live on a wage that is less than the annual fee to keep one royal child at a private school. It is also a decision that has political implications. Every member of the Royal Family, every royal child, has been opted out of the state educational system, and in so doing a conscious *political* choice has been made: that the state system of public education is not for them or for theirs. (Labour Cabinet Ministers have done so too.) Care is thus taken that the royal children remain uncontaminated by contacts with children whose experience of life is radically different from their own. The public-school system has bolstered if not created the present class structure of British society, and the Royal Family has, by its patronage, given it a respectability and status that it does not deserve.

Perhaps, with his great (and carefully calculated) talent for putting his foot in it, we might consider Prince Philip to be the most eloquent, literate and classless member of the Royal Family. Certainly his 'bluffness' has made him the white hope of the British middle classes: a man who 'speaks his mind', who has the 'common touch'. No matter if his sometimes refreshing outspokenness can also turn into arrogance and bad manners. It has made him the best PRO in the Palace and a useful salesman to have around – not only for the Anglo-French flying white elephant,

Concorde, but also, and to better effect, for firing salvoes on behalf of the officially approved conservation lobby.

But Philip's public statements have also revealed a typical conservatism coupled with astounding political ignorance. 'I am not anti-socialist, but I regret to say that it was nationalism and socialism which produced Nazis and Fascists,' said the Duke in August 1973. It takes a political ignoramus to create such nonsense out of Hitler's use of the term 'National Socialism'. The forces and classes that nurtured and sustained that monster in power were far closer to Prince Philip and his family than they were to any continental Socialist – of whom those who failed to escape from the Nazis were put into concentration camps, tortured and murdered. Prince Philip's political reflexes probably represent his whole family's attitude to anything remotely radical or which threatens the *status quo* – despite the efforts of such Labour leaders as Ramsay MacDonald, Attlee and Wilson to prove how safe the Establishment actually is in their hands.

One attempt to change the class image of the Monarchy may be seen in the extension of the Royal Garden Parties to make them national appeals to the vanity of local mayors and their wives – especially the wives – from such provincial backwaters as Middlewich and Downham-on-the-Moor. They turn up in droves in their chains of office and their brand-new Co-op hats and dresses. Few of them actually 'meet' the Queen: to be 'there' is the thing. Some members of the Royal Family may actually tout for customers to talk to. The story has been told of how, not long ago, a librarian from Transport House, the Headquarters of the Labour Party, was invited to a Garden Party. Once there, she was pulled out of the tea queue by a flunky in fancy dress and asked, would she like to meet a member of the Royal Family? As soon as she had succumbed to this blandishment, the equerry hurriedly briefed himself on her credentials. 'From Transport House,' he introduced her to a gangling, lonesome Princess Anne. Quick as lightning, the Princess seized on the three-word brief. 'What,' she asked, 'do you think of the London Ring Road proposals?' The librarian was not too well versed in such matters. That she worked at Transport House did not mean she knew anything about ring or any other roads. Undeterred, for the whole three minutes of the interview the Princess plied her hapless client with further transport posers. She had done her duty. So much for the benefits of her expensive education.

What more is being done to nurture the common touch? Well, there has been the innovation of the royal walkabout when various members of the Royal Family get out of their official cars and actually chat informally to members of the commonalty standing about thirsting for that waxen smile. It always gets a spot on the telly. And talking of the goggle-box, for relaxation the Queen watches programmes like *Coronation Street*. What better way of looking at the working classes through the wrong end of a telescope? This popular parody of north-country working-class life must produce many a royal belly-laugh. It might even lead its royal viewers to realize the enormous gulf which exists – unbridgeable and incomprehensible – between themselves and that which *Coronation Street* purports to represent.

The fact remains beyond dispute that each member of the Royal Family *behaves* like a member of the English upper class. They speak with the characterless, bored vowels of a prissy public-school dialect. The way they dress and react to others, the intimate friends and associates they admit into their circle, are rife with a sense of 'apartness', wealth and privilege.

Who has the *real power* in modern Britain is sometimes difficult to determine. A century ago, *property* meant influence; and influence meant political power. It is as true today as it was in the nineteenth century, though the landed proprietors are no longer as powerful, in the Lords or elsewhere, as they were a 100 years ago. The *nouveau-riche* class has obtained its affluence, influence and power through the exploitation of the former British Empire, now a part of the so-called Third World (of poverty, ignorance and squalor), through giant multi-national corporations.

Despite this metamorphosis in the individuals and organizations who wield influence and power, and so govern people's lives, the class *structure* of British society has remained basically unchanged. Mass education and improvements in communications may have blurred the dividing-lines and created a greater mobility between the classes than ever before. A 100 years ago it would have been unthinkable for British princesses to marry trendy, arty photographers or cloth-capped, part-time soldiers whose families have done well in trade by making meat pies and pork sausages. Doesn't it all prove that today's Royal Family is 'with it'; not so much above the common herd as a very respectable part of it?

Not exactly. The princesses concerned were relatively remote from the succession. Princess Margaret, the photographer's wife, is only fifth in the line, while Princess Anne is only slightly better placed at number four. It is not much more than a convenient simulation for democratic change.

One widespread superstition still encountered is that the Monarchy, and, to a lesser extent, the aristocracy, does not soil its hands with actual commerce. It is true that, at the centre, the Royal Family is untainted by directorships; but the periphery has in fact quite a few, and some are very juicy ones. Said Mr Angus Ogilvy, husband of Princess Alexandra, on the difficulties of being married to a royal princess, 'It's bound to be inhibiting. One has to be much more careful. If I get caught in a normal business risk it would be difficult. Big money is in my view made by backing small men who are going to be big, but imagine what would have happened if I'd backed a crook. You have to be fairly careful, otherwise one could inadvertently damage the Monarchy.'

'It's bound to be inhibiting'? Is it? Not evidently unduly so. Of course being caught in 'a normal business risk' is something to be avoided – whether or not your wife's cousin is likely to be embarrassed. And what *would* happen if Mr Ogilvy 'backed a crook'? Probably very little.

But there is a giant mining corporation called Lonrho which makes much of its money by plundering Africa. Like other big European firms operating in Africa, it can hardly fail to benefit from large-scale corruption in the southern part of the continent. Angus Ogilvy numbered Lonrho among his seventeen lucrative directorships – until Edward Heath, as Tory Prime Minister, described Lonrho as showing 'the unacceptable face of capitalism'. Then, and only then, did Mr Ogilvy resign from the board. In a fit of uncharacteristic charity, the press stayed silent. No harm accrued to the Monarchy.

Meanwhile the Royal Family's own investment portfolios remain among the most closely guarded of secrets outside the Kremlin or the offices of the KGB. We can only know that they must run into many millions of pounds. No wonder the Queen is the darling of the City and of the aristocracy. The institution she represents is a bulwark against revolutionary change. The Monarchy is the shining, glittering mask that conceals, so far successfully, the ugly face of a class system that is based on avarice, social injustice and inequity. It is hard to see how it could hope to survive the forces which must eventually destroy that system. That day, however, is not yet.

6. HONOURS AND PATRONAGE GALORE

'Gentlemen receive titles whom no decent man would allow in his home' – House of Commons debate, 28 May 1919

Thailand may have its Order of the White Elephant and France its hordes decorated with the Legion of Honour. Even the Soviet Union has its awards by which the state acknowledges worthy achievement, ranging from the Order of Lenin at the top to the Order of the Glory of Motherhood at the bottom. But no other country in the world has perfected a more sophisticated package of genteel and cheap corruption and snobbery than the British have with their Honours system. It is like a gargantuan pig trough, into which everybody, or nearly everybody, tries to get his snout. A set of letters after your name is as much a status symbol as living in a castle or owning a couple of Rolls-Royces.

The history of the system is a mixture of hilarious comedy, covert commercialism and occasional tragedy. But the game continues to be played with glee and earnestness, not least by prime ministers and monarchs. The dispensing of patronage is one of the buttresses of our deferential society.

To start with, we need look no further back than James I of England (James VI of Scotland). He came to the English throne in 1603. After his penury in poverty-stricken Scotland it was like striking gold in the Klondike: a Klondike created by his own business – the sale of honours, especially of knighthoods. Present-day Tory MPs and squires would have loved it: 906 knights were created within four months; an average of seven or eight every day of the week (including Sundays)! Not even Harold Macmillan could equal that. Knighthoods were bought and sold like second-hand cars; family trees were happily faked up.

In 1603, or thereabouts, the new English king summoned all persons possessed of Crown Lands worth £40 per annum or more to present themselves for knighting, or, in lieu, to pay a heavy fine. Then, when the knighthood coinage became debased, James had to look for other sources of revenue. So baronetcies were born – for sale at over £1,000 apiece. The King's cottage industry in just over twenty years netted him more than half a million pounds, worth many millions in today's money – royal avarice has ancient roots. As the Divine Right of Kings still needed bolstering with filthy lucre, James I's son, Charles I, sought to purchase his own survival – by continuing his dad's do-it-yourself Honours business. The last year before the Civil War saw Charles creating 128 new baronets to try and buy himself a life-belt. He failed. He was awarded the CHOP.

But Cromwell's republic didn't last long. Its arrogant, military tyranny expedited the return to the monarchical system which we have had to endure ever since. The Honours Industry grew apace: 68 Knights of the Bath at Charles II's coronation; the very next day an unknown number of peers.

When the Hanoverians eventually attained the throne by default and dubious claims and motives, their sordid story inevitably became interwoven with the continuing swindle of the Honours system. The German female camp-followers who crossed the water with George I wished for English titles. This baggage of valkyries, together with their Teutonic king, felt time wasn't on their side. A speedy return to Hanover could be imminent, so quick profits had to be made. Not knowing a word of English, the German dullard had to secure his base in the cabinet and in the Commons. He found a willing and wily tool in Robert Walpole. George immediately made two of his mistresses Duchess of Kendal and Countess of Darlington, while Walpole controlled the parliamentary machine by stuffing it with paid hacks. He created forty dukes, and controlled the Commons by packing it with nominee MPs of the peers he created. What bliss it was, to be the King's favourite and saviour, and to hold the keys to the patronage coffers. (Such are the origins of the modern parliamentary system.)

As we come closer to the present day, we can see how the Honours lark has become one of Britain's major lucky dips. Even Brigadier Sir Ivan De La Bere, Secretary of the Central Chancery of the Orders of Knighthood from 1945–60, felt obliged to complain, in an excellent bumper fun-book, *The Queen's Orders of Chivalry* (1961), that 'there is in this country now a far greater variety of orders, decorations and medals . . . than is either necessary or desirable'. There was 'a pronounced tendency,' he continued, 'to give too many knighthoods . . . to persons who have not deserved such high awards'.

By 1961 the New Year's Honours List alone was containing 1,000 names. Until the latter part of the nineteenth century there had only been one Honours List a year, containing only about 100 prize-winners. By 1938 it had become necessary to hold four small investitures – two in state dress at Buckingham Palace and two morning-dress occasions at St James's. Today there are seldom less than a dozen investitures a year. What anxieties must precede each prize-draw day – New Year and the Queen's official birthday – to know whether this recommendation has got through or that word in the right ear has had effect. Thus does the royal work-load increase.

Inevitably, as quantities have proliferated, so has the quality declined. Not the quality of the Honours holders so much as the quality of the material their badges are made of. In the good old days, we were on a gold standard in royal insignia: nothing but gold and silver. Today it's silver gilt. Tomorrow it could be plastic – if we can get the oil to make it. The value of the metal in the 1918 Mons Star was 2½d. Today's awards are worth a bit more than that – as scrap metal.

When it came to dishing out Honours, Lloyd George was, if not the most honest, the most realistic Prime Minister we have had. He sold them – at anything from £6,000 for a knighthood to £150,000 for a peerage. Big money in those days; but it swelled the coffers of the Liberal Party. It troubled George V a bit. It worried Parliament too. In 1922 a Royal Commission was set up, and in 1925 the Honours (Prevention of Abuses) Act was passed. The Act provided for up to two years in Her Majesty's jails, or a £500 fine, or both, for anybody *caught* buying or selling an Honour.

Then, on to the Honours scene, came something of a mystery in the shape of Mr Maundy Gregory – the first, and the last, broker in Honours to be charged and punished. He had been in business as an Honours tout for years, with an office in Parliament Street, a club and a magazine, the *Whitehall Gazette*, to impress clients and make social contacts, before, in 1934, he was accused of attempting to procure a title for one Lieutenant-Commander Leake in return for cash. At first he pleaded 'not guilty', but subsequently changed this to 'guilty', was given three months' hard labour and fined £50, and ultimately retired to live in France – as 'Sir Arthur', of course. The case was thus effectively glossed over, presumably by Mr Gregory's anonymous establishment paymasters, but it remained symptomatic of the disease that can still affect government and Monarchy in Britain: that scandal and corruption must be covered over and silence bought.

The hunger for knighthoods is still insatiable today. Lesser citizens scramble for OBEs, CBEs and other worthless trinkets of recognition that they feel are their due. Everybody loves an Honour: the patrons who dispense and the recipients who receive. And at the head of the patrons is the Crown. What else is a Crown for, except to put on top of something? And the more disreputable and indefensible that 'something', the more necessary it is to have the Crown at its head. The one supports the other while the system plays on the weaknesses, irrationality, vanity and snobbishness of every citizen. Not for nothing has every monarch down the ages sought to intervene in and control the dishing out of robes and ribbons, medals and titles, and varying combinations of letters. All tastes are catered for. All classes are suitably fed. And still they flock like seagulls round a municipal rubbish tip.

The Making of the Dukedoms

The British Duke is a fascinating species of noble animal. Apart from the royal dukes, where there seems to be a need for a new one from time to time, no new dukes have been created since 1874. Of the twenty-six hereditary dukedoms in the land today, only two, Marlborough and Wellington, were created for merit alone – in 1702 and 1814 respectively. The Wellingtons have been well looked after. The original Duke became a reactionary Tory prime minister. He had before that been the handsomely paid ambassador at Paris and Vienna. After the battle of Salamanca, he had been voted a fortune of £100,000; after Toulouse, of £400,000; and after Waterloo, of £200,000. He was given a service of plate from Portugal worth £400,000; he received large rake-offs from the contractors who clothed and fed his armies. Spain had given him an estate worth £10,000 a year *then*, and he drew monies from an estate given to him by Portugal, as well as monies from a Dutch estate. On top of all this, he had received his salary as Field Marshal, his salary as Commander-in-Chief of the British Army in Europe, and a further salary from the Allied Powers as Commander-in-Chief of the Army of Occupation. Four British dukes are descended from the bastard sons of Charles II: St Albans out of Nell Gwynn, Grafton out of the Duchess of Cleveland, Richmond out of the Duchess of Portsmouth and Buccleuch via Lucy Walters. Charles was a busy lad. The results of his endeavours still hang round our necks today, 300 years later, their bastard origins proudly borne on their coats of arms, though there is some dispute over the heraldic symbol for illegitimacy. One learned tome, A. C. Fox-Davies's *Complete Guide to Heraldry* (revised edition, 1969), weightily states that the assertion by the ignoramus that the heraldic sign for illegitimacy is a 'bar sinister' is 'an utter misnomer. To anyone with the most rudimentary knowledge of heraldry it must plainly be seen to be radically impossible to depict a "bar sinister", for the simple reason that the bar is neither dexter nor sinister . . . The earliest marks of . . . illegitimacy for which accepted use can be found are the bend and the bordure.' There you have it; or not, as the case may be.

The dukes remain all of a kind: heavily landed, groaning with wealth, and mostly educated at Eton and Oxford, Cambridge, or Sandhurst Military College. The Scottish dukes are traditionally loathed by their people, especially Argyll, Sutherland, Lovat, Montrose, Hamilton and Buccleuch. The immorality, cruelty and avarice of their forebears have scarred Scots' souls forever. Their descendants still hold sway, owning thousands of acres and clinging to a feudal landed power that was won by men with the morals of tomcats.

The families of two other dukes, Bedford and Devonshire, created in 1694, had acquired their enormous wealth from the sacking of the monasteries by Henry VIII. Fighting against the ravages of death duties, and down to his last million or two, the Duke of Bedford became the ducal whiz-kid of the 1950s and 1960s. With the panache of a circus ringmaster, he opened to the common gaze his stately Woburn Abbey and acres stocked with herds of rare animals. American tourists paid £10 a head to have lunch with him, and pop groups decorated the ducal scene in the early 1970s. The bandwagon had been set in motion. The others or most of them, have reluctantly followed his example.

Only the daddy of them all, Bernard Marmaduke Fitzalan-Howard, KG, PC, GCVO, GVE, RV and Chain, the Earl Marshal and the 16th Duke of Norfolk, has held aloof. When, in the late 1950s, he tried to ease his tax responsibilities by a private Bill put before the House of Commons, he came and sat in the Public Gallery only to hear his ploy blown to pieces. The fact that his family came across with William the Conqueror 900 years ago no doubt fostered a nostalgic longing for power. The dukedom was created in 1483, and the duke's salary of £20 a year as hereditary Earl Marshall of England has been frozen ever since – the longest wage freeze in history. But he earns it, and since he still has 15,000 acres tucked under his belt, we need not squander our commiserations. And what could have been more delightfully British than that Norfolk, the most senior lay Roman Catholic in Britain, should have produced two of the leading TV spectaculars of the century in the Coronation at the headquarters of the Church of England and the funeral of Winston Churchill, not to mention the quaint Investiture of Charles as Prince of Wales in 1969?

Most ladies of ducal families continue to find jobs and sinecures in the Royal Households. The Duchess of Grafton (created 1675) is the Queen's Mistress of the Robes. The Queen Mother's equivalent is the Duchess of Abercorn (created 1868). Lady Elizabeth Cavendish, of the Devonshire clan, is an Extra Lady-in-Waiting to Princess Margaret; and so one could go on, slotting top-drawer ladies and gentlemen into royal palaces and households.

But while these families have been given by history a long run of power and influence in British politics – the Devonshires right up to Harold Macmillan and Lord Salisbury, the Marlboroughs up to Winston Churchill and Christopher Soames – their power is on the wane. Like the Royal Family itself, they are becoming relics of a bygone age, loved like family heirlooms, but most useful as museum pieces.

Knights, Peers and Lordships

In considering our antique chivalric survivals, let us start at the top of the pecking order – with the Most Noble Order of the Garter. According to a Central Office of Information handout, this is 'the most esteemed of the nine British Orders of Knighthood'.

The Order was founded over 600 years ago by Edward III. The tale goes that King Ted wanted to create an Order as romantic as the legendary company of Arthur's Knights of the Round Table. One day he is supposed to have picked up a lady's garter at a Palace 'knees-up'. Those who witnessed the memorable occasion made the ribald comments you would expect, to which the King riposted, as they often do, '*Honi soit qui mal y pense*.' Which, roughly translated, means, 'You are all dirty-minded old men.'

The story is as authentic as Alfred's *gâteau*-burning or Canute's sea-dip, but that is how our history is made. And to this day every Garter recipient must wear, on his left leg, below the knee, a dark-blue velvet garter, though Lady Garters wear theirs on the left arm, between elbow and shoulder.

With the Garter goes a collar – a kind of dog chain. The 'Great George', it is called: a badge of gold and enamel. When the gear proved a bit heavy for some of the more senile recipients, Henry VIII introduced the 'Lesser (i.e. lighter) George' – with a riband. (The Queen likes to wear the riband and Lesser George when in evening dress – as you've surely noticed.) Charles I added the star to the Garter garb. It's an eight-pointed silver star, with, in its centre, encircled by a Garter in blue enamel, St George's Cross in red and white enamel. The idea initially was to wear the star on a coat or cloak, but it does look nice with evening dress. Finally comes the really fancy bit: a blue velvet mantle lined with white taffeta. And a crimson velvet hood, also lined with white taffeta. And a black velvet hat, with a plume of white ostrich feathers and a black heron's feather. You won't mistake a Knight of the Garter if you meet one in the street.

However, the chances of ever becoming a Knight of the Garter yourself are extremely slender. You do have to call yourself a Christian. Agnostics or atheists, Commonwealth Sikhs, Muslims, Buddhists or Hindus, are out. Apart from the Sovereign and other members of the immediate Royal Family, the Order is limited to twenty-five carefully chosen Knights, who are each allotted a stall in St George's Chapel, Windsor. Some foreign Royals may also be admitted.

This may lead to some embarrassment, as at the outbreak of the First World War in 1914, when it was suggested to George V that the German Kaiser, and eight other foreign KGs whose countries were also at war with Britain, should have their British Honours cancelled. George, being of German stock himself, demurred. But public opinion ran strongly against him. He gave way, and the enemy insignia were removed from St George's Chapel. But the stall plates remain in place to this day.

Then, in 1939, the Second World War similarly led to the annulment of Honours of all those at war with us. King Carol of Rumania and Prince Paul of Yugoslavia were, however, excused. Both were in exile at the time, and neither of them ever got back to rule in their kingdoms. A perilous profession, kingship.

Once the war was over, George VI sought to revive interest in the momentous subject of Orders of Knighthood. He had his limitations, but here was something he could understand. He was anxious that, like the OM and RVO (to be discussed shortly), the Garter and the Thistle should be in the personal gift of the sovereign. (The 'Most Ancient' Order of the Thistle is a Scottish Order that comes next one down from the Garter. It isn't all that ancient, having been instituted by James II in 1687.) So, in July 1946, Mr Attlee, the Labour Prime Minister, and Mr Churchill, the Tory Opposition Leader, sagely agreed that henceforth those two 'great' Orders should be non-political Honours, conferred by the sovereign without previous formal submission for the Prime Minister's advice or approval. In 1948, George VI issued a proclamation that that year was to be considered to be the sexcentenary of the foundation of the Order, celebrated on St George's Day. And so it came to pass.

In recent years, it has been usual for the Garter investiture ceremony to be held in the Throne Room at Windsor Castle on the first day of Royal Ascot Week in June. The Queen is then in the area, and so it becomes a kind of Horses and Garters week! After the ceremony, there's a right royal nosh-up in the Banqueting Room – off gold plate and antique china. Altogether, a great tourist attraction. Modern Britain still has some feudal tricks to show the pushing, materialistic foreigners. Let them land on the moon, if they like. We'll stick to our Garters and Thistles.

Naturally, as Mistress of the Honours Pump, the Queen makes sure that she and her family come in for their own whack of ribbon, medal and title. She made her naval bridegroom a duke and a prince at a stroke – and an earl and a baron to boot. Her children automatically become princes and princesses, of course, but the eldest son, besides becoming Prince of Wales, is also Duke of Cornwall, Duke of Rothesay, Lord of the Isles, Baron of Renfrew and Earl of Chester. Our heir apparent is indeed a man of many parts. Her nephew, then Prince Richard, now Duke of Gloucester, got a KCVO in early 1974. Nobody knew why, or bothered to ask.

But now, descending the scale a little way – if not too far – we come to those who are entitled to sit in the so-called 'Upper' House of Parliament, the House of Lords. These are the Peers of the Realm, and they include dukes (whom we have already met), marquesses, earls, viscounts and barons. Until 1958, it was still the highly reactionary preserve of the hereditary peers together with archbishops and some bishops. Then, in that year, another important rung was added to the ladder in the shape of the Life Peerages Act. Between then and July 1973, 226 life peers were created. That only twenty-nine of them were women was a squalid piece of sex discrimination, rationalized by the fact that there are too few peeresses' lavatories in the Palace of Westminster. Of the total, thirty-eight were known Conservatives, seventy-seven Labour; there has been a spattering of Liberals, and the rest have been political 'don't knows' or 'won't tells'. The average age on selection was 61 – though a quorum of only three nonagenarians is needed to conduct the business of State there. Ear trumpets can be obtained on request.

Few political careers *start* in the Lords. It has become rather useful for putting out to grass and 'rewarding' the former favourites of party leaders and those whose political careers are finished, and for kicking upstairs and neutering those whose presence in the higher echelons of government has become an embarrassment. A postman may become a peer; as may a drunken miner, a Methodist preacher, a Communist or any other left-wing 'revolutionary'. Overnight they will be found to have become the staunchest defenders of our House of Lords, which can tame the wildest of men or women. Firebrand Jennie Lee – widow of Aneurin Bevan and with her origins in a militant Scottish coal-mining background – becomes the smooth, suave, contented Baroness Lee, taking her place in an institution which, a few years before, she would cheerfully have dynamited. Labour's elder statesman, Manny Shinwell, swore he would never go to the Lords. But not even he could resist the smell of moth-balls and ermine.

Once a place of power, like the Monarchy, the House of Lords may now, also like the Monarchy, be being adapted in the hope of survival. And, like Buckingham Palace and Windsor Castle, the House of Lords is more of a tourist attraction than anything else. A symbol of an effete *élite*: colourful, irrelevant, harmless.

Since a peer can only claim £8.50 expenses a day on days when he attends, there are many who feel that those who do take the trouble to attend are grossly overworked and underpaid. Not all of them are rich men. But they can clock in one minute, clock out the next, and clock up £8.50 tax-free expenses. Harold Wilson wanted to improve their lot in 1969. An all-party backstage agreement was reached to foist on the nation a second Chamber to have first- and second-class Lords on a *salaried* basis. This unsavoury manoeuvre was strangled by an unholy alliance of a handful of backbench MPs from all parts of the Commons, and by the massive and suffocating indifference of the rest. Like the Monarchy, the Lords was regarded as a harmless political eunuch, possessing no power and little influence. The need for British Prime Ministers to dispense their patronage so as to juggle and balance the dubious power of the Upper House is a depraving canker in the body politic that cries out for major surgery.

'*Work for the Knight is Coming*'

There may not be a great deal of obvious corruption in the Honours system, but there is still a lot more corruption of a subtler kind than many people think. Massive gifts to charity, given out of shadily obtained wealth, may be made with knighthoods or peerages in view. Some Tory MPs are still willing to put names forward to the Prime Minister for titles provided a payment of cash is made to sustain some cause dear to the heart of the MP concerned. Or dear to the heart of the PM himself.

A knighthood is much coveted by the Tory MP – and especially by his wife; because they may then be addressed as 'your ladyship', which sounds far nicer than plain 'Mrs'. So, over the years, the prospect of 'Sir' has been dangled as a means of discipline in the Tory ranks. 'Behave yourself or say good-bye to that Knighthood'; or, even worse, 'Toe the Party line, or your local Party chairman in the shires will lose out on his title, and his Mrs won't be able to call herself "Lady".' Sometimes the knighthood is used as a consolation prize for those Tory MPs whose ambitions to Ministerial office have been thwarted; or who have given at least ten years of faithful if barren lobby-fodder service to the Party.

The Prime Minister who most enjoyed playing the Honours game in recent years was Harold Macmillan. Between coming to office in January 1957 and leaving it in October 1963, he wielded his patronage like a political Casanova. Knighthoods or peerages were given to every Tory MP who showed signs of life (as may be seen from Appendix E), and averaged one a month throughout his premiership.

Out of a total of 232 Tory MPs or former MPs given titles between 1952 and 1973, 46 had been to Eton, 12 to Harrow, and 116 to other fee-paying 'public' schools. Only two had been to a state elementary school, and 27 to a secondary or grammar school.

Knighted dullards dominated the Tory benches in the Commons in those halcyon days. In the period 1959–70, 122 political Honours went to the Tory party, while, for comparison, only 60 went to Labour (of whom 46 were life peers).

The knighthood game seems more like a game of snakes and ladders, with a good many snakes and only one ladder. And it is all wrapped up in a fancy box that has the Queen's portrait of approval on the front.

Other Orders and Honours

In these 'democratic' days, who knows what good fortune tomorrow may bring to any one of us? Overnight, a fresh-faced Navy midshipman may become a duke and prince; or a smart off-beat commercial photographer may become a lord – if they each marry the right wench. As we have seen, one of the few remaining powers left to the Queen is the awarding of certain Honours at her discretion. Successive monarchs, as their other powers have melted away, have clung the more anxiously to the title trivia. The Garter, the Order of Merit, the Companionage of Honour and the ten-a-penny Royal Victorian Order (RVO) are all the sole prerogative of the Queen.

Perhaps, of these, the Order of Merit (OM) is the most genuinely prestigious – precisely because it goes to people of proved personal merit, including writers, composers, painters and scientists, with only a smattering of politicians and military men. But it is limited to twenty-four members at any one time, so worthy aspirants must wait for dead men's shoes. It also usually goes to people who have won high esteem in the eyes of the Establishment, though some of the artists who have accepted have been known to have previously treated the idea of a knighthood with the contempt it deserved.

The RVO is, however, a different kettle of fish. The Queen's Household is crammed to the gunwhales with its variations of status among the Royal camp-followers, from the GCVO of the

Lord Chamberlain, to the KCVO of the Queen's Private Secretary, the CVO of the Librarian at Windsor Castle, and the MVOs of a multitude of minor dignitaries, including clerks and secretaries and the Royal Bargemaster. The curious may look it all up in any current edition of *Whitaker's Almanack*. When the Queen makes her sorties into the Commonwealth, she hands out medals, usually the RVO, to every acolyte in spitting distance. Thus many overseas luminaries also glow with an RVO – until their assassination. Rumour has it that the Victorian Order medals are made on a production line in Neasden, a West London suburb – out of used railway lines disposed of by British Railways.

Personal service to a Prime Minister can be as sure a road to an Honour as personal service to the Queen; even the maker of Gannex raincoats has found the truth of this, as has one Prime Minister's private solicitor. In an effort to create a new swinging image, Harold Wilson gave the Beatles pop group medals as big as their guitars – much to the disgust of other holders of the same frying-pan. Today it is footballers, cricketers and brain-damaged boxers. We will not have long to wait for decorated bingo players. Democracy is hard at work.

But, to prove the democratic nature of the system, it has been necessary to devalue. Mrs Mopp, twenty-five years scrubbing floors at the Ministry of Defence, could get a BEM, the local Gas Board official the MBE. Each Public Corporation gets its annual allocation, arbitrarily distributed and presented, not by the Queen, but by National Coal Board officials or Ministers of Power.

The OBE is today as common as sliced bread. Well over 150,000 are locked away in 150,000 homes up and down the land. The insignia still swears 'For God and Empire', though most of us have opted out of both. For home civil servants especially, the CBEs, MBEs and OBEs used to come up with the rations: 228 in 1957, but down to 179½ by 1966, and slashed to 112 by Mr Wilson in the 1967 Birthday List.

But the game goes on. Pitiful letters dribble in to MPs, begging for some decoration, some medal, some status totempole. A letter to a Labour colleague in December 1966 went typically: 'Seeing that Honours cannot be bought and that they are to be given for public work I was wondering if I come into being given an Honour for the New Year. I started in public life when I was 18 years old.'

The writer had served in the Labour Exchange for twenty-two years, on the Board of Guardians for twenty years, on the public Assistance Board for twelve years, as a local hospital trustee for twelve years, on the local port and harbour committee for ten years and as governor to a local secondary school. He had founded the local old people's welfare, he had served on twenty-eight committees, had been over thirty-two years on the town council, and had twice been mayor.

'I was wondering if I have qualified for an Honour,' he concluded. 'Hoping you will be able to look into the matter. Yours in Labour . . . '.

Difficult, pathetic and hilarious letters. Some years ago, a small burgh in my constituency celebrated its 500th anniversary. Its population is less than 4,000: a quiet wee Tory enclave, with a dedicated minority Labour-Independent on the Council. 'Wouldn't it be a nice gesture,' wrote the Town Clerk, 'if you, as the MP, could get some Honour for the Tory Provost and the Labour leader?' Just to show it's all non-party, he said. In twenty-four years as a Member of Parliament, I have never recommended anybody for an Honour, and wrote to tell them so. 'Good for you,' replied the Town Clerk – in his private capacity.

The fact is that, when it comes to knighthoods and the lesser fry, anybody can apply, for himself or for anybody else. But the choice effectively lies with the Prime Minister and his Patronage Secretary (the governing Party's Chief Whip in the House of Commons). Top Civil Servants used to get top Honours automatically – for keeping their noses clean. Harold Wilson put a stop to that in 1967, when, as Prime Minister, he announced there would be a reduction in the number of knighthoods, CBEs, OBEs and MBEs awarded to those in the civil, diplomatic and defence services. Earlier, on 27 October 1966, he had announced that he proposed 'to discontinue the practice of making recommendations concerning Honours for political services of the kind which have been a feature for so many years past' – except that Honours for local government service would remain as recognition for *public* service, 'irrespective of party'.

But, in the dissolution honours of August 1970, Mr Wilson, as defeated Prime Minister, shovelled out life peerages wholesale to faithful party officials and ex-MPs. His own private secretary, Mrs Marcia Williams, had a CBE. The Labour Party General Secretary had a knighthood, and the senior lady at the Party's Headquarters became a Dame. There were others.

And why not? If you can't beat them, join them. After his minority government came into office in early 1974, Wilson appointed the same Marcia Williams a life peeress, despite some much-criticized land speculation in which she had been involved.

But, to be fair to Harold Wilson, no Honours went to sitting MPs, except 'automatic' knighthoods to the Law Officers of the Crown. Why these should be automatic nobody knows: the two Labour Law Officers in 1974 refused them. Yet no hereditary peers were created in Wilson's six years as Prime Minister; and none were created by Edward Heath during his 1970–4 term of office, to the consternation of some of his backbench MPs who have only social ambitions left to them as they fade into the autumn of their political careers. (They also fear for the Monarchy should the hereditary principle die elsewhere.) But, in November 1970, Mr Heath did put the political Honours game back to square one. Work for political parties *would* qualify. He had told the Queen – and, of course, she had agreed.

The Queen holds fourteen Investitures a year, as Sir Michael Adeane told the Parliamentary Select Committee, and presents 'some 2,000 Orders, Decorations and Medals'. Hard graft. So goes the Hons. production line. It provides a lucrative trade for Moss Bros. as well as never-to-be-forgotten days in humdrum lives.

'I felt incredibly proud,' recalled Private David Bennet, BEM, of the Queen's Regiment. 'My father said there were no words to describe it.' 'I've never seen such shiny armour,' he said, referring to the glistening Household Cavalry Troopers on stair duty at the Palace on his day of glory in February 1972.

Divisional Officer J. H. (Jack) Brown, BEM, of the City of Portsmouth Fire Brigade, said, 'I thought it would be just another ceremony, but now that I've been, it's something I'll remember for the rest of my days.' Jack's BEM, for gallantry in fighting fire in a blazing oil tanker, will be a precious memory among his grandchildren's children, though the intrinsic value of the medal can't be more than £10 – and the British Empire is non-existent.

But that is to miss the point. That an Honour, however tawdry, can mark the peak of a humble life's ambition, should give us pause for thought. There is a fundamental, patronizing insult behind the notion that a moment of dignity and meaning in a man's life can be bought so cheaply. It is a cynical exploitation of decency. Meanwhile, few outside the Honours factory of the Central Chancery of the Orders of Knighthood (close by Buckingham Palace) have any idea of the relative, subtle shifts in scale of prestige between various combinations of letters or ribbons – or have any wish to know.

What is the future to be of the annual prize chaos in Honours? The simplest answer would be to have done with them altogether.

A referendum on such a proposition might produce interesting results. At the moment, abolition has little hope of being accepted by any Prime Minister, still less by the Queen. Two attempts to apply a dose of weedkiller to the whole paraphernalia of the Honours List were made in 1964 and again in 1968 by the late Emrys Hughes, the republican Labour MP. His second private enterprise Bill sneaked through the Commons for its Second Reading one idle Friday. Everybody who knew anything about the House of Commons knew that that would be the end of the matter. But the Queen grew worried and alarmed. She had sleepless nights. She wished to see the Bill defeated. She begged Ministers, especially Mr Richard Crossman, then Leader of the House, to ensure its demise. Crossman could give no such guarantee. So the Queen consulted the Prime Minister, Mr Wilson. He, of course, agreed. He sent for Crossman, who had meanwhile summoned the support of Roy Jenkins, the Chancellor of the Exchequer. In the end, the Bill died a natural death. Most Bills introduced by Private Members do. The Queen didn't know until told by a Minister. She hadn't, she said, read about it in the *Mirror*!

Though the Labour Government in Australia may have rid itself of the British Honours system, as has the Liberal Government in Canada, British Prime Ministers continue to love their patronage, as the Queen delights in her prerogative and the chance to spellbind a thousand or two every year at her Palace (and tot up her total of 'public engagements').

If you abolish the system, people may ask, what will you do with the House of Lords? Well, the House of Lords could be renamed the Senate, indirectly *elected* by members of the House of Commons, with the political parties represented in the Second Chamber in proportion to their relative strengths in the Commons. The hereditary peers would no longer have the right to sit in the Legislature, and the creation of further hereditary peers would cease forthwith. The scope of patronage presently available to the Queen and to the Prime Minister would thus be drastically cut.

Satisfaction from the performance of public service should ideally be its own reward. To play up to and exploit vanity and self-esteem is a pandering to people's least attractive characteristics. The present system of Honours is so capricious in the way it distributes its rewards, so open to misuse and petty corruption, as to have little merit or meaning. To end it, together with the hereditary system in the Lords, could indeed be the beginning of the end for the Monarchy itself. The prospect fills me with anticipation.

But the day is not yet. We may expect to see further attempts to make the Honours racket appear fairer and more democratic. Honours may be more severely restricted than hitherto – to those who genuinely perform public service beyond the standard for which they are paid. If it can't be abolished immediately, our national fancy dress ball should certainly be modified, simplified and taken out of the field of personal patronage, whether exercised by the Queen in Garters or by the Prime Minister in bishops and life peers.

During the thirteen years of Conservative power from 1951 to 1964, Churchill, Eden, Macmillan and Douglas-Home dished out to Tory MPs 2 earldoms, 19 viscountcies, 32 baronies, 40 baronetcies and 84 knighthoods. And that excludes the Garter, the Victorian Order, Privy Councillorships, Companions of Honour, and advances to various categories of the Orders of St Michael and St George or the British Empire.

The social and political morality of purely party patronage on that scale is an unhealthy aspect of the contemporary political scene. The dealers of the cards love the game. The winners enjoy it. But some refuse to play. Others, I think a vast majority, would prefer it if the sqalid game was not played at all.

A Word on Royal Warrant Holders

Have you ever wondered how some commercial and industrial concerns display the sign 'By Royal Appointment'? Like White Horse Scotch Whisky, for instance? Or Barrow Hepburn, manufacturers of Royal Maundy Purses? Or Wafood Ltd, dog-food suppliers? Or Hawker, James & Co. Ltd, purveyors of 'Pedlar' sloe gin? Or Kleen-Way, the Berkshire chimney sweepers?

The brokers in these commercial honours are the Royal Warrant Holders Association, 7 Buckingham Gate, London SW1. Apparently the Government Department of Trade and Industry knew nothing about this particular racket. They weren't sure whether the association came under the control of the Lord Chamberlain – and, if so, to whom he was responsible.

Royal Warrants are granted to tradesmen by the Queen, or the Duke of Edinburgh, or the Queen Mother. A tradesman obtains an application form from the Secretary of the Royal Household

Tradesman's Warrants Committee, Lord Chamberlain's Office, St James's Palace, or from the Royal Household whose Warrant he is seeking. The names of successful applicants are published annually in the *London Gazette* in late December.

Warrants are only granted after three consecutive years of satisfactory service to the Royal Household. Roughly twenty have been granted in each of the last few years, and an equivalent number cancelled. The companies named above were listed in the *London Gazette Supplement*, 1 January 1972, as a kind of capitalists' New Year Honours List.

There is still a short list of firms holding Royal Warrants of Appointment to the late King George V, who died in 1936. The whisky and wine merchants are there, as well as cutlers and suppliers of Welsh mutton.

On George VI's list of fourteen survivors, six are hard-drink merchants and three supply Bovril, condensed milk and flowers respectively.

Nearly 700 firms are on the list of Elizabeth II, ranging from suppliers of crushed chalk, racing colours and cattle dips to bagpipe-makers and reedthatchers, not to mention saddlers, hairdressers and motor-horsebox makers, purveyors of pork pies, muffin-makers and candlemakers, and Messrs Walls, suppliers of sausages.

Top of the chart come the booze companies – about forty in all. Some tobacco companies enjoy the Royal Warrant prestige too. Yet two of our killer diseases are alcoholism and lung cancer, caused by excessive drinking and smoking. It would seem a welcome contribution to the nation's health if the royal symbol of respectability were to be withdrawn from these companies whose goods contribute to the deaths of so many loyal subjects.

The Duke of Edinburgh's stamp of approval has been given to firms making guns, medals, hats, polo sticks, soap, ties and Gannex raincoats! But, up to the end of 1971, there was no drink firm on his list.

Early in 1974, according to the *Essex County Standard* of 18 January, Prince Charles ordered two miniature chastity belts from a Halstead firm which has built up an international market in such gimmicks. The Prince evidently proposed to use them as toilet-paper holders. The firm's director, Mr Hugessen, realized that this was not enough to get him a Royal Warrant, but he lived in hopes. 'I have had several inquiries from the Palace for my leather goods,' he said.

Though the grant of a Warrant sanctions nothing more than

the right to use the Royal Arms 'in defined circumstances', there is little doubt that it has commercial value for the firms who obtain it. When the tragedy of the Thalidomide children was revealed in all its stark reality, the Distillers Company, which had retailed the drug, presented us with one of the ugly faces of capitalism. But pleas to Buckingham Palace to withdraw the Royal Warrant fell on deaf ears.

Whatever commercial value it may have to the firms concerned, this form of royal patronage is not in the public interest, and it should cease. There is no public accountability, and no democratic control. And, like so much to do with the Monarchy, it is deliberately shrouded in mystery and therefore gives rise to doubts and suspicions.

7. CANUTE AND THE COMMONWEALTH

King Canute, as England's Danish King early in the eleventh century, left one apocryphal tale for the unofficial history books. Every schoolboy knows that it was Canute who sat on his throne on the seashore and commanded the tide to stop – and, as a result, got his feet wet. Another version has it that the King carried out his demonstration to show his sycophantic and fawning courtiers how foolish they were in claiming that he was so powerful that the elements would obey his command.

Tides, like winds of change, are natural forces that hold no respect for any human being, however exalted their status. The presence of the Throne in Britain is usually paraded as the cohesive force that somehow keeps the Commonwealth together. But, so far as the Commonwealth is concerned, the tide has been considerably on the ebb – ever since 1945.

Years ago, we had what was known as the British Empire. Geography and history lessons were invariably coupled with one essential visual aid: a map of the world, half of it coloured red. The red showed the British Empire: the greatest empire the world had ever seen; the empire on which the sun never set. The red colouring symbolized the blood spilt in empire-building. But, more important, Britain's standard of living rose as the abundant cheap raw materials of the overseas colonies were exploited. British merchants and trading companies waxed fat at the expense of the natives throughout the African continent, in India, Malaya and the West Indies. The 'White' Empire had a different basis. Canada, Australia, New Zealand and South Africa were founded mainly by white refugees and emigrants from their native homelands of England or Scotland – driven out by religious intolerance, or through other assaults made on individual freedom by piratical feudal landlords and unrepresentative governments, or shipped abroad by a barbaric criminal law.

The final turning-point may be taken as the end of the Second World War. After 1945, the post-war world came to be increasingly dominated by the two major powers: the United States and the Soviet Union. Britain lay unbowed, but virtually bankrupt. Western Europe was divided and shattered. The Commonwealth was a remote concept for a nation beset with mind-boggling internal problems. The tenuous ties with the Indian sub-continent were the first to be snapped. If Britain hadn't left India in 1947, she would have been swept out by the raging torrents of nationalism. Churchill's oratorical fury against the liquidation of the Empire was itself a Canute-like fantasy.

The liquidation was in full spate by the 1950s and 1960s and a royal visit a week could have done nothing to stop it. Under Labour and Conservative Governments alike, emergent nationalism in Africa, Asia and the Caribbean had flexed its muscles, the common factor among all the nationalists being a contempt of and hatred for Britain's former colonial ruling *élite*. And the British Crown was the clear symbolic head of that alien rule and foreign yoke. But, as the tides of history remorselessly flowed, we were meant to pretend it wasn't happening. The late Lord Salisbury, as an epitome of Empire, bitterly castigated Iain Macleod as 'too clever by half' when, as Colonial Secretary in a Tory Government, Macleod was able to read the writing on the wall. During the post-war decades, written constitutions for the 'Coloured' Empire countries became one of Britain's major and more futile exports. The Westminster plant does not root easily in foreign soil. It was, all too often, like trying to grow tea in Wick. In India, Nehru, once jailed as a dangerous nationalist, became one of the most distinguished of Commonwealth Prime Ministers – but as the political head of a Republic. Nkrumah, who had also been behind British bars, led the Gold Coast to a free Ghana, only to end as an exiled, discredited dictator. It was a story that was repeated many times: in Kenya, Cyprus, Uganda.

Thus, the idea of the Commonwealth was largely a pretence from the start: an illusionist's attempt to compensate the brainwashed British citizen for having lost 'his' Empire, and a bid to retain some of the trading advantages that had belonged to it.

But, as an article by 'A Conservative' said in *The Times* of 2 April 1964, 'it is dangerous to prostitute to the service of a transparent fiction [i.e. the Commonwealth] the subtle emotions of loyalty and affection on which that heritage depends . . . A great and growing number of the people of these islands do not like to see the Sovereign whom they regard as their own by every chain of history and sentiment playing an alien part as one of the characters in the Commonwealth charade. If Kingship and the British Crown can be reduced to this [they feel] will it long stand for anything to anyone?'

If Britain continues to be seen by the rest of the world as clinging to a fantasy, we will unsentimentally and rightly be left alone in our dream world as others move on. The dilemma became crystal clear in the excruciating parliamentary debates on British entry into the EEC of the 1960s (with tedious repeats in 1972–3). Labour and Tory MPs joined in wet-eyed sentiment over our 'kith and kin' in Canada, New Zealand and Australia, disregarding the fact that these independent states are being increasingly populated by Poles, Czechs, Germans and all peoples east of Dover. The Commonwealth, they implied, should be preserved forever as a source of cheap food and raw materials. The emigration of unemployed Britishers to the other side of the globe was infinitely preferable to their working a few miles away in Europe. The Labour Party stood on its head as usual, taunting imperialistic Tories for ratting on the Commonwealth. It was nothing new. Mr Wilson and Mr Gaitskell, as successive Labour leaders, had consistently flung jibes at Tory Prime Ministers for presiding over the steady decline of Commonwealth trade. Not that the decline had showed any signs of reversal during the six years of the 1964–70 Labour Government. And though the Royal Family might span the globe perennially like a gilded, glittering sales team, the figures spoke for themselves. (See Table overleaf.) In 1950, UK exports to the Commonwealth as a whole had represented nearly half our total to the world (48 per cent). By 1972, it had fallen to less than 19 per cent. And, over the same period, total imports from the Commonwealth fell from 42 per cent to only 19 per cent.

It is significant that, even though South Africa withdrew from the Commonwealth in 1961, the pattern of Britain's trade with that country does not markedly differ from that shown in the figures given. This, alone, implies that the idea of 'a Commonwealth' is not as relevant as is usually made out. For investment, a similar pattern emerges. Over the past decade, UK investment

	1950		1971	
	Exports to UK	*Imports from UK*	*Exports to UK*	*Imports from UK*
Australia	38·7%	51·9%	11·2%	21·4%
New Zealand	65·5%	60·1%	34·4%	28·9%
Canada	22·7%	12·7%	7·7%	5·4%
India	25·8%	17·6%	11·1%	7·8%
Nigeria	79·0%	22·0%	59·8%	32·0%

in Australia, Canada and New Zealand has increased, especially in Australia, but it is far outstripped in those countries by US investment. By 1968, the American 'stake' in Australia had more than trebled compared with 1960, and it had more than quadrupled by 1971. The same is broadly true of New Zealand.

So far as trade with the Common Market was concerned, even before British entry the proportion of total exports increased from 22 per cent in 1960 to 32 per cent in 1972, while that with the Commonwealth fell from 34 per cent to 18 per cent. This trend can only accelerate, and all the undeniable evidence points to the fact that the bonds intended to hold the Commonwealth together are steadily being broken or eroded. The process can only continue. The populations of the older 'White' Commonwealth countries become less British-orientated all the time. In Australia between 1947 and 1966 (the latest available figures), the non-British-born population increased from about 39,000 to 511,000, or nearly one in twenty of the total Australian population. The vast majority of Australians were born in Australia and have never set foot in Britain. Over 97 per cent of New Zealanders were born in New Zealand, the numbers having been born elsewhere having increased from 18,000 in 1945 to more than 73,000 in 1966. As for Canada, 10 per cent of the population have no connection with Britain at all, and another 84 per cent were born in Canada.

In 1973, the advent of Labour Governments in New Zealand and Australia saw a further weakening of links with Britain. New Zealand has been moving towards regional development in the Pacific. Her trade with that area now equals that with the enlarged European Community. Before the Second World War, 80 per cent of New Zealand's trade was with Britain. Today it is less than a third.

New Zealand has not yet dispensed with 'God Save the Queen' as the National Anthem; Mr Kirk, as Labour Prime Minister, accepted membership of the Privy Council; and gave no indication that New Zealanders' names would cease to be recommended for the Honours List.

On the other hand, Mr Whitlam, as Labour Prime Minister of Australia, declined to become a Privy Councillor. He jettisoned the Honours system along with 'God Save the Queen' and the Union Jack. Opinion polls in Australia confirmed public support for his gestures of contempt towards the trappings of colonial servility. The slavish royalism once indulged in by the former Conservative Prime Minister, the late Robert Menzies, has disappeared forever from the Australian scene at least. There is still a great affection for the UK, and family links will naturally last for a long time, but these have nothing to do with the Crown. As William Davis wrote from Australia in the *Guardian* at Christmas 1972: 'On television we'll have the Morecambe and Wise Show and the Queen's Christmas Day message – twice. "This scintillating ten minutes is awaited eagerly by anything up to a dozen viewers," says one television critic. "I fear I'm not one of them. Nothing could keep me away from that beach – not even Her Majesty the Queen." '

That just about sums it up, as did the reaction to some remarks made by Prince Philip when he gave a televised press conference in Canberra early in March 1967. He would not be surprised, he said, if Australia did become a republic. ' . . . The British Commonwealth is changing. It is an association of peoples of different languages, races and cultures.' But, he went on to claim, 'In the Monarchy we have something that brings them together. It would be silly to chuck it over.' 'A bloody bore,' was the verdict of one Australian journalist.

And what of Canada? That swinging Liberal Prime Minister, Pierre Trudeau, said in a speech of December 1969: 'The values of the new generation and tremendous technological changes may lead Canada to give up its connections with the Royal Family in the coming decade.' In early 1967, the liberal Toronto *Daily Star* had a leading article headed 'Monarchy Divides Us. A Republic Would Help Canada.' The editorial stated bluntly, 'We believe that the monarchy no longer serves any useful purpose in the task of nation building that lies ahead.' It went on to say that the institution fed the illusions of some Canadians that Britishness defined the country's identity, but, the fact remained, Canada is no longer a British country.

Today there is in Canada at best a massive indifference towards the Monarchy, except among the older generations of British stock in the genteel quarters of 'British' Columbia. In any case, 30 per cent of the population is French Canadian and jealous of its own legitimate cultural origins. About another quarter is Italian, German, Dutch or Ukranian. Far less than half the Canadian people have any British connection whatsoever. As Professor Gerald S. Graham wrote in *The Times* on 12 December 1972, 'The majority of the Canadian people under 50 are simply unconcerned about Britain.'

The 1967 visit of the Queen and the Duke of Edinburgh to Canada for the centenary celebrations was one of those flops that is known as a brilliant royal success. The Canadian Broadcasting Company did its best, for it, too, has its nasal, awestruck courtiers of the air: 'There we see her, the Queen of Canada, adding her own stroke of splendour to our birthday celebrations.' While the French Canadians turned their backs, Canadians of Ukrainian or Italian extraction could only have found the idea of their nation genuflecting to this foreign lady faintly ridiculous. German Canadians cannot have felt much different, despite the British Crown's German origins. And, whatever she was (and whatever her titles say she is), she was demonstrably *not* Queen of Canada. She lived in *England.* She belonged to *Britain.* She spoke with an impeccable, genteel *English* accent, which English aristocracts and class-conscious Britons may lap up, but not rugged Canadians of mid-European extraction. For them the gilded coaches, the colourful tin soldiers and their accompanying military buskers, must have been like ghosts from the past long discarded.

The British Monarch is a foreign intrusion in Canadian affairs, and Canadian newspapers have gone so far as to claim that the British Crown forms a divisive force in their country – as, indeed, it is. Under Mr Lester Pearson's Liberal Government, the Canadian national flag became a single red maple leaf on a white background. 'God Save the Queen' followed the Union Jack down the drain. Royal emblems have been obliterated from mail trucks and post offices – to appease the French Canadians in Quebec, said some pro-Royalists. There is something called the Monarchist League in Canada, which exists to 'counter criticism of the Monarchy by Government, the media, or any other source'. It issues instructions on what can be done to stop the rot from spreading: 'Buy *only* stamps with the Queen's portrait on them. *Demand* them, if necessary speaking to your Postmaster.' 'Try to have your Minister, Priest, or Rabbi say a prayer every service for the Royal Family.' 'Ask all groups of which you are a member to open or close all meetings with the singing of "God Save the Queen".' 'Do not support a republic-orientated group.'

Signs of the times: but much, much more royalist canvassing would be needed in the prairies and the Provinces for the British Monarchy to retain its foothold on the other side of the Atlantic. A lot of ground is lost already, and it is late in the day, as the Monarchist League bemoanfully recognizes: the removal of the Queen's picture from Government buildings, 'notably the Embassies in the Middle East'; the reference to 'Canadian Government Publications' in place of 'the Queen's printer for

Canada'; 'Statistics Canada' instead of the 'Dominion Bureau of Statistics'; the decision of the Canadian Prime Minister or other Cabinet Ministers not to attend Prince Charles's investiture as Prince of Wales; the vote of the Quebec Liberal Party to abolish the Monarchy and set up a republic; the abolition of many 'royal' regiments.

The increasing hostility or indifference to the Monarchy in Canada is always blamed on the activities and attitudes of the French Canadians, but this is only partly true. More and more English Canadians are beginning to feel that the royal connection represents a conservative, enervating influence, sapping desire for change, making the increasing numbers of non-British immigrants feel like 'outsiders'. The emotional concept of 'mother country' and 'daughter nation' is running out of sap.

But the process that is known as 'keeping the family together' goes on. *No* royal visit to *any* part of the Commonwealth at *any* time is *ever* reported as having been less than a splendid triumph. No qualifications. No doubts expressed – except, maybe, that the Queen has worked too hard, has had her gloved hand pumped too profusely. But, like package-holiday tours abroad, all there seems to be to show for it afterwards are the pictures for the family album: 'The Queen's off-the-face hat makes a direct contrast to her daughter's as the royal visitors study a feature of interest on the Beach of Passionate Love at Kota Bharu in north Malaysia yesterday,' said a caption in *The Times* on 3 March 1972.

It is, of course, an absurd sentimentality to pretend that the countries of the Commonwealth hold together for any other reasons than those of self-interest: the advantages in terms of financial and technical aid. What remote or grotesque connection can ever be made between an Indian starving to death on the streets of Calcutta and a wealthy white queen thousands of miles away in London; or between a black African farmer scratching a living from harsh, sun-baked soil and an ageing prince playing polo in Windsor Great Park, England? There is no sign, for instance, that the British Monarchy has had any influence on General Amin's despotic and paranoic régime in Uganda, except that when he sought an invitation to Princess Anne's wedding, he didn't get it. Why not? He *is* the head of a Commonwealth country. His policies *are* no more cruel or repressive than those of Portugal, our 'oldest ally', have been in her African colonies; and no one had any compunction about sending Prince Philip off on an official jaunt to Lisbon in 1973 to celebrate the 600th anniversary of the Anglo-Portuguese alliance.

When Prince Philip was asked if he thought that the Crown was a unifying force in the Commonwealth, his reply was that he could think of few others (see page 236). Quite so. The Commonwealth has no common purpose and can never be a cohesive political union in world politics. It is a loose federation of states which has its uses, though these also must be kept in perspective. The pseudo-mysticism of a continuing common historical destiny is sentimental nonsense, but there are still those who romanticize and who would echo the words used by Winston Churchill in Coronation year: 'The Crown has become the mysterious link, indeed I might say the magic link, which unites our loosely bound but strongly interwoven Commonwealth of Nations, states and races.' Or who would say, as the *Daily Mail* said on 2 September 1952, 'But for the Crown the Commonwealth would have fallen to pieces years ago . . . The British Commonwealth is one, and its inhabitants are one.' They will have to be left to take comfort in a taste for empty rhetoric and meaningless verbiage.

But to look at the Commonwealth on a strictly realistic basis, there is some justification for the claim that it remains the most extensive multi-racial, multi-coloured organization in the world. Its record of achievements, as outlined in the current *Commonwealth Year Book*, is an impressive example of international co-operation not exceeded by the United Nations. But, as a 'free association of peoples, not a collection of subject nations', as Mr Attlee put it in 1947 when he was Labour Prime Minister. It does not, and cannot, speak with one voice.

Meanwhile the Commonwealth has a right to expect that since Britain is the only Commonwealth nation in the world's richest club, the EEC, she should at least defend the interests of her former colonies as determinedly as France and Holland do theirs. The 'Coloured' Commonwealth belongs almost wholly in the poverty-stricken Third World and has an 800 million population or thereabouts. In riches and rags terms, the Commonwealth therefore quite accurately reflects the world at large. The problems are not just those of selling such primary products as cane sugar, cocoa, coffee, tea, or lamb and butter. As developing countries which depend on these commodities, they must be able to develop trade freely, according to need, with Japan, the United States, or whatever. They have no wish to be bound as tightly to the EEC as are, say, the former French colonial territories. In these crucial matters, Britain must be a bold and, if need be, bloody-minded defender of legitimate Commonwealth interests in Brussels.

The Queen may still read from her script for a Commonwealth Day Message: 'The Commonwealth is not for governments or statesmen alone. It is for the people, for all the people of the Commonwealth. The Commonwealth asks us to live up to its ideals of friendship and understanding . . . ' Yet the realities of history now beckon her to look more towards Brussels and Paris. With or without a Monarchy, the problems will remain. And, with or without a Monarchy, the Commonwealth will continue to develop and adapt in a world context, according to its needs and interests. None but the most extreme of romanticists can dream that the Crown has any real role to play in this evolution. Any more than a parish priest can play the part of Prime Minister.

8. FAMILY PORTRAITS

Starting from the top down, England's Queen is now a middle-aged, upper-middle-class lady: a monarch who has seen six Prime Ministers come and go, from Churchill and Eden to Macmillan, Douglas-Home, Wilson and Heath. She had an upbringing akin to that of a novitiate in a convent: more comfortable and luxurious, but almost as exclusive. She never saw the inside of any school or mixed with ordinary mortal children. Only by accident was she cast in the role of up-and-coming leading lady of the Royal Ruritania Light Opera Co., when the wheel of fortune was rocked by Mrs Simpson. By choosing to abdicate to marry his double divorcee from America, Edward VIII ensured that Princess Elizabeth would one day be Queen.

The prospect was probably not relished. It had not been foreseen, or prepared for. If the choice had been open, Elizabeth would doubtless have been happy playing third, fourth or fifth fiddle in the Court orchestra. But it was not to be. Elizabeth II would succeed her father on his early death in 1952, and the new Elizabethan era would be heralded in with trumpets.

Princess Elizabeth had clocked up a considerable, well-publicized record before she came to the Throne: a broadcast to Commonwealth Children when she was 14 (as usual, perfect); at 16 a Colonel of the Grenadier Guards, inspecting the Regiment;

at 18 a Counsellor of State. She had learnt madrigal singing and the piano, been a Girl Guide from 11, quickly rising to patrol leader of the 1st Buckingham Palace Guide Company and, eventually, a Sea Ranger. By the special wish of her dad, however, the Princess was not called on to do wartime National Service when she reached her eighteenth birthday. But she was keen to join the Auxiliary Territorial Service (the ATS). She was duly gazetted as a junior officer in March 1945, and soon qualified as an army truck driver. Newspapers and women's magazines were choked with appropriate photographs of Britain's future Queen in her army uniform, 'doing her bit'.

Early in 1947 her engagement to her cousin, Prince Philip of Greece, was announced. Like the rest of the 'Greek' Royal Family, he was largely a mixture of Danish and German stock, had a good war record in the British Navy, and was a nephew of the Earl Mountbatten. The wedding of November 1947 would produce two children before Princess Elizabeth became Queen. The alliance was a brilliant *coup* to cement 'the new Royal Family' firmly in the hearts and minds of the British people. Rarely had the Crown been stronger in the nation's affection.

At the Coronation, the new Queen was young, recently and romantically married and well-equipped with the good looks of an English rose. Yet one felt a pang of sympathy for her as, shy and withdrawn to an embarrassing degree, she faced a prospect of unknown years of grinding boredom, meaningless chores and endless soporific speeches prepared by Court flunkies more anxious not to offend than positively to please.

How could she possibly begin to fulfil the hopes of the romantics who wrote and spoke glowingly of the onset of a new era? Britain was flat on her face; finished as an international power with a world role (though the realization would take decades to sink in). There was little left except tattered memories of Empire hung up like relic flags from the Battle of Waterloo. With a clear destiny lost, the nation fell back on idolizing this innocent, tense, young lady, whom it feudally crowned as its powerless Head of State in the most expensive and long-drawn-out exercise in national euphoria of the twentieth century. The Establishment worked a mass hypnosis on the nation, and Her Majesty Queen Elizabeth II was their submissive tool. She played the role well: modest, nervous, dignified, so obviously vulnerable. Forces likely to challenge the royal fortress stayed far beyond the horizon, if they even existed. Mild complaints were made about the cost; and the anachronistic nature of the Coronation as our national tribal ritual. Never a word of criticism was uttered about the Queen as a person. Yet, by training and upbringing, she didn't have, and couldn't have been expected to have, the remotest idea of how the great mass of 'her' people struggled for survival. Their lives were another, alien world. Her first Prime Minister, Winston Churchill, was old enough to be her great-grandfather. She could advise him on nothing, warn him on nothing. The air was clear of constitutional crises, like those which had plagued the early days of the kingship of her grandfather, George V. She was able to settle down cosily into the role of wife, mother, guardian of the nation's rapidly slipping morality, and the yearly, unchanging round of horsey high-society events, the breaking of bread at Royal Garden Parties, and periodic forays into outlying remnants of Empire and Commonwealth.

Few would question that the Queen works hard: facts and figures are churned out to prove a point which needs no proof. She's probably shaken the hands of more nonentities than any other living mortal. She's had to sit through more deadly dull rituals than anyone has a right to impose on his worst enemy. And, understandably, she often finds it impossible to hide her weariness. Only her supreme desire to do her *duty* has ensured her physical survival. Many a Goliath, let alone a frail lady, would have long since wilted and died under the senseless strain. But, like Tesco, or Marks & Spencer, she aims to please the customers. She's in business for the nation; and shareholders are ready to swear that the dividends are fabulous.

It was the powerful persuasion of Winston Churchill, combined with the acquiescence of Labour's Leader Attlee, which saw the 1952 Civil List safely and almost silently through the Commons. By 1954 the late Richard Dimbleby was already saying that Elizabeth II was one of England's greatest Queens – and making it sound as if it meant more than it did. As the struggle for national survival still went on, with post-war food rationing still in force, the royal routine remained unchanged. The débutantes' Presentation Parties continued to flourish as the high point of the social year, for they provided a marriage mart for the progeny of the upper classes. The Court functionaries continued to be drawn from the same old social *élite*: qualifications were the right public schools or Guards regiments and a wealthy Tory background – preferably from the hunting set.

The Queen herself was dignified but distant, unbending in public. Even in those early days she projected extreme wealth: a bejewelled symbol and anchor for the British class system. Today, twenty years on, there is little evidence that either the Queen herself, even less her advisers, wish to change her position in any unsuperficial way. The sickening parade of débutantes may have been lopped away, public relations may have been professionalized, but there the revolution stops.

It is not easy to assess the *political* role that the Queen has played in the years since the beginning of the reign. Inquiries on these subjects draw blanks from the Palace, as the questions and answers given on pages 230–39 of Appendix F indicate. Nor can much reliance be placed on the objectivity of autobiographical versions of constitutional events by successive Prime Ministers – from Attlee to Macmillan to Wilson.

Eden's succession to Churchill in 1955 had seemed to present no difficulties. Eden was the accepted Crown Prince, groomed for the job. That he would turn out to be a calamity at the time of the Suez crisis in the following year no one could have foreseen. The full story of that criminal fiasco, which seems in retrospect like the last lunatic death spasm of the old imperialism, during which Ministers of the Crown lied to deceive the Commons, the Cabinet and the Monarch herself, cannot as yet be known (much vital evidence is still officially secret). But, shortly after those disastrous events, the Queen exercised her prerogative of conferring the Garter on Eden. Only twice has the Queen given the Garter to politicians still in active politics, and both were Conservatives: Churchill and Eden. Little public comment followed, and none of it was adverse.

Harold Macmillan's illness and resignation in 1963, however, provoked an entirely different situation over the prime-ministerial succession: an episode of skulduggery and blood-letting in the Tory party's hierarchy. This, of course, brought Lord Home out on top, who disclaimed his peerage and became Sir Alec Douglas-Home on 23 October 1963. As Macmillan points out in his memoirs, the only remaining unqualified executive privilege of the Monarch is the right to select and appoint the Prime Minister. Macmillan (on his sick-bed) was duly consulted by the Queen about his successor. She saw his arithmetic – the voting in the Cabinet, among Tory MPs, and among local party chairman. Not that the Crown is under any obligation to consult, or to accept the advice given. The Cabinet never saw the 'advice' or the document which were presented by a very sick Macmillan to Her Majesty. Macmillan's sums came up with Sir Alec as the answer, though the Queen must have been aware of the strong views against him.

In the circumstances, one might think she would have been better advised to seek a second opinion from someone other than a fading Prime Minister. But she (or her advisers) chose not to do so. The late Iain Macleod had been the prospective Tory successor whom the Labour Opposition most feared, for he was a brilliant politician. In his own version of these events, he wrote, significantly, that there was no criticism whatsoever that could be made of the part played by the Crown. But, he made clear, the procedure used to select a new Prime Minister had been both wrong and unsatisfactory.

From the point of view of Macmillan and the Queen's advisers, there had been very good reasons behind the choice. It had been Macmillan, tending always to boast of his phoney Scottish crofting background, who had put the politically obscure Scottish landlord and aristocrat, Lord Home, into the Foreign Office in the first place, despite fierce opposition from his own party. The Queen must herself have seen in Douglas-Home a man after her own heart: Scottish, wealthy and landed, out of the top drawer; part of what Iain Macleod bitterly called the 'Tory Magic Circle'. Now, Macmillan says, he would have preferred it if Hailsham or Macleod had succeeded him, for they had *genius*. Instead, we were landed with Sir Alec as Prime Minister, foisted on us by the joint machinations of the outgoing Prime Minister and the Palace – the old-boy network in action with a vengeance. And if, as Macleod said, the choice of Douglas-Home had been wrong, then the Queen had shared in the mistake, and it *was* a political one.

Subsequently the Conservative Party was compelled to look for a more democratic method of electing its Leader. They opted for the method that had been used by the Labour Party since its inception: election by the Party's parliamentary members. So, in practice, for the 'Queen's prerogative' we should today read 'Hobson's choice'. When I asked Sir Alec Douglas-Home, 'What would happen if, tomorrow, Mr Heath [then Prime Minister] should fall off his boat and be drowned? What would the Queen do?' 'She would,' he replied, 'probably ask the Home Secretary to act as interim Prime Minister until the Tory MPs elected their new leader. Then he would be invited by the Queen to be her Prime Minister.'

In 1968–9, a move was afoot by some Labour MPs to oust Harold Wilson as Prime Minister. The Palace had been left in no doubt as to the procedure the Queen would be *obliged* to follow in the event of Wilson's removal. She would have to refuse him a dissolution of Parliament (a threat which he occasionally used in those traumatic days). She would have to accept the interim Premiership of the Deputy Leader of the Party, and await the outcome of the subsequent election of a new leader by the Parliamentary Labour Party. Thus we may illustrate the myth of the prerogative divorced from the realities of party politics.

In all other respects, the Queen has done her duty impeccably if unimaginatively. She has striven mightily to maintain the unity of the Commonwealth as it disintegrates inexorably, though its romantic illusions of grandeur are a long time a-dying. Now the end is being hastened by Britain's entry into the European Economic Community. On the Government's instructions, the Queen went to Paris to mouth sentiments about the Common Market which, she must have known, were not shared by a majority of her subjects. She became the clockwork doll, the political puppet, for the political ambitions of Edward Heath, her Prime Minister.

Other Prime Ministers have used her for their own political purposes, including Harold Wilson, with his efforts to bring rebellious Rhodesia to heel and his traipsing up to Balmoral to see her on the eve of a Conservative Party Conference. Politically she is now little more than a pawn on the national chessboard. But she is still socially valuable to those who believe in the *status quo*, and politically useful to the Conservative Party, which seeks to identify itself with the Crown and, conversely, dubs anyone mildly critical of the institution as a Bolshie who ought to take himself off to Russia or be locked in the Tower. (Erskine May, the bible of parliamentary procedure, still provides for the latter punishment. It is my last ambition.)

The Queen works on slavishly at her royal treadmill, as Sir Michael Adeane told the Parliamentary Select Committee in excruciating detail. She receives an average of 120 letters a day (over twenty years, a mighty lot of mail). She answers them all, except those from crackpots. She trudges off to parties, receptions, hot meals, cold meals. She's read over 1,000 speeches to spellbound audiences all over the world. She's pinned medals and ribbons on 35,000 proud chests. And, God help her, she's seen her Prime Ministers on over 1,000 occasions. She can never, according to Sir Michael, enjoy a complete holiday. She's the only person in the land who can never retire. And yet she's never too tired to deal with her official papers at the end of the day.

There may be little merit or worth in what the Queen actually does, unless it be that the pomp, colour and pageantry of regal activities give harmless pleasure to millions whose lives are otherwise as drab and sombre as events in a graveyard. The general consensus is that the Queen goes out of her way to put people at their ease, that she is truly professional at her job. At the drop of a curtsy she will talk about horses, for she remains much more at home with the tweedy country gentry than with town folk or artisans. With great ceremony and dignity she will confirm things that have already happened, officially open hospitals that have been at work for months. She, or her representative, will lower the Union Jack when a colony is ready to go it alone. To the horror of Ian Smith, Enoch Powell and the right-wing Tory Monday Club, she will dance gracefully with a black Prime Minister – as she did with Nkrumah in Ghana, before he was dispatched into exile.

Unfortunately, she is surrounded and penned in by an old-school-tie network of courtiers (from her Private Secretary down) who are as reactionary and blinkered as any in history. It is this, as a lot of her most loyal subjects sense for themselves, that cocoons her in a world of unreality and keeps her in a web of her own creation: a web of flattery and flummery, and as far from ordinary people as the outermost planets. The fault may not lie wholly with the Queen herself. But, if she does not like it, she shows a remarkable capacity for concealing her displeasure. Many would not be sorry to see a start made on the dismantling of the Court's ultra-élitist clique tomorrow.

The complexity of Prince Philip's family tree makes the mind boggle. His grandfather was King George I of Greece, the son of a Danish king; his grandmother a Russian grand-duchess. His father was thus a Greek prince while his mother was a German great-granddaughter of Queen Victoria. But, whatever the blood mix, however complex the family tree, Philip speedily climbed to the top. His family had been exiled from Greece in 1922, and his education was divided between Cheam private school in Berkshire, Salem in Germany, posh Gordonstoun in Scotland. He served in the British Royal Navy from 1939 and throughout the Second World War. He was naturalized as a British subject in early 1947, and adopted the surname of Mountbatten. The Germanic 'Battenberg' had been buried by the English branch of the family in 1917.

Lieutenant Philip Mountbatten married Elizabeth Windsor on 20 November 1947. The day before the wedding, at the touch of a magic wand, he became His Royal Highness The Duke of Edinburgh, and Baron Greenwich, Earl of Merioneth; and, of course, a Knight of the Garter. The housing problem was a little longer in finding a solution, as well it might when hundreds of thousands of families up and down the country were clamouring for somewhere to live. The couple squatted in Buckingham Palace for a year or so, while a week-end bolt-hole was provided at Sunninghill Park, Ascot. Such slumming could not be tolerated for long. The House of Commons, under a Labour Government, gave assent to the spending of £50,000 to make Clarence House shipshape; and, to ensure that the struggling couple weren't without a bob or two, they voted £10,000 a year for the Duke and an extra £25,000 for his missus. At the 1952 Civil List, Philip was put on his £40,000 a year, which was increased to £65,000 from 1 January 1972 (and which, before the 1970s are out, will undoubtedly be increased again with scarcely a blink from the House of Commons). According to the Treasury's information to the 1972 Select Committee, 80 per cent of what Philip received on the previous Civil List counted as tax-free expenses. Since 1 January 1972, when the annuity was increased, there has been no fixed percentage of official expenses. It is now based on actual official expenditure, which in 1972 came to £40,000, i.e. 61·54 per cent. The Duke himself forecast that tax paid by him for 1973/4 would be in the region of £14,350.

What do we get for our money? What is the Prince's role in our constitution. Apart from being the Queen's husband, the father of her children, and a sponsor of various good causes, his main function seems to be to popularize an institution in which he has a considerable vested interest. The Duke is publicly accountable to no one for his activities. It has been rumoured that he would dearly like to have played the role of a Prince Albert to his Victoria; but those days have gone, and for ever.

By royal standards, he works very hard, from choice. He could stay as idle as his sister-in-law, but he chooses to beaver away. He can down a pint of beer in the local pub or take part in the annual Garter pantomime at Windsor with equal relish. He has a refreshing and, in Royalty, unusual habit of making off-the-cuff, 'sensible' speeches. These are on a variety of topics, usually interspersed with salty humour and barrack-room expletives. He can make a fool of himself cheerfully, and put his feet in it with gay, unselfconscious abandon. He is the HP sauce for the royal fish and chips. He will do anything as the desire moves him, and everything the Government of the day tells him to do: like visiting the Portuguese dictatorship; or flying in the elephantine extravaganza Concorde in an attempt to boost its commercial credibility.

He has the casual superiority and self-assurance of his caste. He does not argue or debate. He *asserts*. He'll tell businessmen to get their fingers out, suggest men on the dole might consider emigrating. He can pontificate about the population explosion, and, having sired four children himself, tell others that they should settle for two, as he did in Edinburgh on 17 December 1971:

> We now subsidize people to have children. You could argue that it might be possible to tax people for having children. That is not to say that it will stop them, but it makes it more expensive. There is a certain amount to be said for this, because a couple with eight children, it is estimated, costs society £30,000 in ten years, and this only for education and family allowances.

Well, just *one* of his own children, Princess Anne, is currently in receipt of £35,000 *a year*. She, alone, has already cost the state over £100,000. And, when his two younger sons are 18 in a few years' time, they'll get £20,000 apiece a year, increased to £50,000 when they marry. As a letter in the *Guardian* commented on 23 December 1971:

> It is time that someone reminded HRH that he has produced four offspring, far above the national average number of children per family; and it is doubtful whether during his periods of procreation he once considered the cost to society in the form of the burden which falls upon the taxpayer. It seems glaringly obvious that his is the most outstanding example of an oversized, State-subsidized family.

The writer was being over-polite.

'We're encouraging them to breed like rabbits!' appropriately roared a respected senior colleague on the Civil List Committee during a discussion of the Royal Family Allowances.

No wonder the Prince was described in a London newspaper in 1967 as 'the gabby Duke', after he had said that he was 'sick and tired of making excuses for Britain'. Tory MPs put down a Motion in the Commons deploring the Duke's attack on British industry. The right-wing weekly *Time & Tide* waded in on 1 March 1967 and produced hard facts and figures about Britain's exports, strikes and technology to show up the nonsense the Duke had talked. As the *Daily Express* chipped in, 'This country needs neither Prince Philip's lectures nor his excuses. It is hard to imagine any Jack being more all right than the Prince. If he finds making excuses for us abroad so wearisome he should spend more time in his adopted country.' The Duke eloquently described the *Express* as 'a bloody awful newspaper'.

He has, certainly, spent a lot of time floating around the Commonwealth. But what good it has done is anybody's guess. In Canberra, on 2 March 1967, he himself said that 'these mammoth all-purpose tours . . . don't really achieve a great deal and they are very exhausting, and in the end even the people who comment on them, who have to come round, get equally exhausted and then get bored with them'. There we have it, straight from the horse's mouth. Royal Commonwealth tours are 'exhausting' and 'boring' to everybody concerned – and achieve very little anyway.

Nevertheless, the Duke's role as a foil to Court feudalism, stuffiness and 'apartness' has been invaluable to the Monarchy at its present stage of entrenchment. His interest in science and technology, the youth of Britain, and conservation problems, and his occasional forays into the minefields of political cautioning, have made a striking contrast to the rather pointless maunderings and mutterings of other members of his family, not excepting the Queen herself. But an Australian columnist, reviewing the Duke's tour as president of the Australian Conservation Foundation early in 1973, touched brutally on his weak point in the weekly, *News Review*, when he commented that the Duke, 'Without a prepared speech . . . proves to be even more of a fatuous ninny than with one: the brains of a polo pony.' Rather an over-harsh judgement, perhaps.

Basil Boothroyd, in his *Philip, an Informal Biography* (1971), tells us that the Duke paid out over £20,000 in salaries in 1969; that he rides around in a 1961 car; that he pays the rent and rates of the members of his Household – who numbered eight according to the *British Imperial Calendar* for 1973.

By all accounts, the Prince is not personally a rich man. Some have called him the royal pauper. Let us hope that, if he survives the Queen, she will have made adequate provision for him, for that contingency was overlooked when the royal finances were dealt with in 1972–3. Meanwhile, as consort to the Queen, his is a heavy cross to bear. With his salary having increased from £8 a week as sailor to £10,000, £40,000 and then £65,000 a year, he's done his best to prove himself worthy of his hire.

Cash apart, as a benevolent busybody, Prince Philip is as near to being a professional politician as anyone on the non-party cross-benches in the House of Lords. As an automatic member of that decorous mausoleum, he might seriously consider, as he gets on in years, taking a more active part in its proceedings. There his utterances could be just as controversial, and they would moreover be open to immediate cross-examination and challenge. He might, for instance, be persuaded to give us his real views on race relations and racial prejudice, since the bulk of the Commonwealth consists of coloured people, and there are two million of them in Britain. His apologetic, defensive mumblings on this issue have been in stark contrast to his breezy self-assertiveness and arrogance on so many others. Asked about it on Tyne Tees Television, he said he thought it was 'a dreadfully difficult problem', that 'racialism is peculiar', and that 'without God only tribalism was left'. The Duke's limitations become obvious in a personal, impromptu interview, which is perhaps why he is so cagey in granting them. (See Appendix F, page 238.) He has recently taken to the reins of horse-drawn carriage competition.

So what does the future hold for the Duke? He'll probably go on making speeches about the wisdom of keeping him employed as the official hot-gospeller of the monarchical creed. There's no reason why he shouldn't maintain his skill on the grouse moors, blasting birds out of the air with one hand while he supports wild-life preservation with the other. Ascot is for all ages, though he may begin to find the Cowes Regatta somewhat strenuous.

The future seems safe enough, if less intense. As his queenly wife grows older gracefully, the Duke's future will depend almost wholly on what she decides to do. There have been rumours, from time to time, that she would abdicate early, before Prince Charles grows too old. But that would depend in some degree on how soon Charles marries and produces a successor, and so, at the moment, lies in the realms of conjecture. For the moment the Consort soldiers on to nowhere in particular.

The present Prince of Wales, born in November 1948, was christened Charles Philip Arthur George, the names providing a reminder of the Greek, Coburg, Hanoverian and Teck origins of his family. He is the third Prince of Wales we have had in this century. In 1952, following his mother's Coronation, as Duke of Cornwall he came in for one-ninth of the net annual revenues of the Duchy of Cornwall: £9,497 tax free. A Member of Parliament was then paid £1,000 a year gross, a Cabinet Minister £5,000, but those same MPs and Cabinet Ministers eagerly agreed an income several times greater than their own for a child of four. The system of financing Prince Charles is the system of wealth, advantage and privilege writ large in brazen letters.

Some attempts were made to educate him, but always in the private, privileged sectors of the educational system. It is significant that his father sent the lad to Gordonstoun School in the Scottish Highlands – a select school founded by a refugee German and noted for its Teutonic disciplines. Equally significant was his taking a Cambridge University degree in archaeology and anthropology – two subjects studying the venerable past. He had failed – twice – to pass 'O'-level mathematics.

A high point of ridiculous grandeur was reached with Charles's investiture as Prince of Wales on 1 July 1969, run with all the panache a Labour Government in a tight corner could muster. Attempts to get Labour Welsh MPs to go led to a derisory response. The official budget for this jamboree was £200,000, or 'over £2,650 a minute', as the *Observer* commented on 16 March 1969. Local landladies cashed in – £250 for window space for one newspaper cameraman. There were special seats for invited guests inside the Caernarvon Castle at £12 a bottom, cheaper seats in the moats outside at 5 guineas and 10 guineas a time. There was £5,000-worth of free paint dished out to local property owners to tart up premises. Chains of souvenir shops were stuffed with junk selling at Bond Street prices. Hundreds of manufacturers churned out souvenir medals and mugs. The Prince himself took a crash course in Welsh, taught by a Welsh Nationalist.

But the lad acquitted himself well on the day, for he had always had aspirations to be an actor. He once excelled as a singing dustman at Cambridge University.

Today that investiture is a half-forgotten can of royal history in the television archives, and the Prince is still trying to find a new role. Few avenues are open. He could hardly join the Board of ICI, Unilever or Lonrho. If he went into the Church, it might be a long time before he became a bishop. And he can't spend the next twenty or so years just opening things, eating things or visiting things. The best traditional escape-hatch in such circumstances has always been into the comparative oblivion of the Armed Forces. So now he follows the family tradition as an officer in his mum's Navy.

Yet he does find time to do other things. In the autumn of 1972 he wrote a Foreword to a biography of his ancestor George III, by Mr John Brooke, senior editor of the Royal Commission on Historical Manuscripts. The story runs that Prince Charles took an interest in that crazed ancestor and volunteered to do the Foreword. He wrote, 'Much has been written by learned scholars to the effect that George III was manic depressive, and suffered from sexual frustration, a difficult wife, and hideous family problems . . . If this was so, why didn't the King "go mad" far earlier than 1788?' After all, the Prince points out, three years earlier the King had discovered that the then Prince of Wales had married his mistress, Mrs Fitzherbert. 'Enough to crack any remotely unstable character!' Charles doesn't go so far as to say George III *wasn't* as mad as a hatter, only that we tend 'to judge people too quickly'. Well, 150 years after George died it seems of little consequence whether or not his illness lost him the few wits he had. If some members of the present Royal Family showed some signs of genuine eccentricity it might help to make them less dull.

As Margot Asquith wrote in her diary on 20 April 1908:

> Royal persons are necessarily divorced from the true

opinions of people that count, and are almost always obliged to take safe and commonplace views. To them, clever men are 'prigs'; clever women 'too advanced'; Liberals are 'Socialists'; the uninteresting 'pleasant'; the interesting 'intriguers'; and the dreamer 'mad'.

Alas, it seems unlikely now that Charles will blossom into someone with genuine originality or the vision to question the values of his upbringing. It is always encouraging to see an individual break through the straitjacket of what their birth has made them, whatever their social origins, but that takes exceptional qualities of imaginative courage and sensitivity, and is perhaps a lot to ask. It is a pleasant fantasy to think that he might fall in love with the daughter of a miner or steelworker – or even of some rich socialist. It is as highly unlikely that he will fall for a black girl or a Roman Catholic and land us in a major constitutional crisis.

To help protect us all against such disasters, there is kept at Buckingham Palace, according to the *Western Daily Press* of 24 November 1973, something called the 'Blue File'. Any girl in whom the Prince takes more than a passing interest is likely to find her parents and her employer phoned as the dossier-compiling begins. They will be asked about her educational background, her spare-time interests and whether she has any political views. Charles, it is said, has been warned off a girl only twice. 'The last occasion was apparently two years ago and concerned an aristocrat's daughter with violent left-wing leanings, whom Charles had first met at Cambridge.'

Under an ancient Royal Marriages Act those in succession to the Throne must seek the Monarch's permission before they marry. As the immediate successor, Prince Charles knows what is expected of him. In a televised interview, when asked about marriage, 'You've got to remember,' he said, 'that when you marry, in my position, you are going to marry somebody who perhaps one day is going to be Queen. You've got to choose somebody very carefully. The one advantage about marrying a princess, for instance, or somebody from a royal family, is that they know what happens.' Poor Charles. Royal princesses are scarce these days. When Prince Charles has been interviewed on television it has always been by sycophants who would never dream of asking a hostile question. Personal interviews are only granted to crawlers. To my *written* questions (Appendix F, pages 239–41), the royal answers were, as usual, skilfully uninformative.

One thing that is certain is that Charles, whether prince or king, will, before he is 50, be among the wealthiest men in the world. We have already seen the actual and potential wealth of those lands known as the Duchy of Cornwall of which Prince Charles is very much the absentee landlord, while the Duchy's satraps suck their lifeblood in his name and earn themselves a good living into the bargain. The case for declaring the Duchy lands as the public property that they are may grow overwhelming in the next few years, especially if royalties from mineral exploitation become a reality.

On his creation as Prince of Wales at the age of 9 years, 8 months, Charles automatically became a Knight of the Garter. It was only in 1968, however, that his mum physically touched his shoulders with her sword and gave the Knight a garter of his own. Meanwhile his dad has, naturally, taught him to exercise a taste for shootin' and fishin', as well as for polo, that curious relic of the imperialist days of the Indian Raj. It sounds just the training needed for an acceptable member of the country gentry and county squirerarchy. Possibly that is exactly what he will become in the end.

The Queen's second child was born in the grace and favour residence of Clarence House on 15 August 1950, and was baptized at Buckingham Palace on 21 October. Thus her Royal Highness The Princess Anne Elizabeth Alice Louise took her place in the divine order of things. Her early education took place behind the hermetically closed doors of Buckingham Palace, where Miss Katherine Peebles, former governess to Prince

Michael of Kent, gave private tuition to her and her brother Prince Charles. Both learned to play the piano under Miss Hilda Bar. There was a weekly dancing class at the Palace from Miss Vacani. When Charles went off to school, Anne continued in her cloistered upbringing, taking lessons with other highly select little girls in the Palace. None from Wapping, Bermondsey or Brixton were included.

At the age of 9, she and her privileged friends began their adventures around London: off they went to the Tower, the Planetarium and other tourist attractions. When she was 12, she made a 'private' educational visit to France and, naturally, stayed among aristocracy: the family of the Marquis de Saint Genys, friends of the Comte de Paris. Then, the next year, she visited the House of Commons during Question Time. So, once upon a time, she actually saw democracy in action.

In 1963, it was off to Benenden, the posh boarding-school for girls in Kent. She quickly forgot her academic non-qualifications when she left in 1968 to take a crash course in French at the Berlitz School of Languages in London. In that year she qualified for her very first pay packet of £6,000 – or about £115 a week. So, to justify her well-paid existence, the Princess began her round of meaningless royal visits; once she drove a double-decker bus. Soon, however, she was showing a marked preference for four-footed transport. In her wild-oat days she was twice caught speeding on Britain's crowded roads – and twice let off by the police. Similar preferential treatment later appeared to be shown to her fiancé when he, too, committed a motoring offence. Any ordinary driver could have been fined at least £10 and have had his licence endorsed.

In due course the Princess's undoubted horse-riding ability and courage led to romance in the saddle. At one point the tittle-tattlers were linking her name with that of the dishy Richard Meade, leader of Britain's horsey Olympic team. Then a Lieutenant Mark Phillips, an officer in the 1st Queen's Dragoon Guards and a sprig of the Wiltshire yeomanry, appeared on the scene. There was the inevitable tittering rumour, gossip, speculation and statements of denial from the Palace that no one believed. After a hot, secretive, sometimes bad-tempered love-affair in stables and horseboxes, their engagement was announced.

During those hectic months of courtship, Mark, a part of our NATO armoured defences in Germany, had more leave from Army duties than any other soldier gets in ten years. Following the announcement, lo and behold, the Lieutenant quickly became a Captain. A transfer to the Army's public school at Sandhurst was as speedily arranged.

The pre-wedding public relations were forthwith handled by the most stupid and insensitive mules in the British public service. An instruction was sent out by 'the authorities' to the effect that the Army and other members of the Armed Forces might like to buy wedding presents for Princess Anne. Suggested contributions were 5p from each soldier and 30p from each officer. Anybody who didn't want to pay had to put his 'contracting out' within 48 hours *in writing*! All hell broke loose in the press. Quick as lightning the Ministry of Defence issued a *second* instruction. Contributions were to be purely 'voluntary' (though, as we all know, nothing in the Army is voluntary – a soldier is a slave in uniform). In the event, the response was comic – £1,100 from the entire Navy; less than £5,000 from the entire Army. The Air Force had decided to make a contribution from their own collective funds – raised from airmen's contributions made for quite other purposes than buying wedding presents for total strangers.

The usual bilge issued from the media in torrents. Competitions were run by papers, the prizes varying from getting a car 'like Mark Phillips's' to free travel to London for the Wedding Day. The souvenir manufacturers churned out their junk by the cartload, and, for the well-heeled, there was patriotic investment in silver and gold plaques, plates, goblets and medals. As a new Middle East conflict threatened to engulf the world in nuclear holocaust, Britain choked on a heady diet of royalist romance and royalist insensitivity to the perils, fears and hardships in the *real* world.

Nor was the College of Arms idle. Mark Phillips's father was a director of Walls, the ice-cream and pork-sausage makers. His family had made a packet out of 'King Coal' and the industrial tragedies of so many miners' lives in earlier days. But the industrious gnomes of the College of Arms burrowed back down into the bowels of heraldic history and emerged in triumph with Mark's line traced back to Edward III. They actually proved him a distant relation of his bride-to-be.

Even Mark's granny, Mrs Evelyn Tiarks, got into the news when she reported breathlessly that they'd 'even had a call from Australia'. 'All I hope,' she said, 'is that the ordinary people are pleased', adding that, 'It's quite a feather in the family's cap to have a member become engaged to a Royal.' And, just to show the common touch, 'I spent yesterday evening drinking sherry and I've lost count of how many I had.'

'I don't give a damn whether Lieutenant Mark Phillips's granny goes shopping with two dogs in an Austin 1300,' fumed John Gordon in the *Sunday Express* of 21 January 1973. 'Nor do most people. I don't give a damn either whether his sister carries a bucket and horse lotion to the stables. Or even whether he marries Princess Anne. But I do get rather het up that the Army supplies a 24-year-old lieutenant with a groom to attend his two Olympic horses. Who pays for Corporal Johanson when he goes to the Phillips family farm for weeks on end, lives in digs and looks after the horses? We should be given a straight answer to that. We should also be given a straight answer to the question why a man who is a qualified and expert Chieftain tank driver should be wasting his time playing around with horses.'

Similar seedy stories abounded like weeds in a neglected garden. One, reported in the *New Statesman* in February 1973, told of how Princess Anne, after opening a bridge, was asked by the contractor what she wanted for a present. She asked for, and got, a full set of horse harness. No one could be blamed for thinking that the primary motto of the British Royal Family in the modern world is grab what you can while the going is good – an attitude no one hesitates to deplore in the working population.

On their wedding day, 14 November 1973, the entire British nation went through one of those emotional lump-in-the-throat spasms, the like of which can be matched by no other nation in the world.

The Army laid on for the young couple's occupation a splendid and elegant five-bedroomed Georgian house at a bargain rent of £8 a week, or £400 a year. Meanwhile, from the day of her marriage, the Princess's annuity was increased to £35,000 a year. Then, to rub salt in the wounds, the royal honeymoon was spent cruising in the sun of the West Indies on their Royal Yacht (well it's *our* yacht, actually), *Britannia*, financed once again by the taxpayer. 'No extra expense will be involved' ran the utterly unconvincing and untrue official ministerial guff. Ministers of all political persuasions are ready to tell the biggest of lies whenever an awkward question is raised about a royal spendthrift. Who, asked the *Daily Mirror*, had been 'the nameless donkey who landed them with this absurdly expensive yacht trip when all that newly-weds need is a love nest?'

> Who is the anonymous functionary who thought it a good idea to provide a member of the Royal family with yet another home at the taxpayers' expense?

And who, above all, is the catastrophic chump who decided to announce this preposterous perk on the very day that less conspicuous lovers were faced with a 10 per cent mortgage rate? . . . The Britannia love-cruise, with its sailors in rubber-soled shoes lest the occupants of the Royal cabin be disturbed, makes a seaside-postcard mockery of romance in 1973. . .

The £8-a-week house (hasn't the Army heard of an economic rent?) is a blunder of classic proportions.

In a year when mortgage rates were to rise to 11 per cent and council-house tenants were to have to pay their way to the hilt, thousands of other newly-weds, struggling to find *any kind* of shelter, must have read of the privileges being handed on a plate to this very ordinary girl with justifiable dismay and bitterness.

Yet one cannot help feeling a degree of sympathy for Princess Anne. She couldn't help being born a princess. She maybe didn't even want the bloody job, as some of her past actions have implied. But the pressure of 'duty' combined with £35,000 a year have no doubt narrowed the options. She may, in time, become more up to the job's limited intellectual requirements and less painfully ill at ease in coping with people whose experience of life is different from her own. It is to these difficulties that we may charitably put down her occasional public displays of bad temper and understandable boredom. It was no wonder that, in the middle of 1973, she shared with Auntie Margaret the bottom spot in the Royals' pop chart.

Perhaps, one day, she will welcome the advent of a genuinely radical government that will declare her redundant and allow her to settle into a life of married bliss, horse-riding and relative obscurity. But she will miss the £35,000 a year.

She nearly lost everything when an attempt to kill or kidnap her was made in mid-March 1974. On the way back to Buckingham Palace after an evening engagement the royal car in which she and her husband were travelling was ambushed in the Mall. Nine shots were fired. HRH's bodyguard was seriously wounded – happily not fatally. The episode was front-page headlines for days. Royal security became a matter of supreme governmental concern. Meanwhile, British soldiers were being killed daily in Ulster; no headlines for them, just headstones.

If a personal public image is the thing to cultivate today, then the Queen Mother is among the best of gardeners. The words drip like honey from the printing presses of the land, with never a stray hornet to be seen with a sting in its tail.

'A Queen Dowager perhaps unique in British history, a character who has firmly and fondly implanted her charm on the public imagination,' said the *Daily Mail* of 16 December 1971. 'She brims over with unforced charm . . . In Clarence House, the racing dowager has a bookmaker's blower system installed to give her rumours and prices at [race] meetings all over the country. [And already has over 200 National Hunt winners in the bag.] . . . She is blessed with vitality and sparkle, a sense of fun, and a wit which she probably has to curb, like her daughter . . . People are such fun to her.'

Lady Elizabeth Bowes-Lyon has travelled far since she married her stammering young man, the Duke of York, later pushed unwillingly into Buckingham Palace to be King George VI. They produced two daughters, the elder destined to be Queen.

The Bowes-Lyons were poor by landed aristocratic standards, but they were filthily rich by comparison with the urban working-classes, and politically as reactionary as they came. It is not surprising that a very prominent, right-wing ex-Labour Cabinet Minister once described the Queen Mother as the most reactionary member of the Royal Family.

She makes no speeches of any consequence. She gets through her public relations by pleasing facial exercises, or by purposely chatting to 'the lads in the back row' and taking a drop of the hard stuff, her native Scotch whisky. Yet, behind the matey tipple and the ever-ready smile, there lurks the mind of a shrewd businesswoman. Her investments are naturally among the world's best-kept secrets. We do, however, know that she has collected an annuity of £70,000 between 1952 and 1 January 1972, when it was increased to £95,000. Thus, by the year 1974, she has garnered £1,590,000 in wholly tax-free 'expenses'. No one knows, no one will tell, how these figures of £70,000 and £95,000 were arrived at. Mr Barber told the 1972 Select Committee that higher figures were in mind; and Mr John Boyd-Carpenter wondered why the £95,000 wasn't rounded up to £100,000. The Committee *was* told how hard she works for her money: 211 official engagements in 1970. Of these, 47 were 'audiences', seldom lasting more than a few minutes each, 32 were lunches and dinners, 13 were church services and 31 were classified as 'Other' (which included portrait sittings). Then, in addition to her annuity, the old lady, when she's not living in her own 'privately bought Castle of May', lives in Clarence House completely free of charge. In short, she has a life of gaiety, luxury, and elegance, surrounded by the inevitable retinue of male and female employees or status-loving leeches. Thirteen members of her Household are salaried, though the Private Secretary refused to divulge the salaries and no accounts were presented to the Select Committee.

The Queen Mother's Household is second in size only to that of the Queen herself. The list in the 1973 *Imperial Calendar* shows a total of thirty-two including five full-time clerks. Only five of the thirty-two are not titled or honoured in some way, and three of these are female clerks. She has three lords, one duchess, five dowager viscountesses, countesses and ladies, five plain 'ladies', one lieutenant-colonel, four majors and two captains. No mere corporals or plain misters in sight. There are three KCVOs, nine DCVOs, six MVOs, and a spattering of other Christmas-tree ornaments: thirty-five honours in all among thirty-two people.

The two Ladies of the Bedchamber are a dowager viscountess and a countess. The three Extra Ladies of the Bedchamber are two dowager countesses and one dowager lady. The *Women* of the Bedchamber consist of one dowager lady, one plain lady, one even plainer Mrs, and a slightly less plain Honourable Mrs. Then, in the reserves, are the Extra Women of the Bedchamber -- five of them, every one a lady except for one poor Honourable Mrs. No one seems to know how the distinction arose between Bedchamber *Ladies* and Bedchamber *Women*. There doesn't appear to be any career structure.

But here we have what is clearly just a Household of ordinary people. As the Queen Mother's Private Secretary was quick to point out to me, not everybody has a title, and anyway, a title is not a qualification for appointment to the Household. *Anybody* can apply, though I doubt if you will find it much use going through the local Employment Exchange.

The lady is cheerful, contented and well preserved. She has a lot to be contented about. And who wouldn't be well preserved and cheerful on a tax-free income of about £2,000 a week?

In November 1965, our royal lady Margaret made an 'official' visit to the United States. It was an odd event. For long it had been known that Princess Margaret was keen to see the pop culture of the States, but her wishes had come to naught. She had personal friends in America, especially Miss Sharman Douglas, who had been a sparkling light of the 'Margaret Set' when Sharman's father was American Ambassador to Britain.

By the early summer of 1965 her persistence paid off when she suggested that, if she attended two functions organized by the English Speaking Union, and two fashion shows laid on by the Incorporated Society of London Fashion Designers, in San Francisco and Los Angeles, the Foreign Office might plausibly foot the bill. The Labour Foreign Secretary, Mr Michael Stewart, yielded to these blandishments.

Of course, the Princess's trendy husband, Lord Snowdon would have to go too, with his valet and his second footman (whatever he does). The Princess herself was aided by a Lady in

Waiting, a Private Secretary, a Lady Secretary, a police officer, the Deputy Captain of the Queen's Flight and two others, plus René Moulard, her hairdresser, and two maids: a total retinue of twelve. In the event, the actual itinerary, timed to the minute, day by day, from the moment they left Britain to the moment they returned, told a completely different story from the propagandist official handout prepared by *Labour* Ministers. This made no mention of the fact that, during the entire tour of three weeks, the total time spent on official engagements was under forty-eight hours.

The event was utterly typical of our Margaret's haughty life-style. For her the people of Britain must seem like so many milch-cows. But their traditional patience and indulgence towards anything that has a royal tag attached should not perhaps be treated with such flagrant contempt. Public opinion could harden disastrously where she is concerned: not without reason is she bottom of the current royal pop chart.

Her American jaunt provoked an acid *furor* in the Press. The *Sunday Citizen* of 28 November 1968 carried its headlines: 'Jet Set Parties and Private VC 10 Complete With Own Hairdresser. "Who Pays?" Row over Snowdons' Luxury Tour.' The article underneath demanded to know how 'a whirl of high society dinners and receptions fitted the image of a Britain battling for higher productivity and bigger exports'. The *New Statesman* weekly had already commented on the 26th:

> They departed, tastefully, on the eve of Thanksgiving, which commemorates the Pilgrims' deliverance from the tyranny of the British Crown as well as the abundance of the American wilderness . . . They had sumptuous meals and lavish receptions wherever they went, but if they fulfilled their desire to 'meet all kinds of Americans' they must have done it on the sly . . . In San Francisco they met descendants of late nineteenth-century robber barons, in Los Angeles they met movie stars and Barry Goldwater, in Arizona they met bankers and a prominent member of the John Birch Society, and in Washington they met the gay young fun set. Our every-other-inch-a-Queen was going to show off Britain's new fashion consciousness. The Royal wardrobe contained a white wool coat with bronzed seal lapels, yellow feather toque, and sky blue organza gown with diamanté embroidery for Her; patent leather jodphur boots with high loops, fitted blue jacket and cuffless pegged pants for Him. For a while the couple began to act like Barbie and Ken,

> the real-life dolls for children who can afford to buy miniature clothes costing hundreds of dollars.

The Sunday *Observer* of the week remarked tartly:

> Expense apart, the exact purpose of the trip is under question. Like all Royals on tour the Snowdons were, of course, showing the flag; they were Britain's most prized exhibits on tour . . . The Princess was . . . a front runner for the British rag trade [and] Lord Snowdon made the best of his chances to publicize *Private View*, his new 7 guineas work on modern British artists.

The *Women's Wear Daily*, the most influential newspaper in the American clothes industry, had, in fact, called Margaret's clothes 'a schizophrenic mixture of chic and sheer fashion disaster. Even at her best, her almost perfect, there's always one thing wrong.' The paper had blasted the Princess's hats, had called her dresses 'too fitted', 'ancient', 'matronly', and 'too big', 'too bulky, and too outdated'. 'What image of Britain do the Foreign Office wish to project abroad?' asked Harold Hutchinson in the *Sun* on 3 December. 'If it is one of imperial ostentation, or of royal ornaments to international society, then the visit was successful.' The *New Statesman* had the last word: 'For a so-called official visit that has, in part at least, been a private rubber-necking trip to the American fun centres, a thirty-day tour that has badly misfired in its impact on the American public, the British taxpayer is having to foot a fantastic bill.'

The bill was for over £30,000 as it happened. At least, that was the official figure given to me in the House of Commons. In answer to other questions, Mr George Thomson, now one of the Common Market Commissioners, but formerly an editor of the radical left-wing *Glasgow Forward*, defended the visit as 'an outstanding success'. In fact, he said, the Princess had actually 'proposed a number of additional engagements', and Sir Geoffrey de Freitas, an ex-Labour Minister, sprang to his defence to plead that 'Princess Margaret had really tried to do even more than she was asked'.

During a subsequent adjournment debate in the Commons I was called to order a dozen times by the Speaker for making attacks on the Queen's sister. But this was not the first attack I had ever made on Her Extravagant Royal Highness, nor would it be the last.

In 1960, at the age of 29, Princess Margaret Rose married Anthony Charles Robert Armstrong-Jones, a professional photographer who became Lord Snowdon overnight. A year or two earlier she had had her well-publicized but ineptly handled affair with Group Captain Peter Townsend. Before long Lord Snowdon had got a glossy, colour-supplement photographer's job with Lord Thomson's *Sunday Times* and had fathered two royal children, the first, Viscount Linley, in 1961; the second, Lady Sarah, in 1964. Both now at posh schools, out of mum's way.

The 1952 Civil List had awarded Margaret an annuity of £15,000 – or a total of £300,000 between 1952 and 1972 – in theory taxable, but in practice tax free. It was all allegedly spent on officially accepted expenses for doing her royal job. According to Sir Douglas Allen, Permanent Secretary to the Treasury and Auditor of the Civil List, in his evidence to the Select Committee (Q.398), 'the expenditures of *all*' the Royal Households, exceeded the annuities 'vastly'. So what were they all living on? If my expenses claimed as an MP vastly exceeded my salary, the Inland Revenue would start asking awkward questions. But Princess Margaret was still evidently able to send both her children to those private fee-paying schools. The taxpayers had already paid out over £80,000 on her houses in Kensington Palace. Her earlier honeymoon on the Royal Yacht *Britannia* had, moreover, cost the people of Britain £26,000 *at least* to go to the West Indies.

Princess Margaret has, indeed, remained a frequent visitor to the sunny climes of the West Indies, especially during our nasty cold damp winter months. I am sure it is good for her health. Wouldn't it be for all of us? The lucky girl has a luxury house on the tiny Caribbean island of Mustique, on Gelliceaux Bay, where she can enjoy the company of many wealthy escapees from British weather and taxes. The house is said to have been a wedding gift from the island's owner Colin Tennant (Lord Glenconner's heir). He bought the island for £45,000, and now sells it off in parcels at £15,000 an acre. There have been plenty of buyers, including the Queen's photographer cousin, the Earl of Lichfield, among forty others.

In early March 1973 Margaret paid an 'official' visit to the British Virgin Islands, to attend the tercentenary anniversary of the British connection. The invitation had come from the local Government. The Princess 'was accompanied by her suite with a consequent charge to the Foreign and Commonwealth Vote', stated a letter from the Foreign and Commonwealth Office of 10

April 1973. She stayed four days, then flitted off to her private haven. 'The cost was £3,175.05', which included air fares '*and a sum for expenses* [my italics]'. That's the way the money goes. But expenses for what, in heaven's name? The lady was already getting £35,000 a year expenses.

On 12 March 1973, the *Daily Mail* reported:

> Here, amid the still of the tropic Caribbean night, a clear and resonant voice could be heard singing that old hit tune 'Walk On By' – to the vocal accompaniment of local islanders. The singer? A very tanned and relaxed Princess Margaret performing happily away – the high point of an impromptu cabaret at a party this week-end marking the end of her month-long stay in Mustique.
>
> The previous night the Princess – looking noticeably younger then her 42 years – had been the mainstay of a 'Jump Up', local jargon for a festive dancing party.

The dole figures in Britain in the dark winter of 1972–3 were to soar to a million, but no matter, our royal, plumping Princess by that time had had her salary uplift to £35,000, or to about £100 a day, Saturdays and Sundays included. It represented an increase of 133 per cent; a bigger increase than that given to any other royal annuitant. This had been because, as witnesses to the Civil List Committee explained, the original £15,000 had been too low. How the poor girl had suffered!

The day after the pay award was announced, she took delivery of her brand-new Rolls-Royce. Then, immediately, she insisted on some changes, as the London *Evening Standard* reported on 8 March 1972:

> The position of reversing lights and side-indicator flashers, things even the most avid motor enthusiast might overlook, were among those which offended her artistic sensibility. She ordered the flashers to be removed, and instead of two individual reversing lights, she asked Rolls to fit the rear lights in a cluster. Neither was she happy with the highly polished woodwork traditional in a Rolls. A matt-finish wood replaced it. The £11,000 car, finished in regal red, replaces the five-year-old black Rolls the Princess traded in part exchange. It has now gone into service for her official work, bearing only one item from the old vehicle, the number plate 3 GXM to which she had become attached.

So exactly what are the advantages that the people of Britain gain from their middle-ageing Princess who happens to be the Queen's younger sister? On 11 February 1973, the Scottish *Sunday Post* reported that she was cutting down on her public engagements, partly because her migraine was getting worse, and partly because, at 43, she felt it was time some of the younger Royals took over some of the work. Cutting *down* on her work-load? During 1970 she had 177 official engagements, or about three a week. Twenty-three of them were 'audiences', or hand-shakings; another twenty-four were attending 'Charitable Performances'. In all she spent only thirty-one days outside London. During 1972, the score dropped to less than 150 (see Appendix F, page 244), or little more than two public engagements a week.

No wonder people do not think much of her. The *Sunday Mirror* Public Opinion Poll of 16 September 1973 placed her with her niece, Princess Anne, at the bottom of the popularity league. She makes no attempt to conceal her expensive, extravagant irrelevance and it is impossible to make out any honest case for her being much use to anybody. It is even said that she makes her husband pay rent for the rooms he uses in their grace and favour residence in Kensington Palace, even though *she* pays no rent at all.

Lord Snowdon, in fact, showed some sensitivity to my criticisms of the public costs of housing him and his wife. He made his views known to the Right Honourable Mr Charles Pannell when he was the Minister responsible for making 1A Kensington Palace all right for the royal couple. With typical generosity, Mr Pannell offered to arrange and pay for a lunch where Snowdon and I could meet face to face. But nothing came of it. There were equally unsuccessful efforts to bring us together in 1972. Lord Snowdon had talked to Mr Ron Brown, Labour MP for Shoreditch, at some social function, and had indicated that he would like to have a meal with me so long as certain matters were excluded from our discussions. Correspondence and telephone calls were exchanged, but it soon became obvious that the lad was being warned off. The exercise ended when he sent me a picture postcard from his stand at the Ideal Home Exhibition in early 1973.

Tony is a man of many parts. He has been a waiter at Brighton and a £2 a week tout for a London bedsitters' agency. Money-grabbing capitalist instincts emerged early, while he was still at Eton, where he flogged hand-made crystal wireless sets in matchboxes at five bob a time. Yet, in the entire Royal Family, he is the only one with any real creative talent of his own. He is an impressive photographer with a professional eye for detail. He has made bird cages for the London Zoo. He has designed a useful mechanical invalid chair. He would undoubtedly have made a good living and a name for himself without marrying a Princess and becoming a Lord. But that was what he did, and before you could turn round, a family tree had been produced showing that he was a distant relation of King Edward I, the Emperor Charlemagne, and the playwright Sheridan.

His individual talents must actually place him at odds with the all-pervading emphasis on conventionality in the reigning dynasty. From time to time the continental gossip magazines have hummed with rumours that the Margaret-Snowdon marriage is on the rocks, that the possibility of divorce proceedings is even being discussed in the Royal Family. The British press can only comment on these stories at second hand. If the rift exists, it has evidently for the moment been skilfully papered over in the best tradition.

In 1972, Snowdon admitted to a newspaper interviewer that he wished he had the courage to speak in the House of Lords. He has since done so in a debate on invalid chairs in early April 1974. I wonder if he drew his £8.50.

In March 1974 the rumours of divorce were again appearing in an American magazine. No firm denial was made, though reports had it that the Queen had advised them just to go their own ways. A royal divorce would be a damaging blow to the public image of a happy, model Royal Family – as well as an affront to the Established Church.

The elderly Duke of Gloucester finally died in early July 1974 after years of inactivity due to a long illness, the nature of which has never been disclosed. Neither the late Duke nor his family are likely to merit a footnote in the history books. Though he had done little worthwhile in his lifetime, the House of Commons nevertheless decided to increase the £35,000 annuity of 1952 to £45,000 in 1972. Apart from that, and for the first time, provision was made for the widows of the Duke's two sons at £20,000 apiece. This bold suggestion had come from the Queen herself and Parliament meekly acquiesced.

The elder son, Prince William, was killed in an air crash in September 1972. He was a batchelor, not yet 30, but he left over £400,000, though his exact will cannot by law be published for 100 years. How did he make so much in such a short time? The family estate of 2,500 acres at Oundle near Peterborough had been managed by Prince William. He owned two of the six farms on it, sharing the others with his parents, no doubt to avoid death duties.

The Prince, having twice failed the Civil Service examinations, was nevertheless given a job at the Foreign and Commonwealth Office. Hostile questions were asked in the Commons about such indefensible patronage, and in 1970 he resigned to become a royal estate farming manager until his death.

On the demise of his father, the younger brother, Richard, succeeded to the title. An unassuming young man, an architect by profession, and married to a Danish girl, he would probably have been content to live in his grace and favour house at

Kensington Palace and get on with his career – secure in the knowledge that he was now the heir to a large estate. It was not to be. As the new Duke of Gloucester he automatically receives his £45,000 a year. Let's hope he does something to earn it. It could make a nice change.

Not much is known of the Kents, for they keep themselves out of the limelight. The former Duchess of Kent, Princess Marina, was left a widow on the death of her husband during the Second World War. No provision was made for her in the 1952 Civil List, but, from 1953 until her death in 1968, she received £15,000 a year out of the £25,000 which Parliament had provided for the Queen to dispense as she wished among her more deprived relations. She was also provided with a rent-free grace and favour residence at Kensington Palace, and she owned a magnificent country house, Coppins, near Iver, in Bucks, on the western outskirts of London.

Princess Marina was Greek by birth. As an active Royal, she had personal charm and did much good work. The public often assumed that she was the 'poor relation'; and, by royal standards, she was. Between 1953 and 1968 she was paid a tax-free £242,000; and when she died in August 1968, she left £54,121 – the most meagre royal legacy in the last twenty years. Few of Britain's workers leave one tenth of that.

The Duchess's daughter, Princess Alexandra, had been in receipt of £1,500 a year from 1955, a figure increased to £1,750 in 1957, to £2,000 in 1958, to £3,000 in 1961, to £4,000 in 1965, to £10,000 in 1969, and no one knows what it is now. Alexandra had married, in 1963, the Honourable Angus James Bruce Ogilvy, second son of the 12th Earl of Airlie. Mr Ogilvy's father had been a Lord-in-Waiting to George V, and, until 1965, Lord Chamberlain to the Queen Mother. And Mr Ogilvy's grandmother was a Lady of the Bedchamber to Queen Mary. There's nothing like keeping things in a family.

Princess Marina's son, the present Duke of Kent, first began to dip his fingers in the gravy in 1961 when he started on his £2,500 a year from the Queen's contingency fund. In 1962 he had an increase to £4,000, and in 1969 to £10,000. It is probably £20,000 today. So, between them, the Kents have collected over £400,000 since 1953, and every penny free of tax. In the course of discussions during the 1972 Civil List debates, one member put in some special pleas for the Kents, but they went unheeded. Even the other Tories on the Committee felt enough was enough.

The Ogilvys lived at Thatched House Lodge, Richmond Park – a 'modest' family home, with six reception rooms, four bathrooms, a heated swimming-pool, its own stables and four acres of private gardens. Worth £300,000 of anybody's money. But Princess Alexandra, like many thousands of others, has been bothered by the noise of jets going into London Airport. The abandonment of the Maplin airport scheme has meant that this will grow worse. Lo and behold, the Ogilvys have been offered a rent-free grace and favour residence in Hyde Park – and have accepted without a qualm of conscience. Somebody suggested it might have been cheaper to move London Airport.

The Duke of Kent, only son of Princess Marina, has married into a Yorkshire landowning family – Tories from fingertips to toenails. They moved into the family home at Coppins. The Duke was evidently good enough army fodder, and had served as a junior officer with inconspicuous success for a number of years while receiving his £4,000, and later his £10,000 a year, from a benevolent Commander-in-Chief.

Early in 1972 it was announced that the Duke would sell Coppins and take up residence in one of the Queen's houses in Norfolk. He and his family would also have the use in London of York House – a grace and favour rent-free pad. Coppins went for a quarter of a million.

9. THE FUTURE OF THE MONARCHY

'What we live with today is a Cheshire Cat monarchy, consisting of a bright smile surrounded by nothing, a frightened, timorous monarchy hoping not to be noticed so that the death sentence may be delayed' – Geoffrey Bocca, *Uneasy Lies the Head*

What therefore are the possible scenarios for the Monarchy in Britain in the immediate future? There seem to be three. First, the Monarchy could stay as it is, unchanged and unchanging. Secondly, the Monarchy could adapt itself to an increasingly democratic and egalitarian society. Or, thirdly, the Royal Family could be demoted to the status of private citizens and a republic with an elective head of state in place of the Monarch. The first alternative, though it would, by definition, be preferred by more 'conservative' spirits, would be highly impracticable in a world changing and developing as rapidly as ours is today. The second alternative seems the most probable, given the present relationships between the Monarchy and the British people, but it is likely to involve difficulties as much for us as for them. Readers of this book will realize by now that the much-publicized 'democratization' of the Monarchy has so far been more of a public relations operation than a genuine reform.

More radical changes will be resisted with fierce jealousy by both individual members of the Royal Family and their sinecured advisers. But changes will be essential if progress towards the third alternative is not to be accelerated as a younger generation, less susceptible to hocus-pocus and more realistic in its demands, comes to maturity.

Monarchy has been on the retreat all over the world ever since the First World War. After 1914, thrones began to become more like electric chairs than shrines of worship. Queen Victoria, with her brood of nine, and her thirty-two grandchildren, formed an ambitious regal trade union, nurtured to believe they would inevitably occupy nine of the fifteen thrones in Europe. Then the thrones toppled like skittles in a bowling alley. Only six remain in Europe today, and these could be reduced to four at any time.

But, whatever may happen elsewhere, the British Monarchy seems secure, as long as monarchs keep their noses clean, steer clear of politics, and conceal their wealth. Republicanism in Britain was last at its peak about a hundred years ago. Then it was middle class, born as much out of Victoria's *absence* from the public gaze as from any other cause. Britain has never had any strong republican *party*, organized to overthrow the Monarchy, and none is likely in the immediate future.

Yet public disillusion can only grow as our Queen begins to lose her glamour and her husband his hair and flair. So far, shifts in opinion are subtle. A vote taken from the audience of a BBC Television programme, *These Young People*, on 6 August 1973, showed 76 per cent of the 18 to 25 age-group happy with the Monarchy as it is, but only 43 per cent felt the Royal Family was in touch with ordinary people and the modern world. Then a recent poll taken by a well-known and respected provincial paper, the *Sheffield Star*, showed in October 1973 that 53 per cent were in favour of a republic. And a *Sunday Mirror* poll in the same year provided evidence of similar disenchantment.

Young people increasingly question the usefulness of existing institutions, especially those based on the hereditary principle. Certainly the mystique of royalty is fast disappearing, killed stone dead by television. The pre-wedding TV interview of Princess Anne and her fiancé by two metaphorically kid-gloved reporters, revealed stark limitations in the Princess's intellect, vocabulary and imagination. Such revelations are healthy for the nation. More and more we are witnessing the shortcomings of a very ordinary family for whom extraordinary claims are made by its supporters. These are no more than ordinary mortals cast (and miscast) in the role of superstars; not gods and goddesses, but men and women with painfully obvious limitations.

I hope we have not yet heard the last of the Houghton proposal for setting up a Crown Department of State, details of which were set out in Mr Houghton's Minority Report to the Select Committee (see pages 48–9). This idea, coming from a highly respected former Labour Chancellor of the Duchy of Lancaster, would get rid of much of the secrecy surrounding the royal finances, making everything open to public scrutiny. Expenditure figures would be presented to Parliament each year. Questions could be asked about them. There could even be annual debates on whether we are getting value for money. And the sordid rigmarole of Select Committees on the Civil List would become a thing of the past.

But Treasury officials put all kinds of difficulties in the way. (There are no revolutionaries in the Treasury.) To set up a Crown Department would have been as impossible as walking on the sea. And the more royalist Tories on the Committee had nightmares at the thought that there could be *questions* and *debates* in the Commons! Was *nothing* to be sacred any more? Yet the Houghton proposal was lost by only one vote. Not even all the Tory Committee members were unsympathetic, and one voted against it only on learning that the Queen herself was opposed.

The reasons for this are not hard to find. For one thing, the Queen saw her prerogatives of patronage slipping through her fingers. For another, she hopes to retain the best of both worlds. She wants to maintain the fiction of a Royal (private) Household, where *she* makes all the appointments, but she also wants the taxpayer to foot all the bills, without him or his representatives being able to ask any questions. Parliament is expected to hand over the cash, but may not know how it is spent.

What, therefore, would be the practical consequences of the Houghton proposals? The Monarchy as an institution would remain, with its feudal militaristic pomp, colour and pageantry. The Royal Family, however, would be treated as no more and no less than what they are: civil servants, albeit of a special kind. The Queen, Prince Philip and the immediate successor to the throne, Prince Charles, would qualify for special rates of salary: say, for instance, twice the going rate for top civil servants, which would mean about £30,000 each in taxable income. If they chose to do so, other members of the family could be offered jobs within the new Department at rates of pay equal to that of a Cabinet Minister. Other modest changes might be made, as I had suggested to the Civil List Committee. The scandalous, anachronistic farce of grace and favour houses would be ended, with the Monarch no longer able to nominate the tenants. That would, henceforth, be done by the Prime Minister, who would be answerable to Parliament. The Duchies of Cornwall and Lancaster could be merged with the Crown Estate and renamed the Public Estate, with all net revenues accruing to the Exchequer. The Honours System as we know it today could be abolished. The Prime Minister, advised by a small cross-party committee, would bear the sole responsibility for the granting of any such Honours as may be retained, once a much-modified and more worthwhile basis had been agreed upon, if even that was thought necessary.

Some would say that these proposals, limited and moderate as they are, don't go far enough. Others would be horrified by their revolutionary implications. Such proposals would nevertheless command support from wide sections of the British people. But, whatever happens, the Monarchy must be deeply conscious of its own shortcomings. If it shuts its eyes to these facts, that must be a cause of great concern to all of us. For we, the *people*, must eventually assert our sovereignty over *them*. This is hardly a new principle in British history. *They* are *our* servants. *They*, and the class they represent, must no longer be allowed to hold the reins of power, and the privileges that go with them.

Radical change must come. All the arguments used to justify the institution of Monarchy in its present form are now known to be weak, unsubstantiated or irrational. One by one, the myths are collapsing, the magic dissipated. In twenty years, Commonwealth trade has shrunk by half, and in the next twenty years any *raison d'être* for Royal Commonwealth Tours will finally evaporate like morning dew. The tourists who come to our island take in the Monarchy along with feeding the pigeons in Trafalgar Square, looking in at the Houses of Parliament and other theatrical occasions, or listening to goings-on at Hyde Park Corner or in Westminster Abbey. The 'model family' apologia doesn't hold much water either, when that family is so stuffily and helplessly trapped in its upper-middle-class cast of mind.

What is actually left? Unity, continuity, stability?

Unity? There is no unity in Britain, which is a nation deeply divided on political, religious, social and class grounds.

Continuity? Then why not have hereditary Prime Ministers, too, and hereditary Members of Parliament. And in these days when nations all over the world are legislating to ensure that equal opportunities are open to all and that sex-discrimination is a thing of the past, why don't we get rid of the principle of primogeniture? That would put Princess Anne next in the line of succession – a daunting prospect.

What then of 'stability', meaning, presumably, a state of fixation, of stasis, of standing firm? Even if possible, this would be an argument not so much for the maintenance of the Monarchy as for the maintenance of conservatism, the *status quo* and downright social stagnation. Some *do* want that, but not, by and large, those who are in the political centre or to the left of it.

Finally, we should mention the 'cost' argument: the assertion that our Monarchy is cheap at the price, even a profit-maker. Either way, the case is trivial and irrelevant. It is impossible to make international comparisons, and equally impossible for anybody to put a price-tag on the Royals. Having said that, it is hard to see what we have left except a pleasure-giving symbol, like the neon lights at Piccadilly Circus or a fireworks show, and a totem pole for tribal capitalism.

Every nation seems to want a Head of State, whether elected or hereditary. He may be called a King (or Queen), or a President. He can be the powerful Head of the Executive, as in the United States, or an impotent figurehead. Or, as in the UK, he (or she) can be a hereditary, constitutional Head of State, with no effective political power, seemingly above the heated squalor of party politics, and a force providing an element of continuity and stability which seems completely absent from the United States scene, for instance.

Hence, the question that everyone asks: if you get rid of the Monarchy, what do you put in its place? Frankly, if asked the blunt question: 'Which would you prefer, a Nixon, with his Watergate and a bunch of gangsters, or Queen Elizabeth II, Buckingham Palace, and a coterie of hangers-on?' I would opt for the latter. But then Nixon and the American people both deserved what they got. A bad President is the electors' fault. They can put it right next time. But, saddled with a hereditary Head, you must take what comes. My children and yours are stuck with Charles III, whether we like it or not. We may have had a reasonable run of luck these last sixty years, but our forefathers were not always so lucky and the hereditary principle is less selective than a stud farm. That is one of the reasons why a third of the United Kingdom's citizens would probably vote for a republic if given the chance to do so.

We may turn once again to Tom Paine for a grass-roots statement on what a republic is (or should be):

What is called a *republic*, is not any *particular form* of government. It is wholly characteristical of the purport, matter, or object for which government ought to be instituted, and on which it is to be employed, RES-PUBLICA, the public affairs, or the public good; or, literally translated, the *public thing*. It is a word of good original, referring to what ought to be the character and business of government; and in this sense it is naturally opposed to the word *monarchy*, which has a base original signification meaning arbitrary power in an individual person . . .

Republican government is no other than government established and conducted for the interest of the public, as well individually as collectively. It is not necessarily connected with any particular form, but it most naturally associates with the representative form, as being best calculated to secure the end, for which a nation is at the expense of supporting it.

Paine was writing at a time when the barefaced tyranny of kings was for the first time facing the catalyst of Enlightenment liberalism. He saw no reason to mince his words when, in his 'Address to the People of France' on the occasion of Louis XVI's flight on 25 October 1792, he said:

. . . If we take a review of Europe . . . all the Monarchs there are the very dregs of Humanity. This one is a tyrant; that other an idiot; another a traitor; this last a debauchee; some are collections of all vices . . . In whatever manner we consider it, we find the notion of Hereditary Royalty only foolishness and infamy. What is this office which infants and idiots are capable of filling? Some talent is required to be a common workman; to be a king more is needed than to have a human figure, to be a living automaton.

Royalty is as repugnant to common sense as to the common right . . . of all superstitions, none has more debased men's minds. We seek the cause of abjectness of character in the monarchical system; there it is . . . Royalty, its fanatical éclat, its superstitious idolatry, the false prejudice of its necessity – all these lies have been invented only to obtain from men excessive contributions and a willing servitude.

Paine may have been writing here in a historical context, but other quotes from him, like this one from *The Rights of Man*, still have an uncomfortably up-to-date ring:

Give to any man a million a year, and add thereto the power of creating and disposing of places, at the expense of a country, and the liberties of the country are no longer secure. What is called splendour of the throne is no other than the corruption of the state. It is made up of a band of parasites, living in luxurious indolence, out of public taxes.

Not everybody would agree with Paine's view, even today. One British daily newspaper actually rebuked the *New Daily* in these terms for its criticism of the royal finances: 'We hasten to add that, compared with the fact of its having been divinely established, this [the cash] is of infinitely less importance.' *Divinely* established? The Almighty has then been wayward more than occasionally in His choices. In 1973, it was decided by the City of Bath's Tory Council that, since King Edgar had been crowned in Bath 1,000 years before as the earliest true King of England (where had God been up to then?), celebrations were in order. It would help the local rates, Tory hoteliers, and the souvenir trade. But, the *Daily Telegraph* tactlessly reported, 'Bath's councillors were surprised to find, after naming Edgar the first King of England, that he was reputed to have been married three times, had killed the previous husband of one of the wives, and raped a nun.' Nevertheless, 'The Queen, who is a descendant by lineage of King Edgar, will visit Bath with Prince Philip on 9 August.' We are all likely to be descendants of the lively Edgar; and of Adam and Eve.

My own view of the British Monarchy is that it is our only living museum – a human equivalent of the London Zoo, but giving much less pleasure than the chimpanzees' tea party, and running at much greater cost. Britain's task is to find a new role in the rough, tough world now engulfing us, instead of wallowing in the cloying romanticism of a primitive, taboo-infested institution. Sir James Frazer, in his classic on myth and religion, *The Golden Bough*, referred to those special taboos which cling like barnacles to the royal hulk. It would still be sacrilege today to, say, refer to the Queen as 'Mrs Liz Windsor'. She must never be spoken to first (though I did so when she opened the Forth Road Bridge), and after she has started the patter going, in the first instance you call her 'Your Majesty', though after that it becomes 'Ma'am'. As the American Ambassador said, when the Queen asked him how he was getting on with moving home, 'Very well, Ma'am, except for some discomfiture owing to elements of refurbishment.' As an Ambassador to Britain, Walter

Annenburg is likely to be remembered for little except that anecdote.

In 1973 the satirical magazine *Private Eye* ran a series called 'Love in the Saddle' that held all the royal bullshit up to mockery in what purported to be an account of the courtship of Princess Anne and her husband-to-be Mark Phillips:

> The couple tumble off their horses into a pool of water while Lord Snowdon, hidden in the bushes, photographs them. Mark explains to the Duke of Edinburgh:
>
> 'Well, sir . . . it was an accident. You see, I fell on top of her. Jellicoe was out of control.'
>
> 'Ha, Bloody Ha,' rasped the Duke, his teeth bared in a sarcastic smile. 'Premarital mullarkey – that's what the Press will call it. There's only one way out of this, you know.'
>
> Mark took the Luger pistol from the wall and held it to his head.
>
> 'Not that, you bloody fool,' growled Anne's father, pouring a tumbler of whisky from the exquisite cut-glass Watergate decanter. 'You'll have to marry the gel.'
>
> Anne's heart welled up inside her and warm tears gushed down her rose-petalled cheeks. Before she knew what was happening to her Mark was shaking her hand.
>
> 'Well, old girl. What about it then?'

This skit made its point: royal personages must never be seen to cut loose from the absurd conventions which shackle them. They mustn't be seen to act like ordinary mortals, for did not a recent public opinion poll show that a third of the population still believe they were chosen by God? But God hasn't been playing his hand too cleverly of late, so young Mr Armstrong-Jones and young Lieutenant Phillips have to learn to wear the harness and accept the full weight of the taboos.

How much longer can we afford to go on being treated as a museum, fit only for visitation by dollar- and mark-laden tourists, who come not so much to envy as to wonder at us. If the whole charade were to be ended tomorrow, I would not personally feel any deprivation or any sense of a vacuum in my life. But it seems the most unlikely scenario of all that the Monarchy in Britain will be forcibly deposed overnight. Britain is not a country that is easily rocked by revolution. A violent demonstration in Trafalgar Square is a three-hour Sunday-afternoon wonder. In Britain our institutions evolve. We are a Fabian Society writ large. The one thing we can be sure of is that, if the Monarchy is still with us fifty years from now, it will not be the Monarchy of the 1970s.

But if the seemingly impossible happens, and the Monarchy and all its prostituted entourage are dumped in the garbage can of history (as I believe is likely before the century is out), there will be far fewer sleepless nights on British pillows than many would like to think. In next to no time we would all be wondering why and how we endured the clutter for so long.

Appendix A.

THE PALACE AND THE MEDIA

On 16 May 1972, William Hamilton wrote to Mr Heseltine, the then Press Officer at Buckingham Palace, seeking an interview on the function of the Press Office for his research assistant, Dr Newman. Mr Heseltine replied that he had recently moved over to the Private Secretary's Office, and suggested that Dr Newman should make an appointment to see both him and his successor, Robin Ludlow.

> Perhaps it is worth mentioning that the Press Office at Buckingham Palace is an information office, and as such, we always try to give factual information in answer to specific requests. I am sure that Dr Newman will not be expecting us to offer our own opinions on wider generalizations about the role of the Monarchy.
>
> It would, I am sure, be helpful to us all if Dr Newman were able to indicate in advance of his visit the kind of questions he would like to put.

In a later letter, of 23 June, Mr Heseltine said:

> As I explained in my letter of 23rd May, I have recently been succeeded as Press Secretary by Mr Robin Ludlow, and the Press Secretary is our normal channel of communication with authors and others seeking information about the Royal Family and their official activities, and the organization which supports them. He has now settled down into the job, and I

should be grateful if you would communicate with him if you have any further questions that you want answered for your book.

I know Mr Ludlow will be ready to give you any factual information which should properly be made available to an author writing on this subject. We feel on reflection that such information would best be communicated in written questions and answers, as it ensures that the information given is completely accurate.

The resulting question-and-answer material on the function of the Press Office and Press Secretary ran as follows:

Q.1. How did the office originate? How is the officer appointed? Is the post advertised? What qualifications are looked for? What are the terms of the contract? Is it conceivable that the job would ever be offered to a Fleet Street or BBC man? Is the officer resident at the Palace? What staff has the officer?
A. See notes on the history of the Press Office, already sent to Mr Hamilton. [These notes form the basis of the material on pages 18–21.]

The Press Secretary, like all members of the Household, is appointed by The Queen. The recommendation is made by the Lord Chamberlain, the senior member of The Queen's Household. The post has never, so far as I know, been advertised. The qualifications are those for any similar job. Some acquaintance with the work of newspapers and communications, experience in dealing with people, some knowledge of administration and the usual intellectual qualities required for any senior executive. It is quite conceivable that the job could be offered to a Fleet Street or BBC man. In fact, one of the present Assistant Press Secretaries to The Queen came to the Palace from the BBC, having worked on newspapers and in radio in New Zealand and Australia. The present Press Secretary came to the Palace from *The Economist*, where he had worked for 11 years. Although there is always someone on call from the Press Office (24 hours a day), the Press Secretary does not live at the Palace. His staff consists of two Assistant Press Secretaries and three secretary typists.

Q.2. Does he advise Her Majesty how to handle the public media?
A. The Press Office exists basically as an information office to answer inquiries about the Royal Family and their official activities and to arrange press facilities, so that all the official activities of the Royal Family can be adequately covered by the media. The Press Secretary advises The Queen on all these matters.

Q.3. Does he draw up 'ground rules' to be followed by the BBC and press on royal visits at home and abroad? Is it possible to see a copy of such rules?
A. There are no 'ground rules'. When arranging the facilities, the Press Secretary and his office always attempt to make sure that the press on one hand are given adequate facilities to see, photograph and report on what is going on and, on the other hand, they attempt to make sure that facilities are such that they do not interfere with the dignity or propriety of any formal royal occasion. The only other 'rules' that exist are designed to facilitate this process by limiting the total number of photographers and cameramen present in close proximity to members of the Royal Family at such events. This is done by arrangement with the various newspaper and other organizations.

Q.4. Does he decide when, and in what form, information concerning the Royal Family should be released? Sometimes fairly trivial things which are done by the Royal Family are given great prominence on BBC news. Is this the BBC's own decision or does the Press Officer ask the corporation to act in this way? Who informed the press that members of the Royal Family were to fly in Concorde?
A. Information concerning the Royal Family is given out as and when requested. Releases about engagements and other news items are also made by the Press Secretary at times which he judges to be appropriate, usually as soon as the arrangements for a visit have been finalized. The prominence which television or radio and the newspapers give to these items is governed entirely by their own judgement. The Queen's Press Secretary and his office look after press matters for The Queen and The Duke of Edinburgh and their four children, but not for other members of the Royal Family. Information about official engagements of other members of the Royal Family is given to the press by their own offices. When Prince Philip flew in the Concorde, this information was released by the Press Secretary to The Queen. When, subsequently, other members of the Royal Family made a flight, this information was given to the press by their own offices.

Q.5. What part did the Press Officer play in (a) deciding whether a film about the Royal Family should be made and (b) choosing the form it should take? What happened to the profits?
A. The then Press Secretary was obviously involved in the discussions which preceded the making of the film *Royal Family*, and also in the discussions about the form which this film ultimately took. It was announced that the profits, or that

part of them which was put at the disposal of The Queen and The Duke of Edinburgh, are to be devoted to some charitable or other good cause. They have been placed in a special account, where they have been added to profits made by an earlier film about royal palaces, and have been earning interest. Discussions are proceeding about the use of these monies, and an announcement will be made in due course about the project to which they are to be devoted.

Q.6. Does the Press Officer play any part in deciding which engagements members of the Royal Family should fulfil?
A. The Press Secretary usually takes part in the discussions which precede decisions on their programmes by those members of the Royal Family mentioned above.

Q.7. What is the estimated cost annually of the public relations side of the Royal Family? Is this likely to increase as the children begin to participate more fully?
A. No details are available. Indeed, no salaries of individual members of The Queen's Household are published and there is no breakdown of the costs of stationery, equipment, etc. in the Private Secretary's Office, of which the Press Office forms a part.

Q.8. What liaison, official or unofficial, is there with the media? Does the Press Officer have a 'special relationship' with any newspaper on which he relies to carry particular stories? For example, when the Conservative Party changed its method of choosing a leader, *The Times* carried an editorial which claimed that this did not affect the Monarch's prerogative. Did the Press Officer suggest this?
A. The Press Association has a full-time Court Correspondent, who attends most official engagements of the Royal Family, and who calls for a conference with the Press Secretary at Buckingham Palace every morning. The BBC also has a court correspondent. No newspaper has at the present time a reporter with any special responsibilities to report on royal events and the Press Secretary has no 'special relationships'. All other newspapers or news organizations are welcome to supplement the information which is made available to them through the Press Association either by calling personally on one of the Press Officers, or by ringing up for further information. There is no 'Court Lobby'. The Press Secretary of the day would certainly not have suggested that *The Times* should have carried the editorial mentioned in question 8.

Q.9. Is there any form of censorship exercised over photographs taken of the Royal Family? Is there any restriction on press criticism of the Royal Family?
A. No.

Q.10. How many personages are covered by the Press Officer?
A. Refer to question 4.

Q.11. Has Her Majesty the last word on anything which the Press Officer proposes – for example, on statements to the press? What sort of initiative can the Press Officer exercise?
A. The Queen, of course, has the final decision on anything that is said or done by the Press Secretary in her name, although she is not necessarily consulted about minor matters.

Q.12. Have press conferences ever been arranged? Could they be desirable, for example, before a Commonwealth visit?
A. Yes. During every Commonwealth visit and indeed, foreign visit, there is usually a press conference or briefing meeting attended by the Press Secretary on almost every day of the visit. Prince Philip, too, has given press conferences from time to time on specific subjects which he has been dealing with at that time.

Q.13. Does a public relations officer accompany Her Majesty and other members of the Royal Family on all tours?
A. The Press Secretary, or one of his assistants, normally accompanies The Queen on overseas visits and occasionally other members of the Royal Family as well. Within the United Kingdom the Press Secretary is sometimes in attendance when members of the Royal Family undertake engagements outside London.

Q.14. Why was it thought necessary to improve and increase the scope of the public relations of the Royal Family? Has there been an attempt to change the 'image' of the Royal Family?
A. The only change made in the strength of the Press Office in the last 14 years has been the addition of one secretary typist in 1969, the year of the Investiture of The Prince of Wales. The Press Office does not exist to present an 'image' of the Royal Family, but to respond to requests for information about them and their activities and to arrange facilities for the press to report these activities.

Q.15. Was there advance thought given to the handling of proceedings in connection with the funeral of the Duke of Windsor by the Press Officer?
A. As the papers have reported in recent days, tentative plans for the funeral for The Duke of Windsor began to be made some years ago. The Press Secretary was consulted about arrangements for press facilities.

Q.16. Does the Press Officer have any control of content of Royal speeches – including Prince Philip's controversial

speeches on such topics as family limitation, planning procedures and the Common Market?
A. No. The constitutional position is that The Queen acts and speaks on the advice of her Ministers. It follows from this that Ministers either provide drafts for Her Majesty's speeches or are given the opportunity to see and comment on what she proposes to say. No other member of the Royal Family is in the same constitutional position as the Monarch.

*

On 3 July 1972, Lord Hill, as Chairman of the BBC, replied to a letter from William Hamilton by inviting him to submit questions about the BBC's relations with the Monarchy.

The BBC's relations with the monarchy necessarily involve more than one member of its staff and we shall therefore have to decide who might best provide the information you are seeking. It is of course inevitable that the confidentiality which is attached to these relations will have to be reflected in the framing of our replies to you.

Mr Hamilton therefore submitted his questions on 11 July, and Lord Hill was able to send the BBC's replies in due course on 18 September.

Q.1. How long has there been a BBC official acting as liaison officer with Buckingham Palace? What are the total numbers involved, men and women? Full time?
A. A senior member of the BBC's staff has acted as liaison officer between the BBC and Buckingham Palace since about 1930. The duties have always been additional to the official's other duties. No more than one official has ever been employed at the same time and he has been assisted only by his usual secretary.

Q.2. On whose initiative was the liaison started and why?
A. There is no record of how the initiative arose or from whence it came. It is, however, clearly a convenient arrangement, in view of the size of the BBC, that all matters concerning the Royal Family and the BBC should be channelled through a single office.

Q.3. Is there any [sic] one liaison officer dealing with all members of the Royal Family? Or just the Queen?
A. The BBC official responsible for liaison deals with all the Royal Households.

Q.4. What initiatives are open to the BBC, e.g. in suggesting broadcasts on particular subjects; in presenting Royal news items in the way *they* choose? In suggesting more broadcasts to the Commonwealth?
A. The BBC, like other large organizations, does from time to time put forward suggestions to Buckingham Palace. The BBC reserves the right to present news items, whether about the Royal Family or any other subject, in the way which it considers appropriate to the audience which it serves.

Q.5. How frequently does consultation occur orally with Her Majesty or with other members of the Royal Family?
A. The liaison officer does not deal directly with any member of the Royal Family.

Q.6. Would it be possible to have a copy of the written 'ground rules' governing the behaviour of the BBC when covering Royal Family occasions, e.g. the use of telescopic lenses, particulars of photographs taken etc.?
A. The BBC has no special 'ground rules' for covering Royal occasions, but tries to cover them, as it does all other events, responsibly and appropriately.

Q.7. Is any form of censorship exercised?
A. Normal editorial control is exercised, but no special form of control is applied simply because a programme involves members of the Royal Family.

Q.8. How is the Christmas broadcast organized? How did it start? Did the BBC seek to persuade Her Majesty to continue with the programme after she had announced its discontinuance?
A. The content of the Christmas Broadcast is a matter for the Queen. King George V broadcast the first Christmas Message in 1932, the first Television Message being broadcast by the present Queen in 1957. The BBC did not seek to persuade the Queen to reinstate the Christmas Broadcast after she decided not to give a broadcast message in 1969.

Q.9. Has it ever been suggested that Her Majesty might use the BBC more to get closer to the people, e.g. by talking informally about her job – or her family? Would it be a useful suggestion?
A. The Royal Family film, shown several times by the BBC and the IBA, was considered by many people to have been interesting and informative and possibly to have fulfilled the purpose which seems to underlie the question.

Q.10. Does Her Majesty have any influence or choice of the

BBC's Court liaison officials? Is she consulted? Could a known republican or communist be appointed? Or must they be 'safe' establishment figures?
A. The choice of the BBC liaison officer is a matter for the Corporation to decide. The BBC is guided in its selection by the need to appoint the man or woman who will best do what is required of the post-holder and that might disqualify the ardent monarchist no less than it might the dedicated republican.

Q.11. Could a confrontation be considered between Prince Philip and critics of the Royal Family?
A. If such a suggestion were made, it could be considered by the BBC, but its practicality would depend on circumstances at the time and, above all, on the willingness of Prince Philip to participate. The latter is, obviously, not a matter on which the BBC can comment.

*

On 10 July 1972, Lord Aylestone, as Chairman of the Independent Television Authority, summarized the relationship of the Authority with Buckingham Palace in response to a letter from William Hamilton of 28 June.

We do not have any particular liaison arrangement with Buckingham Palace and indeed contacts between the Authority's staff and the royal household are few and far between. There is an occasional relationship between the Queen's Press Secretary and staff of the Programme Division about such matters as the timing of the Queen's Christmas message on the Independent Television Network but that is all. Of course, if there is some special project, like the production of the BBC/ITV film about the Royal Family, it would be normal for initial contact to be established between the Palace and the ITA but this would then be handed over to somebody working on behalf of the ITV companies.

Independent Television News and the individual programme companies do not appear to have any difficulty in making their arrangements about the television coverage of royal occasions direct with the Press Secretary to the Queen. This officer is at the disposal of ITN and the companies just as he is at the disposal of the newspapers, and all these routine contacts seem to operate quite smoothly.

There are certain 'ground rules' which govern the positioning of advertisements in relation to television appearances by members of the Royal Family, but these, having been agreed

> with the Postmaster General (now the Minister of Posts and Telecommunications) under Schedule 2 of the Television Act, become entirely our own concern and do not involve any relationship with the Royal Household. It is also, I think, normal practice for a company which wishes to make use of any film library material about members of the Royal Family to notify the Press Secretary to the Queen as a matter of courtesy.

As Lord Aylestone's letter is identical, down to the last comma, with one sent by Mr Brian Young on behalf of the ITA to a correspondent in Hertfordshire on 11 July 1972, it is clearly a stock reply to all such inquiries.

Appendix B. TAXATION OF MEMBERS OF THE ROYAL FAMILY. MEMORANDUM BY THE TREASURY TO THE SELECT COMMITTEE ON THE CIVIL LIST

The following information is in amplification of that contained in paragraph 5 of the Chancellor's Memorandum (M.2).

Her Majesty The Queen

2. As part of the Royal Prerogative, the Queen is not liable to pay tax unless Parliament says so either explicitly or by inevitable inference. There is no distinction for this purpose between the private and public aspects of the Sovereign. The tax immunity extends to the Duchy of Lancaster.

3. The following statutory provisions explicitly displace the Crown's immunity from tax:

a. The Crown Private Estates Acts 1800, 1862 and 1873; these make the Sovereign liable to rates in respect of Sandringham and Balmoral. Liability for Schedule A Income Tax no longer arises since its abolition in 1963.
b. Section 119 of the Stamp Act 1891 makes an instrument relating to Crown property (including, by inference, private property of the Queen) liable to the same stamp duty as if it were the property of a subject.
c. Section 44(7) of the Finance Act 1966 makes the Queen liable to pay Selective Employment Tax in respect of both public and private servants.

4. The Queen is not liable to assessment to income tax or surtax

and is entitled to claim repayment of any income tax suffered at source (e.g. on company dividends). She is not liable to capital gains tax, nor is any of her property liable to estate duty. While no tax is payable by the Sovereign on the Civil List, salaries and pensions paid out of the Civil List are taxed in the hands of the recipients.

5. The Queen is not liable to indirect taxation (whether in the form of import duties or internal indirect taxation) in the absence of any special statutory provision to the contrary. Where however (as in the normal case) the indirect tax is levied on goods before they are purchased by The Queen there is no relief from tax. Where goods are imported by The Queen, import duties are charged by long-standing custom. There is however, a special arrangement whereby purchase tax on Civil List purchases for State or ceremonial purposes is refunded from Subhead H of the Vote for Miscellaneous Expenses.

HRH The Prince of Wales

6. The income and the property of the Duchy of Cornwall is exempt from income tax, surtax, capital gains tax, and estate duty. Any other income or property of the Prince is liable to taxation in the ordinary way, as though it were his total income or property.

HRH The Duke of Edinburgh

7. The Duke is not liable to tax in respect of his wife's income. Otherwise he is taxable like any other subject in respect of his income and his property. Under a Treasury order part of his Civil List annuity is treated for tax purposes as properly attributable to expenses of his public duties and that part is therefore not taxable.

Other Members of the Royal Family

8. There are no special tax exemptions, so they are taxable like any other subject on their income and property. Treasury orders are currently in force attributing each of the existing Civil List annuities wholly or partly to admissible expenses, and to that extent not taxable. In accordance with normal taxation practice, any voluntary allowance the Queen may make to a member of the Royal Family does not rank as income of that Member.

The Treasury Orders

9. The Treasury orders referred to have been made under various

legislative authorities; they have been consolidated from time to time and are currently contained in Section 191 of the Income and Corporation Taxes Act 1970 as applied by paragraph 28 of Schedule 14 of the Act.

Appendix C.

ACCOUNTS OF THE REVENUES OF THE DUCHIES OF LANCASTER AND CORNWALL FOR 1973–4

1. DUCHY OF LANCASTER REVENUE AND CAPITAL ACCOUNTS, 1973–4

AN ACCOUNT of the RECEIPTS and DISBURSEMENTS of the DUCHY of LANCASTER for the year ended 29th September, 1973 prepared pursuant to Act 1 & 2 Vict. c. 101, s. 2.

RECEIPTS	£	£	£	1971/7 £
Balance at Bank on 29th September, 1972 ..	56,945			
Loan Deposits	115,000			
	171,945			
Less: Balance due to Capital	2,739	169,206		
Balances in the hands of Surveyors and others on 29th September, 1972		5,963	175,169	143,69
Rents, etc.:				
1. Arrears outstanding on 29th September, 1972	6,209			
2. Rents accrued, 1973	410,647	416,856		
Less: Arrears outstanding on 29th September, 1973	6,663			
Less: Allowances to Tenants	1,345	8,008	408,848	404,55
Mineral Rents and Royalties:				
Rents, etc., accrued, 1973			28,253	33,14
Income Tax Repaid			16,107	12,57
Portion of Law Charges charged to Capital			—	1,14
Dividends on Investments			2,728	2,87
Annuity received from the Consolidated Fund under Acts of 43 Geo. III and 2 & 3 Will. IV for the purchase and surrender of the Duties of Prisage and Butlerage within the County Palatine			803	80
Produce of Devolutions and Forfeitures			109,572	80,24
Interest on Money on Deposit, etc.			54,199	19,46
£			795,679	698,49

DISBURSEMENTS	£	£	£	1971/72 £
Payments made to the Keeper of the Privy Purse (for Her Majesty's use)			295,000	260,000
Expenses of Maintenance:				
Repairs and Improvements chargeable to Revenue		101,092		
Transfers to Capital:				
(*a*) Portions of amounts paid out of Capital in respect of Improvements to the Estates	24,236			
(*b*) Portions of Mineral and certain other Rents	3.014			
		27,250		
Sinking Fund Purchase of Government Securities in respect of certain properties purchased by the Duchy and of certain Special Improvements		1,428		
			129,770	108,943
Deductions under various Acts of Parliament, etc., viz:				
Income Tax	14,059			
Other Rates and Taxes	4,188			
Rent Charges and Tithe Redemption Annuities	1,034			
		19,281		
Proportion of Rent in the Savoy due to the Crown Estate Commissioners		2,794		
			22,075	27,923
Net Expenses of Woods after deducting Receipts on Account of Wood Sales			3,302	8,920
Salary of the Chancellor of the Duchy			2,000	2,000
Disbursements under the following Heads, viz:				
Superannuation Allowances and Annuities ..		17,653		
Sinking Funds on account of charges under Superannuation Act, 1909, etc.		7,580		
Stipends, Donations and Ceremonial Officers		3,341		
Savoy Chapel		6,484		
			35,058	30,525
Expenses of Management:				
Salaries: Administrative Officers, etc..	31,690			
,, Estates Department	31,662			
,, Legal Department	17,750			
		81,102		
Surveys, Valuations and Plans		334		
Contingent Disbursements	19,870			
Less: Fee Fund Receipts	4,555			
		15,315	96,751	85,018
Balances in the hands of Surveyors and others on 29th September, 1973		8,780		
Loan Deposits		50,000		
Balance at Bank on 29th September, 1973 ..		157,624		
		216,404		
Less: Balance due to Capital		4,681		
			211,723	175,169
		£	795,679	698,498

Audited and found Correct,
P. L. FORWOOD,
Chartered Accountant,
Auditor of the Duchy of Lancaster.
15th November, 1973.

CAPITAL ACCOUNT (cash) of the DUCHY of LANCASTER for the year ended 29th September, 1973

RECEIPTS		£	1971/72 £
Balance at Bank, 29th September, 1972		43	43
Balance due from Revenue, 29th September, 1972		2,739	3,766
Received for Grants in Fee		260,990	162,572
Received for Compensation for Manorial Incidents		10,540	560
Sale and Redemption of Securities		1,082,487	750,000
	£		
Transferred from Revenue (see Revenue Account)	27,250		
Less: Expenses of Sales and Purchases of Estates	3,447	23,803	23,079
£		1,380,602	940,020

DISBURSEMENTS	£	1971/72 £
Permanent Improvements to the Estates	64,885	38,690
Purchases of Lands	13,506	3,548
Purchase of Securities	1,297,442	895,000
Balance at Bank at 29th September, 1973	88	43
Balance due from Revenue on 29th September, 1973	4,681	2,739
£	1,380,602	940,020

Note:—At 29th September, 1973 Securities held on Capital Account had a Market Value of £685,268.

Audited and found correct,
P. L. FORWOOD,
Chartered Accountant,
Auditor of the Duchy of Lancaster.
15th November, 1973.

ACCOUNTS OF THE REVENUES OF THE DUCHIES OF LANCASTER AND CORNWALL FOR THE YEAR ENDED 29th SEPTEMBER, 1973

2. AN ACCOUNT OF THE RECEIPTS AND DISBURSEMENTS OF THE DUCHY OF CORNWALL FOR THE YEAR ENDED 31st DECEMBER, 1973

AN ACCOUNT of the RECEIPTS and DISBURSEMENTS of the DUCHY OF CORNWALL in the year ended 31st December, 1973.
Prepared in pursuance of the Act 1 & 2 Vict. c. 101

CHARGE	*1972* £	1973 £
Rents, etc.	*689,456*	739.076
Royalties and Reservations of Dues and Rents of Mines and Quarries	*10,177*	18,059
Produce of Wood Sales, etc.	*221,283*	252,632
Home Farm Receipts	*34,768*	27,577
Annuity received from the Consolidated Fund, under the Act 1 and 2 Vict. c. 120 in lieu of Tin Coinage Duties, Post Groats and White Rents	*16,217*	16,217
Dividends on Securities	*49,788*	59,929
Casual Profits of the Office of Havenor (Proceeds of Sale of Unclaimed Wreck)	—	—
Casual Profits from Estates of Deceased Intestates dying domiciled in Cornwall without kin	*1,449*	5,154
Withdrawn from Mineral Deposits	*154*	919
Miscellaneous Receipts	*10,553*	20,337
Total Receipts	*1,033,845*	1,139,900
Balance on 1st January, 1973	*127,276*	175,046
	£1,161,121	£1,314,946

DISCHARGE	*1972* £	*1972* £	1973 £	1973 £
Outlay for the Benefit of the Estate, viz:				
Repairs and General Upkeep	*209,342*		249,758	
Repayment to Capital in respect of Sums advanced for Permanent Improvements, etc.	*84,634*		90,727	
Expenditure on Mineral Property ..	*154*	*294,130*	919	341,404
Deductions under various Acts of Parliament, etc., viz:				
Parish Rates, etc.	*36,048*		42,649	
Tithe Redemption Annuities	*6,506*	*42,554*	6,124	48,773
Disbursements under the following Heads, viz:				
Superannuation Allowances and Annuities	*30,123*		27,650	
Donations and Subscriptions	*6,544*		8,405	
Fire and other Insurances	*11,598*		11,495	
Miscellaneous Payments	*5,377*		4,737	
Decima Stanni	*17*		17	
Expenditure on Woods	*186,115*		284,812	
Home Farm Payments	*28,103*		42,716	
Duke of Cornwall's Benevolent Fund..	*1,449*	*269,326*	5,154	384,986
Expenses of Management, viz:				
Salaries and National Insurance of the Duchy Establishment in London ..	*39,399*		35,625	
Law and other Professional Charges ..	*11,230*		9,292	
Upkeep of Duchy Office, Printing, Stationery, and other Incidental Expenses in London	*35,913*		29,957	
	86,542		74,874	
Less: Produce of the Fee Fund of the Duchy, etc.	*2,185*		869	
	84,357		74,005	
Surface Property Expenses including Salaries, Allowances and Office Expenses of Land Stewards, Collectors, etc.	*66,278*		77,246	
Mineral Property Expenses	*829*		1,224	
Travelling Expenses and Entertainment of Duchy Tenants on Rent Days, etc.	*11,325*	*162,789*	10,089	162,564
Total Payments		*768,799*		937,727
Payments made on account of His Royal Highness		*217,276*		265,046
Balance on 31st December, 1973		*175,046*		112,173
		£1,161,121		£1,314,946
Audited and found correct, J. H. BOWMAN, *Auditor.* *28th March, 1974.*				
		£1,161,121		£1,314,946

CAPITAL ACCOUNT of the DUCHY of CORNWALL for the year ended 31st December, 1973

RECEIPTS	1972 £	1973 £
Balances on 31st December, 1972	*97,748*	100,634
Sales of Estates	*89,697*	183,033
Purchase Money received on account of Sales not completed	*20,800*	30,000
Sales and Redemptions of Securities	*240,750*	241,052
Capital Distributions on Securities	*1*	—
Repayment of Advances for Permanent Improvements, etc. (under the Acts 26 and 27 Vict. c. 49, s. 8 and 31 and 32 Vict. c. 35 ss. 1 and 2 and 6 and 7 Geo. VI c. 21 s. 72 (4))	*84,634*	90,727
£	*533,630*	645,446

DISBURSEMENTS		1972 £	1973 £
Purchases of Estates		*34,125*	20,078
Redemption of Tithe Annuity		—	5
Expenses attendant upon the Purchase and Sale of Estates		*1,030*	2,327
Outlay for Permanent Improvements, etc. (under the Acts 26 and 27 Vict. c. 49, s. 8 and 31 and 32 Vict. c. 35, ss. 1 and 2 and 6 and 7 Geo. VI c. 21 s. 72 (4))		*135,773*	162,313
Purchases of Securities		*262,068*	244,485
Balances on 31st December, 1973:			
Advanced for Permanent Improvements	17,388		
Held at Bank of England	163,797		
Held at Baring Brothers & Co. Ltd.	35,053		
		100,634	216,238
£		*533,630*	645,446

Note—In addition securities held on Capital Account at 31st December, 1973 had a market value of £904,952 (*1972 £1,204,544*).

Audited and found correct,
J. H. BOWMAN,
Auditor.
28th March, 1974.

Appendix D.
1913 OPINION ON THE DUCHY OF CORNWALL BY THE LAW OFFICERS OF THE CROWN AND MR W. FINLAY

1. We are of the opinion that the same principles which render the provisions of an Act of Parliament inapplicable to the Crown unless the Crown is expressly named, apply also to the Prince of Wales in his capacity as Duke of Cornwall. This result arises from the peculiar title of the Prince of Wales to the Duchy of Cornwall. In other respects the Prince of Wales, as being the first subject of the Crown is, like other subjects, bound by statutory enactments.

2. Taxation is not and cannot be exacted from land; it is exacted from subjects who are tax payers. For the reason given in our answer to the first question, The Duke of Cornwall is not liable to such taxation, but it may be that he will not wish to insist upon his privilege of exemption. In view of the fact that the property in the hands of the Duchy of Cornwall may change from time to time, it is in a high degree inconvenient that valuations should not proceed in the ordinary course in respect of land now belonging to the Duchy, and we think that the Duchy of Cornwall should be strongly urged (without raising any question of legal rights on one side or the other) to make returns and co-operate in getting valuations settled.

3–6. *We would most strongly deprecate the bringing to an issue of questions such as those here set out. It is obvious that if such a matter were litigated the Duchy of Cornwall might find that even though they succeeded their success in the Courts did not conclude the matter. The practice which, as we are instructed, is followed by the Crown itself, is one which avoids raising these awkward and difficult questions* and we are of opinion that representations should be made to the advisers of the Duchy as to the propriety, while expressly saving what they conceive to be their legal rights of exemption, of making concessions as of grace.

Law Officers' Department RUFUS D. ISAACS
18 August, 1913 JOHN SIMON
W. FINLAY

AUTHOR'S NOTE: I later heard from the Library Clerk that this document should not have been released to me; but it was! (The italics are mine.)

Appendix E. HONOURS (PEERAGES, BARONETCIES, KNIGHTHOODS AND D.B.E.s) TO CONSERVATIVE AND LABOUR M.P.s 1952–73

Steps are included, e.g. knight to baron. Honours to law officers, which go with the job, are excluded: there were five knighthoods to Conservative law officers in the period 1952–73: Simon, Rawlinson, Hobson, Howe and Havers.

Name	*Honour*	*Educational background*
To Conservatives 1952		
Brendan Bracken	V	Irish schools; 2 terms at PS
R. S. Hudson	V	E; Ox
Earl Winterton	B	E; Ox
R. V. Grimston	Bt	PS; U
C. L. Ropner	Bt	H; C
J. E. Crowder	K	E; Ox
E. De la Bere	K	PS
E. Errington	K	PS; Ox
G. C. Hutchinson	K	PS; C
E. H. Keeling	K	SS; Ox
S. H. Marshall	K	El
D. L. Savory	K	PS; Ox
E. A. Taylor	K	SS
G. C. Touche	K	PS; Ox
Viscountess Davidson	DBE	nr
To Conservatives 1953		
Sir H. O'Neill	B (Rathcavan)	E; Ox
Sir P. F. B. Bennett	B	PS

Name	*Honour*	*Educational background*
Sir R. Glyn	B	H; RMC
Sir A. Salter	B	SS; Ox
A. C. Bossom	Bt	PS; architect
Sir R. De la Bere	Bt	PS
Sir H. Williams	Bt	Privately; U
W. Churchill	KG	H; RMC
H. W. Butcher	K	SS; surveyor
R. Boothby	K	E; Ox
P. W. Donner	K	Ox
Sir C. Drewe	K	E; RMA
D. Eccles	K	PS; Ox
I. L. Orr Ewing	K	H; Ox
W. Fletcher	K	PS; U
L. H. Gluckstein	K	PS; Ox
H. N. Linstead	K	PS; U
E. G. R. Lloyd	K	PS; Ox
S. F. Markham	K	Ox
V. Raikes	K	PS; C
H. Sutcliffe	K	H; Ox
To Conservatives 1954		
Sir D. Maxwell-Fyfe	V (Kilmuir)	PS; Ox
O. Lyttleton	V (Chandos)	E; C
Sir J. S. Holmes	B (Dovercourt)	PS
R. K. Law	B	PS; Ox
J. G. Braithwaite	Bt	PS
M. Bullock	Bt	Privately; C
R. J. E. Conant	Bt	E; RMC
H. R. Mackeson	Bt	PS; RMC
A. Eden	KG	E; Ox
A. B. Baxter	K	Canada
G. I. C. Hutchison	K	PS; RNC
R. Jennings	K	nr; accountant
W. R. D. Perkins	K	E; C
C. S. Taylor	K	PS; C
J. R. Robinson	K	C
To Labour 1952–4		
NIL		
To Conservatives 1955		
R. Assheton	B (Clitheroe)	E; Ox

Name	*Honour*	*Educational background*
H. Crookshank	V	E; Ox
T. D. Galbraith	B	PS; RNC
Sir A. Gridley	B	PS
H. L. d'Aubigne Hopkinson	B (Colyton)	E; C
M. S. McCorquodale	B	H; Ox
O. Peake	V (Ingleby)	E; Ox
H. Strauss	B (Conesford)	PS; Ox
J. P. L. Thomas	B (Cilcennin)	PS; Ox
Sir R. Cary	Bt	PS; RMC
D. Gammans	Bt	PS; U
L. W. Joynson-Hicks	Bt	PS; Ox
J. G. Smyth	Bt	PS; RMC
W. N. Snadden	Bt	SS
W. G. Bennett	K	nr
R. S. Clarke	K	E; C
A. Colegate	K	U
I. M. Horobin	K	PS; C
N. J. Hulbert	K	PS
D. McCallum	K	PS
F. Medlicott	K	SS; solicitor
R. D. Scott	K	PS; C
W. A. Steward	K	SS
Miss Irene Ward	DBE	nr
To Labour 1955		
C. R. Attlee	Earl	PS; Ox; barrister
To Conservatives 1956		
G. Lloyd-George	V (Tenby)	PS; C
Sir W. Monckton	V	H; Ox
P. Buchan-Hepburn	B (Hailes)	H; C
W. J. Anstruther-Grey	Bt	E; Ox
J. R. H. Hutchison	Bt	H
Sir T. Moore	Bt	PS; U
H. G. Studholme	Bt	E; Ox
A. G. Gomme-Duncan	K	PS
R. H. Rayner	K	nr
A. C. M. Spearman	K	PS; Ox
G. S. Summers	K	PS; C
To Labour 1956		
Tom O'Brien	K	El

Name	*Honour*	*Educational background*
To Conservatives 1957		
P. Agnew	Bt	PS
J. A. L. Duncan	Bt	PS
H. W. Kerr	Bt	E; Ox
F. Maclean	Bt	E; C
D. J. Henderson-Stewart	Bt	SS; U
W. Robson Brown	K	SS
H. Channon	K	Privately; Ox
A. V. Harvey	K	PS
A. Low	K	PS; Ox
M. Stoddart-Scott	K	PS; U
B. Nield	K	H; Ox
C. R. Mott-Radclyffe	K	E; Ox
To Labour 1957		
NIL		
To Conservatives 1958		
Sir R. Boothby	LP	E; Ox
Sir I. Fraser	LP	PS; RMC
Godfrey Nicholson	Bt	PS; Ox
A. E. Baldwin	K	SS
C. Thornton-Kemsley	K	PS; Ox
G. Wills	K	Privately; C
To Labour 1958		
V. Collins	LP (Stonham)	U
D. G. West	LP (Granville-West)	nr; solicitor
George Benson	K	Manchester Grammar
To Conservatives 1959		
James Stuart	V	E
Sir T. Dugdale	B (Crathorne)	E; RMC
Sir C. MacAndrew	B	PS; C
Sir P. Spens	B	PS; Ox
J. Nixon Browne	LP (Craighton)	PS
Dame Florence Horsburgh	LP	PS
K. Pickthorn	Bt	PS; C
H. D. Oakshott	Bt	PS; C

Name	*Honour*	*Educational background*
C. Black	K	PS; surveyor
A. Hurd	K	PS; C
W. Duthie	K	SS
O. Prior-Palmer	K	PS; RMC
A. Noble	K	PS
H. Ashton	K	PS; C
To Labour 1959		
Herbert Morrison	LP	El
To Conservatives 1960		
Sir A. Bossom	LP	PS; architect
Heathcote Amory	V	E; Ox
A. Lennox-Boyd	V (Boyd of Merton)	PS; Ox
A. Head	V	E; RMC
G. Ward	V	E; Ox
D. Kaberry	Bt	SS; solicitor
J. Vaughan-Morgan	Bt	E; Ox
G. Nugent	Bt	RMA
S. Storey	Bt	PS; C
Sir H. Butcher	Bt	SS; surveyor
Sir G. Lloyd	Bt	PS; Ox
D. Walker-Smith	Bt	PS; Ox
H. Nicholls	Bt	SS
Douglas Glover	K	PS
E. Cooper-Key	K	RNC
D. Llewellyn	K	E; C
J. Maitland	K	RNC
E. Keatings (MP 1944–5)	K	PS
H. Legge-Bourke	K	E; RMC
G. Beresford Craddock	K	U
To Labour 1960		
Hugh Dalton	LP	E; C; barrister
Myer Galpern	K	U
To Conservatives 1961		
Sir A. Eden	Earl (Avon)	E; Ox
H. Molson	LP	RNC; Ox
C. Alport	LP	PS; C

Name	*Honour*	*Educational background*
James Harrison	Bt	SS; Ox
O. Crosthwaite-Eyre	K	PS; C
C. Osborne	K	U
I. J. Pitman	K	E; Ox
Tufton Beamish	K	PS; RMC
W. Bromley-Davenport	K	PS
R. Pilkington	K	PS; Ox
Pat Hornsby-Smith	DBE	SS
To Labour 1961		
George Lindgren	LP	El
Tom Williams	LP	nr; coal miner
Alf Robens	LP	SS
Edith Summerskill	LP	London U; doctor
Geoffrey de Freitas	K	PS; C
To Conservatives 1962		
Viscount Kilmuir	Earl	PS; Ox
Sir Toby Low	B (Aldington)	PS; Ox
Sir David Eccles	B	PS; Ox
Sir R. Manningham-Buller	B (Dilhorne)	E; Ox
Sir Geoffrey Hutchison (MP 1937–45, 1950–54)	LP	PS; C
Martin Lindsay	Bt	PS; RMC
Sir G. Touche	Bt	PS; Ox
John Langford-Holt	K	PS
William Teeling	K	PS; Ox
Ted Leather	K	Canada
S. McAdden	K	SS
Edith Pitt	DBE	SS
To Labour 1962		
Barnet Janner	K	U; solicitor
Elaine Burton	LP	Training college
Arthur Champion	LP	SS
Thomas Williamson (MP 1945–8)	LP	U
To Conservatives 1963		
John Hare	V (Blakenham)	E

Name	*Honour*	*Educational background*
Sir W. Wakefield	B	PS; C
Niall Macpherson	B (Drumalbyn)	PS; Ox
Charles Hill	LP	SS; C
Viscountess Davidson	LP	nr
William Taylor	Bt	SS; U
Kenneth Thompson	Bt	SS
Richard Thompson	Bt	PS
Sir E. Errington	Bt	PS; Ox
Ian Orr-Ewing	Bt	H; Ox
Knox Cunningham	Bt	PS; C
G. Nabarro	K	SS
Leslie Thomas	K	PS
John George	K	El
John MacLeod	K	PS
Douglas Marshall	K	PS
William Aitken	K	Canada; U
To Labour 1963		
Charles Hobson	LP	nr
Viscount Alexander	Earl	El; technical classes
To Conservatives 1964		
Lord Eccles	V	PS; Ox
John Maclay	V (Muirshiel)	PS; C
Harold Watkinson	V	PS; U
Lord John Hope	B (Glendevon)	E; Ox
W. Fletcher-Vane	B (Inglewood)	PS; C
Sir A. Hurd	LP	PS; C
Lord Dilhorne	V	E; Ox
F. Erroll	B	PS; C
Sir R. Grimston	B	PS; U
John Morrison	B (Margadale)	E; C
M. Hughes-Young	B (St Helens)	H; RMC
Mrs Emmet	LP	SS; Ox
Sir Hendrie Oakshott	LP	PS; C
Denis Vosper	LP (Runcorn)	PS; C
John Arbuthnot	Bt	E; C
John Rodgers	Bt	PS; Ox
R. Dudley Williams	Bt	PS; Cranwell
Graeme Finlay	Bt	PS; U
F. Pearson	Bt	PS; C
M. Redmayne	Bt	PS

Name	Honour	Educational background
David Renton	K	PS; Ox
F. Bishop	K	SS; U
R. Russell	K	PS; C
J. Henderson	K	PS
J. Foster	K	E; Ox
F. Bennett	K	PS
E. Bullus	K	SS; U
R. Speir	K	E; C
Joan Vickers	DBE	PS
To Labour 1964		
(*a*) *Under a Conservative government*		
G. R. Mitchison	LP	E; Ox; barrister
Hervey Rhodes	LP	El; technical college
Charles Royle	LP	SS
Barnett Stross	K	Leeds U; doctor
(*b*) *Under a Labour government*		
Frank Beswick	LP	nr
William Blyton	LP	El
George Bowles	LP	U; solicitor
Fenner Brockway	LP	PS
Chuter Ede	LP	High school; C
Samuel Segal	LP	SS; Ox; surgeon
Reginald Sorensen	LP	El
Elwyn Jones	K	Grammar; C; barrister
Dingle Foot	K	Ox; barrister
Eric Fletcher	K	PS; U; solicitor
To Conservatives 1965		
R. A. Butler	LP	PS; C
To Labour 1965		
John Haire (MP 1945–51)	LP	Queen's U, Belfast
Albert Hilton	LP	El
Ian Winterbottom	LP	PS; C
To Conservatives 1966		
Sir W. Anstruther-Gray	LP (Kilmany)	E; Ox
Sir R. Nugent	LP	RMA

Name	Honour	Educational background
Sir M. Redmayne	LP	PS
Sir S. Storey	LP (Buckton)	PS; C
Henry Brooke	LP	PS; Ox
To Labour 1966		
Walter Monslow	LP	nr
Arthur Moyle	LP	El; Fircroft college
Arthur Henderson	LP (Rowley)	C
Thomas Jones	LP (Maelor)	nr; coal miner
George Pargiter	LP	SS
Ernest Popplewell	LP	El
Sir Frank Soskice	LP (Stow Hill)	PS; Ox
Bernard Taylor	LP	El
Horace Holmes (MP 1945–59)	K	El
To Conservatives 1967		
Peter Thorneycroft	LP	E; RMA
To Labour 1967		
Frank McLeavy	LP	El
Charles Smith (MP 1945–50)	LP (Delacourt-Smith)	Ox
Edgar Granville (Lib. MP 1929–51)	LP	Australia
George Wigg	LP	SS
Herbert Bowden	LP (Aylestone)	nr
Arthur Irvine	K	U; Ox; barrister
To Conservatives 1968		
NIL		
To Labour 1968		
NIL		
To Conservatives 1969		
R. Grant-Ferris	K	PS
To Labour 1969		
Alfred Broughton	K	PS; C; doctor
To Conservatives 1970		
Lady Tweedsmuir	LP	nr

Name	*Honour*	*Educational background*
Nigel Birch	LP (Rhyl)	E
Sir E. Boyle	LP	E; Ox
Sir J. Vaughan-Morgan	LP (Reigate)	E; Ox
Quintin Hogg	LP (Hailsham)	E; Ox
To Labour 1970		
Sir Eric Fletcher	LP	PS; U; solicitor
James Hoy	LP	SS
Sir Barnett Janner	LP	U; solicitor
Emanuel Shinwell	LP	nr
Joseph Slater	LP	Council school; miner
Alice Bacon	LP	High school; training college
Jennie Lee	LP	U
Eirene White	LP	Ox
George Brown	LP	nr
Harold Davies	LP	SS; training college
John Diamond	LP	SS; accountant
Anthony Greenwood	LP	PS; Ox
Julian Snow	LP (Burntwood)	PS
Leslie Lever	K	U; solicitor
To Conservatives 1971		
Sir Jocelyn Simon (MP 1951–62)	LP	PS; C
Sir I. Orr-Ewing (MP 1950–70)	LP	H; Ox
Sir A. Vere Harvey	LP	PS
Robert Turton	K	E; Ox
To Labour 1971		
NIL		
To Conservatives 1972		
J. Boyd-Carpenter	LP	PS; Ox
Bernard Braine	K	SS
G. Longden	K	PS; C
Harold Stewart (MP 1955–64)	K	SS; engineer
B. Bryan	K	PS; C
F. Corfield	K	PS; RMA

Name	*Honour*	*Educational background*
To Labour 1972		
Leslie Hale (MP 1945–68)	LP	SS; solicitor
Tudor Watkins	LP	El; evening classes
To Conservatives 1973		
D. Dodds-Parker	K	PS; Ox
J. Peel	K	PS; C
To Labour 1973		
NIL		

In summary, the grand total of titles for this period was 232 to the Tories against 68 to Labour. Under the 1952–64 Conservative Government, 207 went to the Tories and only 23 to Labour; an imbalance of 9 to 1.

Key to abbreviations used

Honour

V =Viscount
B =Hereditary baron
LP =Life Peerage
Bt =Baronetcy
KG =Knight of the Garter
K =Knighthood

Educational background

E =Eton
H =Harrow
PS =other public school
El =Elementary school
SS =secondary school (incl. grammar)
C =Cambridge University
Ox =Oxford University
U =Other university
RMC =Royal Military College, Sandhurst
RMA =Royal Military Academy, Woolwich
RNC =Royal Naval College Dartmouth
nr =not recorded in *Who's Who* or *Who Was Who*

(Appendix compiled from information provided by the Home and Parliamentary Affairs Section of the Research Division of the House of Commons Library.)

Appendix F.
A RECORD OF CORRESPONDENCE BETWEEN WILLIAM HAMILTON, MEMBERS OF THE ROYAL FAMILY AND THEIR REPRESENTATIVES

1. Correspondence with the Queen's Household

On 11 April 1972, Mr Hamilton wrote to the Queen's Private Secretary to inquire about access to the Royal Archives for research purposes. On 14 April, Sir Martin Charteris replied:

> The Royal Archives at Windsor Castle consist of the family papers of The Queen. Papers from certain sections, which are chiefly devoted to Government business in earlier reigns, are sometimes, by Her Majesty's permission, released to academic historians and historical biographers who are recognized as authorities in the field concerned. Sections which deal with the personal and private affairs of the Monarchy are not, however, available for release, except to those few authors who are personally selected by The Sovereign as biographers of particular members of The Royal Family, or as editors of royal correspondence for publication.
>
> Papers which have not yet been moved from the current files at Buckingham Palace to the Royal Archives at Windsor cannot be made available for research at any time.
>
> In the light of these restrictions, I regret that I should not be authorized to grant the request in your letter. If, however, there are any specific questions on constitutional (as opposed to private) matters on which you think the papers at Windsor might throw light, I hope you will not hesitate to write to me again.

On 8 May 1972, William Hamilton wrote to Sir Martin to thank him for his invitation to pose questions of a constitutional character. He then asked for enlightenment on four specific questions, 'although I suspect in the nature of things you will not be able to give me much useful information in view of the immediacy of the events on which I seek information'. The questions were as follows:

> Q.1. What part did Her Majesty play in the appointment of Mr Macmillan as Prime Minister in place of Sir Anthony Eden [in 1956]? Did she simply accept the advice given to her by the Conservative Party leaders, or was her role of a more active character?
>
> Q.2. Did Her Majesty influence in any way the decision to appoint Lord Home as Prime Minister in 1963? Again did the initiative come entirely from the Conservative Party leaders and was Her Majesty's role entirely passive?
>
> Q.3. In the period 1968/9 was any advice, or guidance, or initiative received from the Labour Party to Her Majesty as to the procedure she would be expected to adopt in the event of the resignation or ousting of Mr Wilson as Leader of the Labour Party and therefore as Prime Minister.
>
> Q.4. You may recall that in the course of cross-examination of Sir Michael Adeane, then Her Majesty's Private Secretary, appearing before the recent Select Committee on the Civil List, I questioned him about the photograph taken at Chequers of Mr Nixon, President of the U.S.A., Mr Heath and Her Majesty. That photograph was used by the Conservative Party in a subsequent political pamphlet. Was Her Majesty made aware of that fact? Did she authorize any protest about the use of this photograph for political purposes? Did she realize then and does she realize now the political implications if that photograph is put to subsequent political use, either in America or the United Kingdom?

Sir Martin replied on 24 May:

> I fear you are correct in assuming that I am unable to give you much useful information on the questions you ask because of the immediacy of the events to which they refer.
>
> Indeed, in so far as your first three questions are concerned, I can give you no information at all. The papers dealing with these questions do not yet form part of the Royal Archives but are still part of the working papers at Buckingham Palace to which access is never given. Moreover, what passes between

The Queen and her Ministers is, of course, confidential, and information about this is never given by this office, nor is information ever given about any confidential approaches which may, or may not, be made at any time to The Queen or to her Private Secretary by Leaders of any political parties.

In regard to your question No. 4, the facts, as I understand them, are that the photograph to which you refer was one of a number taken by Press photographers who were granted facilities for that occasion in the normal manner. It is, of course, implicit in the granting of such a facility that the pictures taken may be reproduced without further formality in newspapers and other publications. The photograph was available like other press photographs at the time, and those responsible for the publication did not seek approval from here for such publication and, indeed, they were under no obligation to do so.

As Sir Michael Adeane said in his answer to your question No. 247 in the Minutes of Evidence taken before the Select Committee on the Civil List, no protest was made.

*

On 4 July 1972, Mr Hamilton wrote to Lord Adeane, the Queen's former Private Secretary, following up an earlier letter seeking an interview. On 6 July, Sir Martin Charteris replied on Lord Adeane's behalf, from the Palace of Holyroodhouse.

By longstanding custom, members of the Household having retired, do not give interviews to discuss their past work. I fear, therefore, that Lord Adeane does not feel that it would be proper for him to have a discussion with you nor with your researcher.

*

On 27 November 1973, Mr Hamilton wrote direct to the Queen:

Your Majesty,

Some short while ago, I was informed by a very reliable source that there were several cottages which had been standing empty on your Sandringham Estate for a considerable time.

I think you would agree that in a time of grave national shortage of housing among your people, this must be a matter of considerable concern. I would therefore be grateful if you could advise me on how long this accommodation *has* been unoccupied, how many cottages are involved, and when they are expected to be tenanted.

The second question which interests me is your own personal liability for the payment of tax. The answers given to the Civil List Select Committee on this matter were far from clear.

I would be greatly obliged if you could guide me. In answer to Question 370, the Treasury official said 'The Queen cannot be required to pay tax unless parliament specifically says so'.

My simple question is this: Do you *voluntarily* pay income tax, or any other kind of tax? There is considerable interest in this matter, and the position should be clarified.

He received his reply from Sir Rennie Maudslay, Keeper of the Privy Purse.

The major part of the Sandringham Estate is leased to tenant farmers, and I am not in a position to give you any information how the cottages, which form part of their tenancies, are used.

With regard to those cottages used by The Queen for her employees and at present unoccupied, a number are being modernized, some are for sale, and some are beyond economic structural repair.

You will appreciate that a small float is essential to cater for changes and the retirement of employees. As an example, only recently a young tractor driver who is getting married next year has asked to be provided with accommodation.

In addition, you may be interested to hear that The Queen is building a further two pensioners' cottages to add to the many others completed during the last few years.

As regards The Queen's private finance, I do not have anything to add to the answers given to the Select Committee.

On 20 December, Mr Hamilton wrote back to Sir Rennie, regretting that his letter had not been as informative as he would have wished.

I had been informed on very good authority that 16 cottages on the Sandringham estate had been empty for two years. Surely that allegation could have been either confirmed or denied, the more so since any profits that accrue from the Estate are entirely tax free, and recent publicity about the receipt by the Queen of Improvement Grants from the Norfolk County Council show there is considerable public interest in these matters.

Enclosed is just one of the many letters which I have received on these questions . . . I would be grateful . . . if you could let me know how many improvement grants have been received in the last five years, and the total sums involved.

As regards the reply to my question as to whether the Queen pays income tax, I presume from your answer that she pays no such tax.

On 17 January 1974, Sir Rennie replied, apologizing for the delay, as he had been away:

I am sorry you found my reply to your previous letter uninformative but there is really nothing I can add to the details I gave you.

As regards Improvement Grants, the Estate is in a similar position to any other Agricultural Estate and it has never been the policy to sell properties where a Local Authority grant has been received.

2. Correspondence with HRH The Duke of Edinburgh

On 20 July 1972, Mr Hamilton wrote direct to Prince Philip:

You are well known for your blunt and often controversial talk. I admire that.

As you know, my views on the Royal Family and the Monarchy as an institution have been equally blunt and contentious.

Since I am in the process of putting my views into book form, I would regard it as a great favour if you would grant me a personal interview.

As a poor alternative, I would be obliged if you would be prepared to answer a few written questions on your own role in the constitution and government of the United Kingdom.

On the 24th, Prince Philip replied from Buckingham Palace:

I am always willing to oblige a Member of Parliament. However, I think I ought to make it clear that, apart from being a Member of the House of Lords, I have no role or function whatever in the constitution or government of this country.

I would certainly do my best to help you on any other aspect of the subject but, as your mind appears to be made up on the subject of the Royal Family and the Monarchy, I wonder whether it would serve any useful purpose.

On the 27th, Mr Hamilton wrote back to Prince Philip:

Thank you very much for your courteous and prompt reply to my original letter. My mind may be as firmly made up on the subject of the Royal Family and the Monarchy as is yours, but I am open to conversion by persuasive argument. Failing, however, a personal interview, I would be grateful if you could give me answers to the following questions – put, I assure you, in all good faith.

In due course, Prince Philip replied from Balmoral Castle on 24 August. The questions and answers ran as follows:

Q.1. Much has been written about the role of Prince Albert and his influence on Queen Victoria. How differently do you see your role from his – and the role of Her Majesty the Queen from that of Queen Victoria?
A. Times, circumstances and personalities are entirely different. In Queen Victoria's day, the Secretaries of State acted, in fact, as Secretaries to the Sovereign. The Prince Consort acted more or less as Queen Victoria's Private Secretary. Today, things are very different and The Queen has a Principal, a Deputy and an Assistant Private Secretary, who deal with official and government business. The Queen and I do, naturally, work together on many matters, such as the organization of the Household and the public engagements, at home and abroad, we carry out together.

Q.2. Has Her Majesty ever expressed shock when you have made some of your provocative speeches, e.g. on the need for family planning and the taxing of large families?
A. I rather doubt whether anyone has been ever genuinely shocked by anything I have said; surprised, perhaps, but it usually turns out that, within a year or two, the subject has become quite a normal topic. Incidentally, I never made a speech advocating taxing large families. The remark which sparked this off was made while I was summing up a discussion. It was by way of an illustration and was only one point among many dealing with conservation, pollution and population. I enclose a transcript.

Q.3. How far, if at all, do you allow such speeches to be vetted (a) by Court officials and (b) by government Ministers?
A. I frequently send drafts of speeches to various people, both inside and outside the Household, for their comments. It is very seldom necessary to send them to Ministers, except in certain cases when they are to be made abroad.

Q.4. What further steps do you think could be taken towards 'modernizing' the Monarchy, e.g. by coming out openly against racial discrimination, by employing more coloured citizens at the Royal Palaces; blood sports; by financing in a big way two or three big new mental hospitals, by sending the Royal children to State schools, etc.?

A. I do not think your examples have much to do with 'modernizing' the monarchy. We are constantly adapting to changing circumstances, but these changes are seldom big enough in themselves to attract much attention. Many of the more obvious ceremonial activities remain the same because we have reason to believe that people enjoy such things as the Changing of the Guard, the Birthday Parade, the carriage procession on State Visits and so on. At the same time, a number of other activities, such as the Presentation Parties (for debutantes), have been done away with.

There have also been a number of initiatives. For example, the old bombed chapel at Buckingham Palace has been converted into a picture and exhibition gallery. We have regular informal luncheon and dinner parties. In addition, the Countryside Conference, the Commonwealth Study Conferences, the Commonwealth Technical Training Week, the Award Scheme, the Maritime Trust, and so on, are all more or less 'modern' in concept.

I hope you would agree that parents should be allowed to decide how to bring up their own children, without any form of political persuasion. My own feeling is that freedom means freedom of choice.

As to the endowment of mental hospitals, I think it is generally accepted that it is for Her Majesty's Government to decide about priorities and to make the necessary financial provisions for this sort of thing.

Q.5. How far do you think the role of the Monarchy will be affected by British entry into the EEC? Are you anti- or pro-EEC?

A. I doubt whether it will have much effect and I base this on the experience of the Dutch and Belgian monarchies.

The decision to enter the Common Market rests with Parliament.

Q.6. How real is the claim that the Monarchy is the most important unifying force in the Commonwealth? Did you meet with any signs of republicanism in your frequent visits to Commonwealth countries?

A. I know of very few other general unifying forces in the Commonwealth. In addition to the Commonwealth Secretariat, there are, of course, a number of particular Commonwealth organizations, such as the Commonwealth Medical Association, the Royal Agricultural Society of the Commonwealth, or the Commonwealth Parliamentary Association and various Standing Commonwealth Conferences. However, none of these can compare with the fact that all the 'old' Commonwealth countries 'share' the same monarch. Furthermore, The Queen is Head of State of some of the 'new' Commonwealth countries and, of course, Head of the Commonwealth as a whole.

I have seen few overt signs of republicanism in the old Commonwealth countries.

Q.7. Which Commonwealth countries have not been visited by you or Her Majesty in the last 20 years? Would you like to make such visits? And if so, what stops you?
A. I cannot think of any, but I include, as a separate note, a list of Commonwealth countries and dates when they have been visited by The Queen and/or by me.

Q.8. Some while ago you called a newspaper a 'bloody awful paper'. Why did you use such language? What reaction did you get?
A. This was in 1962 at a press reception in Rio de Janeiro. I was having a private conversation with a journalist, who claimed that the *Daily Express* was a splendid newspaper. My reply was spontaneous and never intended for publication. The reasons for my remark are too long and involved to go into here. I can say that the reasons no longer exist.

Q.9. What are your favourite newspapers, magazines and other reading material?
A. I do not think a reply to this would be of any material help. Suffice it to say that I read the popular dailies, weekly newspapers of various shades of political opinion and various technical weeklies.

Q.10. You are a member of the House of Lords. So too is Prince Charles. Why don't you use it more as a public platform and as a useful instrument in your public relations?
A. I have always tried to keep out of the political arena and although I could certainly use the House of Lords for non-political subjects, I prefer to speak outside. In any case, I never made a speech because of any wish to say anything myself. They are all made in response to invitations.

Q.11. Do you feel angry when people like me attack the Royal Family? And more angry because you feel you can't reply?
A. In a democratic country such as ours, most people have the right to express their opinions and there is, therefore, no point in being angry when it happens. We are not the only people who do not reply to criticisms. Actions are inclined to speak louder than words anyway.

Q.12. Would it not be a healthy democratic exercise if, via radio and/or television, you could meet your family's critics face to face – with no punches pulled, and no questions pre-arranged?
A. Sir Robert Menzies once told me a very revealing story. He said he was often challenged to public debate either at a meeting or on television. His invariable reply was that he had his audience and the challenger should go and look for one of his own.

Q.13. You will recall the row in the UK over your remarks on an American television programme about your financial problems. Was that spontaneous or deliberately engineered?
A. They were in reply to an unscripted question on a television interview.

Q.14. Did you make those remarks in the full knowledge that discussions had been going on between the Palace and the Government about those very problems?
A. I did not know that there were any particular discussions going on at that time, although I knew that the Government had been made aware of the problem. However, I am not quite clear why this should make any difference. I was talking about matters of fact, not matters of opinion.

Q.15. Were you made aware of the Cabinet anger at your 'indiscretion'? Did that worry you?
A. No. Therefore I was not worried.

Q.16. In the course of the Select Committee's proceedings on the Civil List, we were told (a) that of all the Royal annuitants you were the only one allowed only 80 per cent of your annuity (then £40,000) as tax-free expenses, that that had remained unchanged since 1952 with no request for it to be increased to the 100 per cent allowable to all the others, and (b) that all the annuitants' expenditure 'vastly' exceeded their annuities. How far was this true in your case?
A. I am in rather a different situation in that I do not have to run a home. Most of my official expenditure goes on the employment of the staff necessary to arrange and help carry out public engagements. In the year 1966/7, expenditure began to exceed income and, as the question of a new Civil List had already been mooted, I decided to make do by cutting down my personal expenditure pending the approval of the new Civil List.

Q.17. Does the £65,000 new annuity mean you can now save?
A. I do not anticipate being able to save very much as a substantial portion of the extra amount received will be returned

in taxes. I understand that this taxation will be reduced yearly as official expenses increase with inflation.

Q.18. Would you personally have been prepared to give evidence before the Select Committee – as I suggested?
A. This is a hypothetical question.

3. Correspondence with the Private Secretary to HRH The Prince of Wales

On 6 March 1973, Mr Hamilton wrote to Squadron Leader David Checketts, CVO, Private Secretary to Prince Charles, enclosing a questionnaire and inviting the Prince to reply. Squadron Leader Checketts acknowledged the letter on 9 March, and confirmed that the questions would be answered as soon as he had had 'an opportunity to consult with The Prince of Wales, who, as you know, is at present serving on board HMS *Minerva* in the West Indies'. On 12 June, Squadron Leader Checketts was able to forward the answers. The questions and answers ran as follows:

Q.1. Is there any possibility of your granting me an interview?
A. There is no chance of granting you an interview in the foreseeable future as The Prince of Wales is away on naval duties in the West Indies.

Q.2. Do you regard yourself as an absentee landlord so far as the Duchy of Cornwall is concerned?
A. It is difficult to see how Prince Charles can be anything but an absentee landlord on an estate covering six counties and a distance of approximately 200 miles.

Q.3. How many meetings of Duchy of Cornwall officials have you attended in the last five years?
A. Prince Charles has attended every meeting of the Prince's Council since he came of age, with the exception of the last meeting on 5th April when His Royal Highness was serving on board HMS *Minerva* in the West Indies.

Q.4. On whose advice did you relinquish half the entitlement to the revenues?
A. It was The Prince of Wales' own decision to make over to the Consolidated Fund, from the date of his majority, 50 per cent of the net annual revenues of the Duchy of Cornwall. The proportion of 50 per cent was agreed after consultation between The Queen's Advisors, officials of the Treasury, and the Government of the day.

Q.5. Why did you take such a course?

Q.6. Was it because the income is tax free?
As. to 5 and 6. The voluntary surrender of 50 per cent of the net revenue of the Duchy of Cornwall is made 'in lieu of taxation'. This follows a precedent set by the previous Prince of Wales.

Q.7. Do you feel your income should be taxed?
A. All income other than the Duchy of Cornwall is subject to tax, including His Royal Highness' Naval pay which, after tax, is donated entirely to the King George's Fund for Sailors.

Q.8. What have been your official engagements in the last 12 weeks and what are they likely to be in the next 12?
A. The Prince of Wales is at present serving as an Officer in the Royal Navy and consequently cannot undertake many official engagements. Nevertheless as Heir to the Throne, he is called upon wherever he goes to undertake some form of official activity, for example, the official opening of The Prince of Wales' Bastion at St Kitts on 1 June, and representing The Queen at the celebrations being held to mark the Bahamas Independence in July.

Q.9. What formal or informal contacts do you have with the Duchy of Cornwall officials?
A. The Lord Warden, the Secretary to the Duchy of Cornwall, and other Duchy Officials meet The Prince of Wales frequently when he is in London, and have occasionally been to discuss Duchy matters with His Royal Highness elsewhere in the United Kingdom. In addition to this, His Royal Highness receives formal and informal correspondence about Duchy affairs to which he always replies at length.

Q.10. Who determines their salaries, expenses, etc.? And what are they?
A. The Prince's Council determines the salary structure within the Duchy of Cornwall.

Q.11. Will you benefit from mineral exploitation in the Duchy of Cornwall? What is its extent?
A. This question is impossible to answer. There are a few prospecting licences in issue at the moment but nothing is yet known about the results of their explorations.

Q.12. What is the total rent from properties in Kennington?
A. The gross rent from the Kennington Estate is £335,000 and the net rent £127,000.

Q.13. How often have you visited the property in the Isles of Scilly?
A. Once.

Q.14. Would you be averse to the payment of a salary and the incorporation of the Duchy of Cornwall within the Crown Estate?
A. No comment.

Q.15. Out of your tax-free income from the Duchy of Cornwall what expenses do you incur?
A. All personal expenses and the cost of the salaries of the staff and the administration of The Prince of Wales' Office.

Q.16. Are you taxed on your investments?
A. Yes.

Q.17. Do you think your education and subsequent training has been adequate to give you an understanding of ordinary people?
A. No comment.

4. Correspondence with the Private Secretary to HM Queen Elizabeth The Queen Mother

On 21 July 1972, William Hamilton wrote to Sir Martin Gilliat, Private Secretary to the Queen Mother:

> As you may know, the Select Committee of the House of Commons which recently investigated the Civil List and Royal Annuities did not have time to probe as deeply as I personally would have liked.
>
> Accordingly, I hope the following questions might be answered by Her Royal Highness, the Queen Mother.

On 24 July, Mr Gilliat acknowledged the letter and confirmed that it had been 'forwarded to Sir Ralph Anstruther, Queen Elizabeth The Queen Mother's Treasurer, who is at present with Her Majesty at Sandringham, as for the most part he has been dealing with the matters which you have raised'. By 15 November Mr Gilliat was able to deal with Mr Hamilton's questions as follows:

Q.1. On what basis was the £95,000 figure reached? Was it suggested by the Queen Mother herself, or was it the Government's figure put to her?
A. The figure was recommended by the majority of the Select Committee, of which you were a member.

Q.2. The Committee was told that Her Majesty's expenses vastly exceeded her £70,000 annuity. Is that still true today out of the £95,000?
A. Information of this nature is not customarily made public, except in the case of the Select Committee.

Q.3. The Queen Mother has a big Household – according to the 1972 Imperial Calendar – a total of 32. How many of these are paid and/or full time? What is the total salaries bill?
A. Thirteen members of Queen Elizabeth The Queen Mother's Household are salaried. The remainder hold honorary appointment after many years of faithful service. The names listed in the Imperial Calendar include 5 full-time clerks. Information about salaries is not customarily made public, except in the case of the Select Committee.

Q.4. What are the differences in function between the Ladies of the Bedchamber and the Women of the Bedchamber and how did the titles originate?
A. Normally the Ladies attend Queen Elizabeth on Ceremonial occasions and the Women are in attendance at all Her Majesty's day to day engagements, and in addition carry out secretarial work. I do not know how the distinction arose between Ladies of the Bedchamber and Women of the Bedchamber.

Q.5. What are the functions of the Lord Chamberlain and the Comptroller?
A. The Lord Chamberlain is head of the Household; the Comptroller is responsible for the day to day administration of Her Majesty's establishments.

Q.6. How many of the Queen Mother's Household occupy Grace and Favour residences?
A. Two.

Q.7. What was the total number of official engagements undertaken by the Queen Mother in the first six months of 1972? How many does she expect to undertake in the second half-year?
A. Her Majesty's official engagements are recorded in the Court Circular, which is published in the press. It is not possible to forecast the number of future engagements.

Q.8. What foreign visits have been undertaken in 1972, and how many are planned for the next 12 months?
A. None. The programme for 1973 is still under consideration.

Q.9. Does the initiative for such foreign tours come from

HMG? Or are some of them at the suggestion of the Queen Mother herself?
A. There is no fixed rule: normally the initiative comes from the Foreign or Commonwealth Government concerned.

Q.10. Why do all members of the Household – except the Clerks – have to be titled? Is this one of the qualifications for appointment? Do they apply for the posts, or how are they selected?
A. It is incorrect to say that all members of the Household have a title. A title is not a qualification for appointment. It is open for people to apply for appointments, alternatively, appointments are made on recommendation and on Her Majesty's choice.

Q.11. How many racehorses does Her Majesty own?
A. This is a personal matter of which I have no knowledge.

On 22 November, Mr Hamilton thanked Sir Martin for his replies:

The answers to the questions I put were not terribly informative but they will serve my purpose. Thank you for your limited cooperation.

5. Correspondence with the Private Secretary to HRH The Princess Margaret, Countess of Snowden

On 21 July 1972, William Hamilton wrote with a questionnaire to the Private Secretary of Princess Margaret:

As a persistent critic of Princess Margaret, I am sure she would not wish to grant me a personal interview in connection with the book I am in the process of writing about the Royal Family. Nevertheless, I would be very grateful if, through you, she might answer the following questions.

On 16 November, Sir Frederick Burnaby-Atkins wrote that it had now been possible to consider the questions and that he had pleasure in enclosing the replies.

Q.1. According to the British Imperial Calendar for 1972, Her Royal Highness's staff numbers 12, of whom 7 are extra Ladies in Waiting. How many of those 12 are full time and paid – and what are the functions of each?
A. Three members of the Household (Private Secretary, Lady-

in-Waiting and Personal Secretary) are full time and paid. The post of Clerk Comptroller no longer exists – we have a part-time Accountant. The Extra Ladies-in-Waiting are not paid.

Q.2. How many public engagements did Her Royal Highness undertake in the first 6 months of 1972 – and how many are planned to the end of the year?
A. Between January 1st and June 30th, Princess Margaret undertook 82 engagements. From July 1st to mid November, Her Royal Highness undertook 27 engagements. This period includes a tour of three weeks of the Seychelles, Singapore and Australia (Western and Northern territory). We have not included audiences and interviews in the total of engagements.

Q.3. How many of these engagements are, or were, outside London?
A. January to June – 43 engagements out of London.
July to mid November (excluding the tour) – 9 engagements.

Q.4. What overseas tours has Her Royal Highness engaged in in the last 12 months; and what was the mode of travel?
A. From September 1971 to October 1972, Her Royal Highness has visited:

Canada	3 days	Commercial flight
British Virgin Islands	4 days	Commercial flight
Florence	3 days	Queen's Flight
Germany	3 days	Queen's Flight
Seychelles, Australia, Singapore	21 days	Commercial and Air Force flights

Q.5. How many of the Household actually live at Kensington Palace, or in other Grace and Favour residences?
A. There are no members of the Household as we understand it either living in the Palace or Grace and Favour Houses, but 8 members of the domestic staff live in.

Q.6. How many cars are provided to Her Royal Highness for official purposes?
A. None.

Q.7. Does Her Royal Highness draw her family allowance?
A. No.

Q.8. Do she and her family use the National Health Service?
A. No.

Q.9. On whose initiative does Her Royal Highness undertake foreign visits, e.g. her recent visit to the Virgin Islands?
A. On the initiation of the Foreign and Commonwealth Office or the host country or organization.

Q.10. Would Her Royal Highness care to explain how in the recent Civil List pay award she received an increase of 133 per cent over the 1952 figure, whilst Prince Philip only got a 62 per cent increase and Her Majesty the Queen Mother a 36 per cent increase?
A. As Mr Hamilton was a member of the Civil List Committee he must be in a position to know.

Q.11. How does Her Royal Highness regard her role in the British constitution?
A. A supporting role.

Q.12. In evidence to the Civil List Committee it was stated that Her Royal Highness's expenses vastly exceeded her annuity of £15,000. Is that still true today?
A. It is not yet possible to say.

Q.13. Did Her Royal Highness ever consider sending her children to a local authority school?
A. No.

Q.14. What personal staff does Lord Snowdon have at Kensington Palace?
A. One secretary.

6. Correspondence with the Private Secretary to HRH The Princess Anne

On 6 March 1973, Mr Hamilton wrote to Mrs B. M. Aston, Private Secretary to Princess Anne, with seven questions. On 19 March Lady Mary Dawnay, Lady in Waiting to HRH The Princess Anne, replied on the Princess's behalf. The questions and answers ran as follows:

Q.1. What public engagements did you undertake in 1970, 1971 and 1972? May I have details of these engagements?
A. I enclose a separate list of Her Royal Highness's engagements for 1970, 1971 and 1972.
[These yielded the following information:

1970
Princess Anne had official engagements on 59 individual days, including film premières, regimental and charitable luncheons and receptions, factory visits, and such fixtures as Royal Garden Parties and the Festival of Remembrance. In addition, from 2 March to 4 May she was away for a tour of Australia and New Zealand. From 26–28 June she was visiting the Army in Germany. On 5–16 July she accompanied the Queen on the

official visit to Canada, followed up by a visit to the White House, on 17–19 July. On 10–16 August she was in the Western Isles. And on 16–17 September she was visiting the RAF at Bruggen in Germany.

1971
There were official engagements on 71 individual days, the mixture much as before. Then, on 6–21 February she went to Kenya for a visit that was partly official and partly on behalf of the Save the Children Fund. From 3–12 May she accompanied the Queen on her visit to British Columbia. From 3–7 June she visited Norway on behalf of the Save the Children Fund. Illness led her to cancel engagements after 9 July and for the rest of the summer. From 5–8 October she was on a State visit to Japan, before leaving on the 12th on official visits to Iran, Turkey and Hong Kong, returning 2 November.

1972
The Princess had official engagements on 59 individual days. Then, on 8 February she left on an official tour of South-East Asia, returning on 5 March. There was a State visit to Holland on 11–15 April, an official visit to the Channel Islands on 22–25 May, a visit to Monte Carlo for a charity concert on 27–30 June, a cruise in the Western Isles from 30 July to 8 August. Finally, a State visit to Yugoslavia on 17–21 October was followed by a State visit to Germany on 24–27 October.]

Q.2. Did you have any influence, or were you consulted, in the fixing of your annuity at £15,000 a year?
A. In the matter of fixing the amount of the annuity Her Royal Highness was to receive, like other members of The Royal Family, Her Royal Highness made available the figures of her expenses on her Office and official engagements.

Q.3. Do you consider this figure is appropriate?
A. This is the figure which the Select Committee on the Civil List and Parliament thought appropriate.

Q.4. Is it tax free?
A. No. See paragraph 5, report of the Select Committee on the Civil List.

Q.5. How do you see your future role?

Q.6. Do you consider your education and training has been adequate to understand how ordinary people live?

Q.7. What would you like to do, if you were free to choose?
As. to 5, 6 and 7, Her Royal Highness does not wish to answer these questions.

7. *Correspondence with the Buckingham Palace Press Secretary*

On 4 and 20 July 1972, Mr Hamilton sent two lists of questions to Mr Robin Ludlow, who was then the Queen's Press Secretary, seeking information on items of general interest. Mr Ludlow replied on 31 October.

(a) Answers to Mr Hamilton's questions of 4 July 1972

Q.1. On whose advice and guidance are invitations sent to the periodic luncheons which Her Majesty gives?

Q.2. When did the practice start and at whose suggestion and why?

Q.3. How many trade-union leaders have been invited to date? How many Labour and Tory MPs respectively? And how many representatives of the respective religious denominations, and of coloured immigrants? Has anyone ever been declared *persona non grata*?
As. to 1, 2 and 3 The Queen instituted these luncheons in May 1956. They are private occasions and I am not therefore in a position to give you any information on how the guests are selected. Their names however have been regularly published in the press, and may be obtained from this source. No one has ever been declared *persona non grata* in so far as these luncheons are concerned.

Q.4. On what basis are guests to Royal Garden Parties chosen? Are the numbers attending kept, and if so, what have they been over a period of, say, 5 years?
A. There are usually three Garden Parties at Buckingham Palace and one at Holyroodhouse each year. Numbers attending were:

1971	29,114
1970	27,406
1969	31,033
1968	29,595
1967	21,213

Invitations are extended to a broad cross-section of the community and in particular to those who contribute significantly to the life of the Nation. There are occasionally special parties to commemorate a landmark in the history of some organization – e.g. Golden Jubilee of the Women's Institute when 9,000 Institute members were asked and with the exception of 24 all came.

Q.5. Are invitations sent to political parties as such, or the TUC or the Co-operative Movement?

A. The definition of those invited given in the answer above naturally includes members of the Conservative, Labour and Liberal Parties, the Trades Union Congress and the Co-operative Movement.

Q.6. How many Royal visits have been paid to 10 Downing Street or to Chequers in the last 20 years, and who were the persons involved?
A. I speak for The Queen and her own immediate family only. Her Majesty and The Duke of Edinburgh dined at No. 10 Downing Street in 1955 at the invitation of Sir Winston Churchill and on the eve of his retirement. The Duke of Edinburgh dined at No. 10 in May 1958 and June 1959.

In 1970 The Queen visited Chequers at the invitation of Mr Heath to meet the President of the United States of America. The Prince of Wales lunched with the Prime Minister at No. 10 in March 1971.

Q.7. How heavily does Her Majesty rely on the advice of: (a) her Private Secretaries, and (b) her Ministers?
A. As a Constitutional Sovereign, The Queen acts and speaks on the advice of her Ministers.

Q.8. What role does Her Majesty play in the compilation of the Honours List? Has she the power to veto any name put forward, and if so has she ever exercised it?
A. (i) The Queen approves the Honours List and, with some exceptions, does this on the advice of the Ministers of the United Kingdom or of Commonwealth countries of which she is Sovereign.
(ii) The Royal Victorian Order, like the Garter, the Thistle, and the Order of Merit, is given by The Queen without Ministerial advice.
(iii) What passes between The Queen and her Ministers cannot be disclosed.

Q.9. Who decides the form of the Christmas Broadcast? Who prepares the contents of the speech and the general format? Why was a decision taken to discontinue the Broadcast and subsequently rescinded?
A. The nature and contents of The Queen's Christmas broadcast which are addressed to the Commonwealth as a whole are decided by Her Majesty.

There was no decision to discontinue the broadcast. There has only been one year, 1969, in which there was no Christmas broadcast.

Q.10. On whose initiative was Prince Charles interviewed on

television? Did he have advance notice of the questions? Who decided who the interviewers should be?
A. In 1969, in view of Prince Charles' Investiture as The Prince of Wales, His Royal Highness was asked for interviews by all sections of the press, radio and television. The interviewers and general lines of discussion were arranged with the organizations concerned.

Q.11. Was any fee paid for the interview?
A. No fee was paid.

Q.12. Princess Anne's visit to Kenya was widely publicized and televised. Who decided that that should be done? What was the total cost and who paid? Were there any fees involved?
A. (i) Her Royal Highness became President of the Save the Children Fund in January 1970. In that capacity she was invited to visit Kenya in February 1971 to see some of the work carried out in Nairobi with the assistance of the Fund. Early in Princess Anne's term of office as President of the SCF it had been suggested that she might agree to take part in a film for television, showing some aspect of the Fund's work. The visit to Kenya provided an opportunity to make such a film. After informal discussions between the Press Secretary, the Save the Children Fund and the BBC, The Princess agreed that her visit to Kenya should be filmed by the BBC's 'Blue Peter' team, and that the film should include some of the other aspects of her visit in addition to the time spent with the SCF.
(ii) I can give you no exact details. Such costs to public funds as there were, were limited to those connected with journeys by air.
(iii) The Princess Anne received a percentage of the royalties from the sale of the film overseas and this is to be devoted to charitable purposes.

Q.13. Does Her Majesty watch much television?

Q.14. What are her cultural tastes and hobbies?

Q.19. Is Her Majesty an inveterate letter-writer like Queen Victoria?

Q.20. Is she interested in political matters? Has she, for instance, strong views on Rhodesia or South Africa or Communism? Or blood sports?

Q.21. Is it fair to say that she is more at home in a rural setting than in industrial areas?

Q.23. Why did Her Majesty see fit to refuse to disclose to the recent Civil List Committee the size of her private fortune? On whose advice was she acting?

Q.31. What are the estimates of the value of The Queen's personal jewellery?
As. to 13, 14, 19, 20, 21, 23 and 31 These questions are personal ones or they concern Her Majesty's personal views on important subjects, and I can give no answers to them.

Q.15. Why do people know so little of Her Majesty as an individual?
A. This assumption on your part is one with which, I think, few people would agree.

Q.16. When a doctor attends Her Majesty or any of the immediate Royal Family – is he paid? or is it on the National Health Service? or does he give his services free?
Are National Health facilities ever used?
A. The relationship that exists between Her Majesty The Queen and other members of the Royal Family and their respective medical advisers is entirely confidential and cannot be disclosed.
No charge for these services falls directly upon the Civil List, although small retaining fees are paid from the Civil List to certain physicians who are available to attend The Queen's Household and staff when required, as is customary in many other large organizations.

Q.17. Are the usual family allowances drawn?
A. No.

Q.18. How frequently does the Prime Minister visit Her Majesty? Is anyone else in attendance? What is the average length of the weekly business visit of the Prime Minister? Are records kept of such visits to the Palace?
A. The occasions on which The Queen gives an audience to the Prime Minister are recorded in the Court Circular. Such audiences normally take place on Tuesday of each week when the House is in Session and The Queen is in residence at Buckingham Palace. No one is in attendance and I cannot give any other details about these audiences.

Q.22. In how many countries was the Royal Family film shown? Is it still in circulation? Is there any estimate available of the profits made from it?
A. The sale and circulation of the Royal Family film is a matter for the television consortium which made it, and those questions could therefore be put to the BBC as a partner in that consortium.

Q.24. On whose initiative was the recently announced decision of a 2 million pound refit of the Royal Yacht *Britannia* made?
A. This question is one for the Ministry of Defence.

Q.25 Is it possible to have a list of all occupants of Grace and Favour Apartments? On what basis are the tenants chosen? How many are occupied by Court Officials or ex-Court Officials and others? Are such homes offered, say, to retired miners, with 50 years national service of constant danger and unpleasantness?
A. I cannot provide you with a list. The houses known as Grace and Favour houses are for the far greater part occupied by those currently in the service of The Queen and other members of the Royal Family. Some of these houses are in London, others at Windsor and Hampton Court Palace. A handful of the houses in London are at present occupied by retired staff, but the practice of allowing people to remain in their houses after they have retired has now ceased. A number of widows of men who have given distinguished service are given Grace and Favour Apartments at Hampton Court.

Q.26. Since it was indicated to the Civil List Committee that £300,000 that Her Majesty now took from the Duchy of Lancaster went to pay staff, etc., and since substantial increases have now been made in the Civil List, will less be taken from the Duchy revenues in future years?
A. Statement VII on Page XXI of the Select Committee Report shows that £300,000 was paid to the Privy Purse from the Duchy of Lancaster revenues in the year ended 29th September, 1970.

On Page 63, Mr Wheeler, the Clerk to the Council of the Duchy, describes how the £300,000 was an exceptionally high payment and £60,000 of it was, in fact, a contribution to alleviate the increasing Civil List deficit, leaving a not abnormal sum of £240,000 to be paid to the Privy Purse. The same allocation was, in fact, made in 1971, since the Civil List Act 1972 had not by then been enacted and increased funds were not available in the Civil List.

With the present inflation of wages and costs, it is unlikely that future requirements from the Duchy of Lancaster revenues will decrease.

Q.29. How many racehorses are owned by Her Majesty?
A. The Queen had 15 horses in training in 1972.

Q.30. (i) In Mr Kingsley Martin's book *The Crown and the Establishment* he said The Queen gave £3 to each mother of triplets. Is this true?
A. This practice has been discontinued.
(ii) And £27 a year for the Poet Laureate. Is the Poet Laureate paid £27 a year? How much is he paid?
A. A small salary is paid to the Poet Laureate from the Civil

List, and has remained unchanged since Ben Jonson, Poet Laureate from 1619 to 1637, who received such a stipend from King James I.

Later King Charles I gave him additionally a terce of Canary Wine and these emoluments continued unchanged until, in 1800, when Henry James Pye was Poet Laureate, the terce of wine was commuted to a sum of £27 per annum, at which rate it has since remained.

Q.32. Is the Stamp Collection still kept up-to-date?
A. Yes.

Q.33. It was said by Mr Martin that the Queen's furniture etc. is catalogued in 75 large volumes at Windsor. Is that still true – and has any valuation been placed on it?

Q.34. Why is not more of this treasure on show to the public?
As. to 33 and 34. The Inventories referred to are Domestic Inventories listing everything in a Palace and inclusion therein does not mean that an article is a 'treasure' suitable for public exhibition.

The Catalogue Raisonné of Paintings and Old Master Drawings in the Royal Collection has been in course of publication since the War – financially supported by The Queen. The publishers are the Phaidon Press who could supply a list of titles.

The Royal Collection has not been valued.

A large part of the Royal Collection is on permanent view to the public at Windsor Castle (State Apartments and Exhibition of drawings by Holbein, Leonardo and other artists), Hampton Court Palace (State Apartments), The Queen's Gallery at Buckingham Palace; Kensington Palace and the Palace of Holyroodhouse.

In the past ten years The Queen has made 196 loans to public exhibitions all over the country and occasionally abroad. These loans vary from individual items to 10, 20 or more paintings as is often the case with the Royal Academy Exhibition. Occasionally, as with the 'Kings and Queens' Exhibition, the entire Royal Academy Exhibition is comprised of paintings from the Royal Collection.

(b) Answers to Mr Hamilton's questions of 20 July 1972

Q.1. What are the duties of the Master of the Horse? Is this a full-time job? Is it paid?
A. The Master of the Horse is the titular head of the Royal Mews, where he makes periodic inspections. It is a part-time

and unpaid position, but the Master is in attendance on The Queen on important ceremonial occasions when Her Majesty rides on horseback or travels by horsedrawn carriage.

Q.2. What are the duties of Gold Stick? How did the name originate?
A. The original order for Gold Stick in 1528 when the Office was instituted was 'that he should wait next to His Majesty's person before all others' the reason being that this Officer was responsible for the Sovereign's personal security.

It is believed that as a result of an incident in the time of Charles II that Sovereign decreed that thereafter the position of Gold Stick should be held by the Colonel of his Life Guard. In consequence since that time the Gold Sticks in England have been the two Colonels of the Household Cavalry Regiments (the Life Guards and the Blues and Royals).

A similar post exists in Scotland where the Gold Stick is held by virtue of Office as Captain General of the Royal Company of Archers.

The name Gold Stick derives from the fact that the Officer concerned receives a gold topped Stick as a symbol of Office.

Q.3. What duties are performed by the Mistress of the Robes? Is she a full-time member of the Household, and if not, how much time per week on average does she perform her duties?
A. The Mistress of the Robes is the senior lady of The Queen's Household, and is usually a duchess. She is responsible for arranging the rota for the Ladies-in-Waiting, and is in attendance on Her Majesty on State occasions, and sometimes on State Visits abroad. It is not a full-time appointment.

Q.4. What is the distinction between Ladies of the Bedchamber and Women of the Bedchamber? How are they appointed? By whom? What qualifications are required? Must they all be titled?
A. The two Ladies of the Bedchamber are usually the wives of Earls and attend The Queen on major public occasions, but do not go into waiting regularly. They sometimes accompany Her Majesty on visits abroad. There is also an Extra Lady of the Bedchamber who more occasionally attends upon The Queen.

There are four Women of the Bedchamber, who in turn for a fortnight at a time attend The Queen on all public and semi-private engagements.

They also deal with some of Her Majesty's private correspondence and reply to letters written to The Queen by children.

There are also three Extra Women of the Bedchamber.

All are appointed by The Queen, and Women of the Bedchamber need not be titled.

Q.5. The 1972 Calendar is obviously out of date in respect of the Private Secretary's Office personnel. Could it be brought up to date?
A. The only changes in the Private Secretary's Office which will differ from the 1972 Calendar are:
Private Secretary – Lieutenant-Colonel the Right Honourable Sir Martin Charteris, KCB, KCVO, OBE;
Deputy Private Secretary – Mr Philip Moore, CMG;
Assistant Private Secretary – Mr William Heseltine, CVO;
Press Secretary – Mr Robin Ludlow [Mr Ronald Allison since 7 May 1973]

Q.6. How many of those listed as being members of the Private Secretary's Office have Grace and Favour residences? Which of them automatically receive the tenancy of such a residence on retirement?
A. Eleven Members, Officials and Staff of the Private Secretary's Office have Grace and Favour or official apartments. None automatically receive the tenancy of such a residence on retirement.

Q.7. Is the Keeper of the Royal Philatelic Collection a full-time occupation? Does he trade internationally?
A. The Keeper of the Royal Philatelic Collection is a part-time appointment, and he does not trade internally or internationally.

Q.8. What is the purpose of the Royal Almonry, and what duties are performed by the High Almoner, the Hereditary Grand Almoner, and the Sub-Almoner? And why 'hereditary'?
A. See enclosed article by Lawrence Tanner.

Q.9. What does the Master of the Household do? What are the functions of his Department? What does the Palace Steward do?
A. The Master of the Household is the permanent head of his department, and his department's responsibilities include interior and domestic arrangements of Buckingham Palace, Windsor Castle and the Palace of Holyroodhouse; domestic arrangements for Sandringham House and Balmoral Castle; Royal and staff kitchens; the Royal Yacht (in so far as it affects catering and entertainments); State Banquets; the Court Circular; Buckingham Palace garden; Court Post Office; Palace Police; Royal Standards; Security passes; wines, plate, china and glass.

The Master of the Household is also responsible for liaison with the Department of the Environment local depots in the Royal Palaces; the purchase of food and most other supplies for the Royal Household, and travel arrangements for the Court and individual members of the Household, officials and staff on official journeys by rail and air. Also the issue of passes to the forecourt of Buckingham Palace for Guard Mounting, The Queen's Birthday Parade, Opening of Parliament etc. and the despatch of wreaths on behalf of The Queen.

The Palace Steward is the senior member of the domestic staff in the Royal Household and is responsible for all the male members of it, and is in charge of the dining room and all serving arrangements at State Banquets, dinners, lunches, etc. given by The Queen.

Q.10. Why should it require a Lieutenant-Colonel to do the work of State Invitations Assistant? Is he a retired Army Officer? What really is his function?
A. He is an Official of the Lord Chamberlain's Office principally responsible for the organization of the Garden Parties, diplomatic Evening Party and other special official parties which may be necessary. This is a full-time appointment. He does not have to be of any particular rank or status; the present incumbent just happens to be a retired Army officer of Lieutenant-Colonel rank. [In 1974 the incumbent was a civilian.]

Q.11. Are all those Lords-in-Waiting, Gentlemen Ushers, Extra Gentlemen Ushers really necessary? Why should so many of them be drawn from the ranks of HM Forces?
A. There are 3 permanent Lords-in-Waiting, and 7 Lords-in-Waiting, (5 of whom are Government Whips in the House of Lords). They represent Her Majesty on a number of occasions, e.g. meeting important people arriving or departing from the United Kingdom, or at Memorial Services.

Gentlemen Ushers and Extra Gentlemen Ushers are part-time, honorary and unpaid positions, and the holders of these posts are only on duty during major official or ceremonial occasions, e.g. Garden Parties, Diplomatic Receptions, Investitures. (See Report of the Select Committee on the Civil List, page 93, 2(b).)

In order to organize the Garden Parties properly quite a lot of people are needed, and the numbers of Gentlemen Ushers etc. are not therefore excessive.

Q.12. What are the precise functions of the Hereditary Keeper of the Palace of Holyroodhouse? Does he live there? When The Queen is not at Holyroodhouse, who is in occupation?
A. The Hereditary Keeper has general oversight of the Palace of Holyroodhouse, and its administration. He has an apartment there. The appointment reposes in the Dukedom of Hamilton and Brandon.

The Palace of Holyroodhouse is The Queen's official residence in Scotland. It is also used as the residence of the Lord High Commissioner to the General Assembly during the meeting of the Assembly. When neither The Queen nor the Lord High Commissioner is in residence the Palace is open to the public.

Q.13. What job is done by the Surveyor of The Queen's Pictures? Does he buy or sell pictures?
A. The Surveyor of The Queen's Pictures is a full time appointment, and he is responsible for the care and hanging of the Royal Collection; he advises on requests for loans, works on the catalogue for exhibitions in The Queen's Gallery, and supervises the care, maintenance and restoration of pictures and the display of special exhibitions.

Paintings from the Royal Collection are not sold. The Surveyor however advises The Queen on any pictures Her Majesty wishes to buy for the Royal Collection.

Q.14. What does the Curator of the Print Room do? Is she full time?
A. The Curator of the Print Room is a permanent Official in the Royal Library at Windsor Castle. The Librarian requires a skilled assistant to administer the valuable collection of drawings by Leonardo, Holbein and other artists.

Q.15. What is the job of the Bargemaster? For what did he receive his decoration of the MVO?
A. The position of Royal Bargemaster dates from time immemorial when barges provided the quickest and safest method of transport. Until 1919 each Sovereign had a Royal Barge, but now the duties of the Bargemaster and Watermen are few.

Each year before the Opening of Parliament, the Bargemaster and four Watermen accompany the coach from Buckingham Palace to Westminster, and they attend upon The Queen when she is present at functions connected with the River.

The emoluments attached to the positions are nominal, and all Watermen are actively connected with the river in day to day employment, either on the docks, barges, tugs or other river craft.

The Bargemaster received his decoration of MVO for services to The Queen.

Q.16. Is the Keeper of the Swans a full-time occupation? What work is done? How was he appointed? Is he paid?
A. This appointment is not a full time one. The holder is in business as a boat builder and boat hirer. He receives an honorarium plus expenses. His duty is to look after the welfare

of swans on the River Thames. He is assisted in this by the Swan Keepers of the Vintners' and Dyers' Companies. In these days of increasing vandalism he finds more to do than he should.

Q.17 What is the cost of maintaining the Ascot Office? What is its purpose?
A. It is the London office of Ascot racecourse, and as such the cost of maintaining it is not available. Its purpose is to issue vouchers for Royal Ascot and tickets etc. for its members.

Q.18. Why is the Ecclesiastical Household so enormous? How did the title Clerk of the Closet originate? What do all the Chaplains and Extra Chaplains do?
A. The Closet was in earlier times 'the private apartment of a monarch' (OED) and although the origins, date and function of the *Clerk of the Closet* are unknown, he was, in the opinion of the late Bishop of Norwich (formerly Clerk for many years), the private confessor of the Sovereign, with access to this private apartment. 'If this is correct' (continues the Bishop) 'presumably the functions changed at the Reformation, and it was still probably advantageous to have a clergyman in the Royal Household'. It may be of interest to note that the first Bishop of Norwich in 1096 was Clerk of the Closet to Queen Matilda, widow of the Conqueror, and the office is thus one of some antiquity.

The College of *Chaplains* (complement 36 in number) consists of serving clergymen of the Church of England with a meritorious record, who are recommended for appointment by the Clerk of the Closet (Head of the College). The College continues historically the entourage of priests who through the centuries served the Sovereign and the Household. The Royal Chaplains receive no stipend, but a preaching fee on the occasions when they are summoned to preach at the Royal Chapels or at Windsor.

The *Extra Chaplains* are those members of the College who have attained the age of 70 (the retiring age) and have been so appointed in recognition of particularly long and distinguished service. Their function is that of the other Chaplains, i.e. to preach when summoned at the Royal Chapels or at Windsor.

Q.19. What is the difference between an Extra Chaplain, a Priest, and a Deputy Priest?
A. Extra Chaplains (see note, question 18).

A *Priest in Ordinary* is not a member of the College of Chaplains but of the Staff of Her Majesty's Chapels Royal in St James's Palace. There are three Priests in Ordinary, appointed upon recommendation from the Dean of the Chapels

Royal (at present the Bishop of London). Their duty is to attend by monthly rota at the statutory Services held in the Chapels Royal, or on such other occasions as are commanded by The Queen. They share with the Sub-Dean (who is also Domestic Chaplain at Buckingham Palace) the responsibility for maintaining these services, and also during his absence on leave, for the pastoral care of Her Majesty's staff and Household. They are paid a stipend for their attendance. Each of them holds a position in the Church or in academic life apart from this appointment.

A Deputy Priest (no stipend) is appointed to fill the place of a Priest in Ordinary when the latter is unable for any reason to fulfil his duties in accordance with the rota. He is remunerated on these occasions by the Priest in Ordinary for whom he is deputizing.

It will be clear that the function of the members of the College of Chaplains is virtually an honorary one. The Royal Chaplains represent a historical link with the community of priests who through the centuries have ministered to the spiritual needs of the Sovereign and Royal Household.

The Sub-Dean and Priests in Ordinary continue the function described above by maintaining at the Chapels Royal the services of the Established Church at the Court of the Sovereign. By permission of the Sovereign, the use of these Chapels is extended each Sunday to the general public and services continue to be well attended. The pastoral responsibility for this congregation now lies with the Sub-Dean.

Q.20. What does the Serjeant of the Vestry do – and the Groom of the Vestry? And the Keeper of the Closet?
A. The *Serjeant of the Vestry* is the resident salaried Verger whose responsibility, under the Sub-Dean, is that of the maintenance, cleaning and general supervision of the Chapels Royal, i.e. the Chapel Royal at St James's Palace and The Queen's Chapel at St James's. He also carries out the normal duties of a Verger at all Services held in these Chapels. His appointment is made by the Lord Chamberlain.

The *Groom of the Vestry* is the assistant to the Serjeant. His functions are confined to attendance at the services and he is not responsible for other duties. He receives a small salary and his appointment is made in the same way as that of the Serjeant of the Vestry.

The *Keeper of the Closet* is an assistant whose special responsibility is that of the oversight of the Children of the Choir and their uniforms. He attends at Services (vide definition above of 'closet') when the Sovereign attends in person. He, like the Groom, receives a small salary, and his appointment is made in the same way as that of the two other officials above.

Q.21. Are the large numbers of the Medical Household available to all members of the Royal Household, or just to the immediate Royal Family? How many are paid?
A. In the Medical Household, doctors holding special appointments to The Queen are normally unpaid, and are not available to the Household.

Doctors holding appointments to the Household are available for the Royal Family, members of the Household and staff to consult, and are paid retainers.

Q.22. What is the work of the Central Chancery of the Orders of Knighthood?
A. The Secretary, Central Chancery of the Orders of Knighthood prepares the formal announcement of the Honours Lists and arranges for recipients of Honours and Awards to attend Investitures at Buckingham Palace, and for the despatch of Insignia and Medals.

He prepares and arranges for Services of the Orders of the Bath and the British Empire.

Q.23. Of the Gentlemen-at-Arms, what does the Clerk of the Cheque and Adjutant do? And the Harbinger? What uniforms do they wear?
A. The Clerk of the Cheque and Adjutant has the same duties as an Adjutant in a regular Military formation. He issued orders for the parading and employment of the Body Guard.

The Harbinger is the junior officer of the Corps and appears on Parade in command of a detachment of the Body Guard as occasion requires. Otherwise he acts as Assistant Adjutant although in ancient times his duties were rather those of a Quartermaster.

Uniform: scarlet coat, blue trousers, gilt metal helmet, white swan feather plumes.

Q.24. How does the work of the Clerk of the Cheque and Adjutant among the Gentlemen-at-Arms differ from that of the Clerk of the Cheque and Adjutant among the Yeomen of the Guard?

Q.25. In the Yeomen of the Guard, how did the names Ensign and Exon originate? And what do the holders do?
As. to 24 and 25. The Clerk of the Cheque and Adjutant of the Yeomen of the Guard carries out the same duties as his counterpart in the Gentlemen-at-Arms, except that he had more than double the Rank and File to deal with and they perform more duties.

The Ensign is so called because he carries the Corps' Colour. This is the same title as is used in the Household Division today.

The origin of the name 'Exon' is not certain. Probably it is an anglicization of the title of those Officers of the French Royal Guard who were known as 'Capitaines Exemptes des Gardes du Corps', i.e. regular officers excused duty with their Regiment in order to serve in the Guard. They are junior officers of the Yeomen of the Guard and command detachments on a duty as occasion warrants.

Q.26. What is the total strength of the Royal Company of Archers? Who buys and maintains their weapons and uniforms?
A. The Royal Company of Archers, which is said to have originated in the 15th century, is a private archery club and also the Sovereign's Bodyguard in Scotland, and currently has a membership of 384. The members buy their own uniforms and weapons and maintain them.

Q.27. What do all the Equerries and Extra Equerries in the Royal Mews Department do for a living? How are they appointed?
A. Of the Equerries, the Crown Equerry alone works in the Royal Mews Department. He is in day to day charge of the Royal Mews and its services: horses, carriages, and cars.

The other Equerries, and Extra Equerries are, presumably for historical reasons, shown in some works of reference as coming under the Royal Mews Department. This, as you will know, is misleading.

The Equerries perform the functions of Aides de Camp.

The Extra Equerries either do a full time job in other departments of the Household, or are retired members of the Household who have been given this appellation in order that they may be able to retain some connection with Court where they have served for many years.

Appendix G.
A MOTION WHICH WAS OVERWHELMINGLY CARRIED BY A MEETING OF THE GENERAL COUNCIL OF THE WOOLWICH LABOUR PARTY IN 1973

This General Council calls upon the Parliamentary Labour Party to support the lone voice of William Hamilton in its criticism of a Royal Family whose wealth is flaunted daily whilst the bulk of the population suffers from massive rises in rents, mortgages, and the cost of food. While people live in slums this family lives in opulence. We urge more Labour MPs to stand up and be counted as Socialists in a demonstration of support for this courageous man.

INDEX